I0010046

Foundations of Blockchain

The pathway to cryptocurrencies and decentralized
blockchain applications

Koshik Raj

BIRMINGHAM - MUMBAI

Foundations of Blockchain

Copyright © 2019 Packt Publishing

All rights reserved. No part of this book may be reproduced, stored in a retrieval system, or transmitted in any form or by any means, without the prior written permission of the publisher, except in the case of brief quotations embedded in critical articles or reviews.

Every effort has been made in the preparation of this book to ensure the accuracy of the information presented. However, the information contained in this book is sold without warranty, either express or implied. Neither the author, nor Packt Publishing or its dealers and distributors, will be held liable for any damages caused or alleged to have been caused directly or indirectly by this book.

Packt Publishing has endeavored to provide trademark information about all of the companies and products mentioned in this book by the appropriate use of capitals. However, Packt Publishing cannot guarantee the accuracy of this information.

Acquisition Editors: Frank Pohlmann
Acqusition Editor - Peer Reviews: Suresh Jain
Project Editor: Kishor Rit
Content Development Editor: Alex Sorrentino
Technical Editor: Nidhisha Shetty
Copy Editor: Safis Editing
Proofreader: Safis Editing
Indexer: Tejal Daruwale Soni
Graphics: Tom Scaria, Sandip Tadge
Production Coordinator: Sandip Tadge

First published: January 2019

Production reference: 1240119

Published by Packt Publishing Ltd.
Livery Place
35 Livery Street
Birmingham
B3 2PB, UK.

ISBN 978-1-78913-939-6

www.packtpub.com

`mapt.io`

Mapt is an online digital library that gives you full access to over 5,000 books and videos, as well as industry leading tools to help you plan your personal development and advance your career. For more information, please visit our website.

Why subscribe?

- Spend less time learning and more time coding with practical eBooks and Videos from over 4,000 industry professionals

- Improve your learning with Skill Plans built especially for you

- Get a free eBook or video every month

- Mapt is fully searchable

- Copy and paste, print, and bookmark content

Packt.com

Did you know that Packt offers eBook versions of every book published, with PDF and ePub files available? You can upgrade to the eBook version at `www.packt.com` and as a print book customer, you are entitled to a discount on the eBook copy. Get in touch with us at `customercare@packtpub.com` for more details.

At `www.packt.com`, you can also read a collection of free technical articles, sign up for a range of free newsletters, and receive exclusive discounts and offers on Packt books and eBooks.

Contributors

About the author

Koshik Raj is an information security enthusiast who holds a master's degree in computer science and information security. He has a background of working with RSA, a network security company. He has also worked as a senior developer in CoWrks, Bengaluru.

Koshik has been studying blockchain technology since he was introduced to Bitcoin while pursuing his master's. He is currently advising an educational start-up looking to implement blockchain technology in the education space. He is also setting up a blockchain incubation center for students and researchers in Bengaluru to aid mentorship and networking, and even the launching and marketing of their ideas.

Writing a book was harder than I imagined, but the support of the talented team at Packt Publishing made this a smooth journey. I would like to thank my development editor, Alex Sorrentino, and tech reviewer, Pranav Burnwal, for helping me to tremendously improve the quality of the book. Special thanks to my patient project editor, Kishor Rit, who kept me on track with proper guidance. I'm also thankful to Savvy and Suzanne for guiding me at the early stages.

I thank my entire family, including my mom, uncle, sister, aunts, and cousins, for supporting me in whatever way possible. Thanks to my roommates and friends for understanding my busy schedule during the weekends.

Finally, I would like to dedicate this book to my late dad, Vasanth Raj, who believed in me and supported me in every decision of my life.

About the reviewer

Pranav Burnwal has a background in research and development and has been working with cutting-edge technologies for a good number of years now. The technologies he has worked with include blockchain, big data, analytics (log and data), cloud computing, message queues, NoSQL, and web servers. He has worked across various domains, including BFSI, HLS, FMCG, and automobiles, to name a few.

Pranav is an active community member in multiple communities, and the region head for **Blockchain Education Network** (**BEN**), a registered NGO and worldwide network of people working with blockchain. He has also organized multiple meetups and a start-up weekend in India.

Pranav has been an active trainer in the blockchain space for three exciting years, for audiences ranging from junior developers to senior VPs. This has also given him insights into how people understand new and complex technologies, which helped him frame the book in the best interests of the readers.

> *To my lovely mother, Glory. Thank you for believing in me.*

Packt is searching for authors like you

If you're interested in becoming an author for Packt, please visit `authors.packtpub.com` and apply today. We have worked with thousands of developers and tech professionals, just like you, to help them share their insight with the global tech community. You can make a general application, apply for a specific hot topic that we are recruiting an author for, or submit your own idea.

Table of Contents

Preface

Blockchain technology can be very intimidating when encountered for the first time. But in reality, the technology itself is just a combination of three popular concepts: cryptography, peer-to-peer networking, and game theory. Although these may seem complicated at first glance, a basic understanding of these three required concepts will help you to build a strong foundation that once you've completed, can be used as a cornerstone for understanding blockchain technology at an advanced level.

This book helps you to understand the concepts of blockchain technology, and introduces you to both cryptocurrency, as well as several blockchain platforms. It also gives an in-depth analysis of the potential and concerns of the technology so that blockchain can be adopted where its implementation actually adds value.

Who this book is for

This book is designed for anyone who is looking to dive into the foundations of the blockchain technology space. Although this book builds a foundation for blockchain technology for beginners, it can also be used by blockchain developers as a quick reference guide and also to gain deeper insights on a few exciting topics of the technology.

What this book covers

Chapter 1, *Introduction*, gives an overview of blockchain technology by exploring some of the basic topics, such as its definition and history, the motivation behind it, its characteristics, and the different types of blockchain.

Chapter 2, *A Bit of Cryptography*, explores the fundamentals of cryptography with regards to blockchain technology, along with a few practical examples.

Chapter 3, *Cryptography in Blockchain*, explains how blockchain technology makes use of cryptographic primitives, such as **hash functions** and **digital signatures**.

Chapter 4, *Networking in Blockchain*, introduces peer-to-peer networking concepts to achieve decentralization in the blockchain network. This chapter also covers how blockchain is maintained in a decentralized network with the help of an example application.

Chapter 5, *Cryptocurrency*, dives into the original and best implementation of the blockchain technology by exploring the concepts of Bitcoin, and helps to differentiate cryptocurrency from traditional digital currencies.

Chapter 6, *Diving into Blockchain – Proof of Existence*, introduces decentralized application development using MultiChain blockchain framework by implementing a use case: Proof of Existence.

Chapter 7, *Diving into Blockchain – Proof of Ownership*, dives further into decentralized application development by introducing the concepts of smart contracts on the NEO and Ethereum blockchain platforms by implementing a use case, looking specifically at Proof of Ownership.

Chapter 8, *Blockchain Projects*, explores the opportunities in the field of blockchain by classifying and understanding some well-known blockchain projects.

Chapter 9, *Blockchain Optimizations and Enhancements*, focuses on the techniques that can optimize blockchain applications, while introducing a few enhancements of existing blockchain applications in order to add interesting functionalities.

Chapter 10, *Blockchain Security*, gives an insight as to the level of security required blockchain technology by pointing out possible attacks and how they can be prevented.

Chapter 11, *When Shouldn't We Use Blockchain?*, lists the characteristics of blockchain technology and explains several decision models you'll need to consider when picking the right use case for a blockchain application.

Chapter 12, *Blockchain Use Cases*, analyzes a selection of genuine blockchain use cases with the help of decision models, and looks at creating implementations for those use cases.

To get the most out of this book

Although this book builds a foundation of knowledge about cryptography and peer-to-peer networking concepts, hands-on Python programming experience and theoretical networking knowledge would be an advantage.

Most of the applications used in this book can be executed on any platform, the examples shown are executed using Ubuntu 16.04.5 LTS.

You should be comfortable with installing applications with the help of package management tools such as APT on Ubuntu or equivalent tools on Mac or Windows.

Since most of the application source code is hosted on GitHub, you should be familiar with the Git version control system.

Download the example code files

You can download the example code files for this book from your account at
`www.packt.com`. If you purchased this book elsewhere, you can visit
`www.packt.com/support` and register to have the files emailed directly to you.

You can download the code files by following these steps:

1. Log in or register at `www.packt.com`.
2. Select the **SUPPORT** tab.
3. Click on **Code Downloads & Errata**.
4. Enter the name of the book in the **Search** box and follow the onscreen instructions.

Once the file is downloaded, please make sure that you unzip or extract the folder using the latest version of:

- WinRAR/7-Zip for Windows
- Zipeg/iZip/UnRarX for Mac
- 7-Zip/PeaZip for Linux

The code bundle for the book is also hosted on GitHub
at `https://github.com/PacktPublishing/Foundations-of-Blockchain`. In case there's an update to the code, it will be updated on the existing GitHub repository.

We also have other code bundles from our rich catalog of books and videos available
at `https://github.com/PacktPublishing/`. Check them out!

Download the color images

We also provide a PDF file that has color images of the screenshots/diagrams used in this book. You can download it here: `https://www.packtpub.com/sites/default/files/downloads/9781789139396_ColorImages.pdf`.

Conventions used

There are a number of text conventions used throughout this book.

`CodeInText`: Indicates code words in text, database table names, folder names, filenames, file extensions, pathnames, dummy URLs, user input, and Twitter handles. Here is an example: "Mount the downloaded `WebStorm-10*.dmg` disk image file as another disk in your system."

A block of code is set as follows:

```
from Crypto.Hash import SHA256

hash_object = SHA256.new(data=b'First')
print(hash_object.hexdigest())
```

When we wish to draw your attention to a particular part of a code block, the relevant lines or items are set in bold:

```
from Crypto.Hash import SHA256

hash_object = SHA256.new(data=b'First')
print(hash_object.hexdigest())
```

Any command-line input or output is written as follows:

```
$ curl -X POST http://localhost:10332 -H 'Content-Type: application/json'
-d '{ "jsonrpc": "2.0", "id": 5, "method": "getversion", "params": [] }'
```

Bold: Indicates a new term, an important word, or words that you see onscreen. For example, words in menus or dialog boxes appear in the text like this. Here is an example: "A different header is created by altering a variable field called **nonce** in the header."

Warnings or important notes appear like this.

Tips and tricks appear like this.

Get in touch

Feedback from our readers is always welcome.

General feedback: If you have questions about any aspect of this book, mention the book title in the subject of your message and email us at `customercare@packtpub.com`.

Errata: Although we have taken every care to ensure the accuracy of our content, mistakes do happen. If you have found a mistake in this book, we would be grateful if you would report this to us. Please visit `www.packt.com/submit-errata`, selecting your book, clicking on the Errata Submission Form link, and entering the details.

Piracy: If you come across any illegal copies of our works in any form on the Internet, we would be grateful if you would provide us with the location address or website name. Please contact us at `copyright@packt.com` with a link to the material.

If you are interested in becoming an author: If there is a topic that you have expertise in and you are interested in either writing or contributing to a book, please visit `authors.packtpub.com`.

Reviews

Please leave a review. Once you have read and used this book, why not leave a review on the site that you purchased it from? Potential readers can then see and use your unbiased opinion to make purchase decisions, we at Packt can understand what you think about our products, and our authors can see your feedback on their book. Thank you!

For more information about Packt, please visit `packt.com`.

Introduction 1

This book was created to help you explore the exciting blockchain technology, and in this first chapter, we're going to dive into its foundational concepts. The idea is to present a fairly broad overview of blockchain, allowing you to be fully prepared for the topics that we'll cover in more depth in later chapters. Since our intention is to introduce blockchain, the following topics will be covered throughout this chapter:

- What blockchain is and isn't
- How blockchains are different from databases
- The history, motivations, and characteristics of blockchain
- The different types of blockchain
- Overview of blocks and how they work
- The influence of Moore's law on blockchain technology

We'll start with the basics of blockchain, including its myths and history. We'll explore the ideas behind some key blockchain concepts, we'll end with an overview of how exactly the blockchain technology works. The topics in this chapter are designed to give you enough motivation and confidence to feel comfortable with the topics we'll be discussing later in the book.

What blockchain is

Although blockchain has a variety of definitions, a blockchain can best be described as a data structure of blocks that are chained together to form a collection of records, called a ledger, with cryptography being a key ingredient in the process. A blockchain doesn't have a storage mechanism; instead, it has a set of protocols that govern the way in which information is forged. So, a blockchain can be stored in flat files or in a database.

Blockchain technology gained popularity due to the fact that its integrity can't easily be compromised. A compromised blockchain can be recognized for what it is, and rejected quite easily by anyone in a network. This integrity is achieved by cryptography, which is what binds the blocks together; we'll study this idea of cryptography in Chapter 2, *A Bit of Cryptography*.

Blockchain's promise of providing such robust integrity is what eventually paved the way for the idea of sharing chains of data in untrusted **peer-to-peer (P2P)** networks. Validation of the blocks in a blockchain is what makes sure that a blockchain has a valid global state that can be accepted by everyone. Due to a blockchain's ability to share information in an open P2P network without any central authority governing it, the technology can have many different applications; however, the technology could not simply just be deployed to these applications immediately without any troubleshooting. Although blockchain technology, from the beginning, had a huge role to play in the decentralization of applications, it still faced several challenges with regards to its application in trustless environments. One of the biggest challenges was keeping a blockchain consistent across all the participants of a P2P network. This was solved by creating a consensus algorithm, which agrees on how the blocks should be appended to grow the chain in a trustless environment.

The term *blockchain* actually entails a number of concepts, including P2P network management, consensus mechanism, and more, all contributing to the creation of a decentralized application.

What blockchain isn't

As we've just discussed, despite blockchain being fascinating due to its cryptography-based security, decentralized nature, and nearly immutable data storage mechanism, it's very important to understand its limitations.

Blockchain's ideal implementation is with atomic events or transactions, where minimal information about an event is stored as a transaction; these transactions can be clubbed together in a single block and added to a blockchain. Although a blockchain network is good at handling a global state, it would not add much value when it comes to storing data in bulk, as there would be scalability issues. It's very important to understand when best to apply blockchain technology to develop an application. We will explore when not to use blockchain in Chapter 11, *When Shouldn't We Use Blockchain?*.

Blockchain definitions

You'll remember that one of the very first things we did in this chapter was note there are several definitions of the word *blockchain*. Before we move on, let's have a look at several definitions of the word:

> *"A blockchain is a peer-to-peer distributed ledger forged by consensus, combined with a system for "smart contracts" and other assistive technologies."*
>
> *- hyperledger.org*

> *"A blockchain is a specific form or subset of distributed ledger technologies, which constructs a chronological chain of blocks, hence the name "block-chain.""*
>
> *- Antony Lewis, the Director of Research at R3*

> *"The blockchain data structure is an ordered, back-linked list of blocks."*
>
> *- Andreas Antonopoulos, a popular Bitcoin evangelist*

How are blockchains different from databases?

A blockchain is a read- and append-only storage methodology. This means that blocks can only be created and read in the blockchain ledger. Blocks in a blockchain cannot be updated or deleted; blocks can only be appended to the end of a blockchain. There is no access control in a public blockchain as it is open for both read and write operations.

On the other hand, relational databases follow the **create, read, update, and delete** (CRUD) operation model. Unlike the case with a blockchain, each database has an administrator when it is created, and they will assign access control to the other users. Relational databases are mostly maintained by a single entity who is in control of all the application data, whereas blockchain technology was designed for decentralized applications.

Figure 1.1 should help you to visualize the difference between a centralized database architecture and a blockchain architecture:

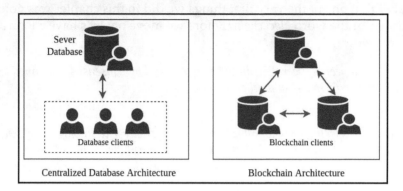

Figure 1.1: Diagrams showing the architectures of centralized databases versus Blockchain

 Note: Blockchain inherently provides **immutability**, **security**, and **redundancy** (**ISR**), whereas traditional databases need additional investment to provide ISR for the data they hold. One of the main advantages of blockchain-based solutions over databases is that little to no investment is required in the management of infrastructure.

History of blockchain

We know that blockchain technology now has its main application where the tracking of transactions or events in a decentralized network is concerned; currently, the greatest scope to be found for this use case is in the area of finance. However, as a matter of fact, blockchain technology didn't appear as we know it and use it today until quite recently. The first ever idea of maintaining a chain of blocks to construct a tamper-proof timestamp of digital documents came about in 1991. But the concept wasn't popularized until an author with the pseudonym of **Satoshi Nakamoto** – whose identity is still not known today – showcased blockchains and their true use in decentralized networks in 2008, by publishing a paper titled *Bitcoin: A Peer-to-Peer Electronic Cash System* (`https://bitcoin.org/bitcoin.pdf`).

Later, in 2009, a reference implementation of blockchain technology was created by Satoshi Nakamoto. This was called Bitcoin. This was the first – and still remains the most popular – implementation of a blockchain-based electronic cash system. Satoshi took inspiration from several previous inventions, such as b-money and Hashcash, to create a decentralized digital currency.

Note: Although Bitcoin was responsible for the cryptocurrency revolution, there were several attempts to popularize electronic cash using cryptographic protocols that predated it. DigiCash is one such popular attempt from an American scientist named David Chaum. There was also a decentralized digital currency called Bit Gold, which was proposed by Nick Szabo, that had a similar architecture to Bitcoin.

Bitcoin was released in 2009 when Satoshi made the first transaction, which was inserted into the first block of the Bitcoin blockchain. This block is called the genesis block, and is the proof of the entire blockchain's legitimacy. Satoshi stopped contributing to the Bitcoin project in 2011 and is now allowing the open community to contribute to the project. Since then, it has grown from being a fairly simple digital currency to a resilient protocol that has become the reference implementation for every blockchain application. Although Bitcoin's market value is volatile, it's nearing the market value of $200 billion US dollars as of late 2018, which is almost half of the entire cryptocurrency market.

Bitcoin was the first decentralized digital currency to solve the problem of the double-spending attack. Maintaining an open distributed blockchain with a consensus for validating the block was the main thing that made Bitcoin a practically implementable decentralized currency. Bitcoin made use of a consensus algorithm called the **proof-of-work** (**PoW**) algorithm to prove that a node has actually worked to create a new block of the blockchain. This concept was also applied in an implementation called Hashcash, which was proposed to limit email spam by forcing the spammer to do some work before sending each email. This system prevented spammers from sending email in bulk, as a computation task was required before each email was sent. All the receiver needed to do was verify the work done by the sender. Similarly, the PoW consensus algorithm implemented in Bitcoin prevents any node from flooding the blockchain with its own created blocks, thus preventing any single entity from dominating the blockchain.

Blockchain 2.0

Bitcoin was what really gave birth to blockchain technology, and since then, several new applications of the distributed blockchain database have emerged, most notably during early 2014. This era is widely known as the era of blockchain 2.0. Namecoin was one of the first concepts to emerge. It expanded the scope of Bitcoin's blockchain and was introduced as a distributed naming system based on Bitcoin. However, unlike Bitcoin, it was able to store data as key-value pairs in the public blockchain. This concept influenced a number of blockchain 2.0 applications that would go on to gain popularity.

One of the most popular enhancements that came with blockchain 2.0 was the introduction of smart contracts. Several blockchain platforms were developed that allowed the user to write higher-level scripts and not worry about the actual blockchain implementation. One of the platforms that was most successful in doing this was Ethereum, which was proposed in late 2013 by Vitalik Buterin. The intention of Ethereum was to make the best use of the technology that Bitcoin used. Bitcoin's initial implementation was intended for the flow of digital currency. Now, although a scripting language was implemented for other applications, such as asset transfer, it was very primitive and only had a few use cases. Vitalik Buterin, the co-founder of Ethereum, suggested that Bitcoin needed a scripting language for decentralized application development in order to increase its scope. Failing to gain agreement, Vitalik proposed the development of a new platform with a more general scripting language. This platform, Ethereum, gained popularity due to the implementation of smart contracts in its environment. Smart contracts are high-level scripts that run on the **Ethereum Virtual Machine** (**EVM**). A number of decentralized applications have been developed using the Ethereum platform.

The Ethereum platform inspired developers to come up with a framework that would use Bitcoin's core protocol and build a platform to develop decentralized applications. This was a revolutionary approach, as the technology would be used to modify any application where having a third party would be both expensive and redundant.

In fact, there are plenty of motives that drive developers to integrate blockchain technology in their existing applications. In the next section, we'll explain this in more depth.

Several blockchain platforms have been created to build scalable decentralized applications; some of the most popular ones are listed here:

- **Corda**: This is a distributed ledger platform designed to record, manage, and automate legal agreements between business partners. It was designed by R3 in collaboration with the world's biggest financial institutions, which makes Corda suitable for financial enterprises shifting toward distributed ledger technology.
- **Hyperledger**: This is an open source effort to advance cross-industry blockchain technologies. It's hosted by the Linux Foundation and achieves collaboration between various industries and organizations. IBM and Intel, for instance, are active contributors to Hyperledger projects. There are a number of Hyperledger projects, all aimed at solving different enterprise-level problems using blockchain.

- **Multichain**: This is a simple and powerful private blockchain framework that is compatible with Bitcoin. It has support for complete asset cycle management. Due to its support for access control, it's an ideal framework for developing permissioned blockchain applications.
- **NEO**: Formerly known as Antshares, this application is often called "the Ethereum of China." It uses blockchain technology and digital identity to digitize assets.

The motivations behind blockchain

Every new innovation is the result of an attempt to solve a problem. Blockchain technology is no exception. It's quite evident after learning about the evolution of blockchain technology that it arose because of a need to address the inevitability of uncertainty in the existing economy.

Uncertainty could never be eliminated, but only lowered: there have always been institutions that have acted as third-party lawmakers to lower uncertainty, or lack of trust, whenever there was a need for an agreement between parties. A typical example would be buying an item on eBay. You would always need as much certainty as possible about the trade. One party expects fair goods, and the other expects agreed money. Now, though the buyer and seller have no reason to trust each other, they complete their trade as they trust the third party, which is eBay, who assures them both of a legitimate trade. Again, there was a need to trust these "medium" institutions. Trusting an institution requires a lot of research and knowledge. Blockchain promised to overcome these issues by implementing applications in a decentralized and secure way, assuring some level of certainty. This was one of the main reasons behind the widespread adoption of blockchain in a trustless society.

We know that blockchain is an ideal technology for implementation in trustless environments. However, the blockchain alone is not responsible for the success of the complete implementation. It's assisted by several other protocols that make it the robust and resilient technology it is. Blockchain can be implemented in trustless networks mainly due to the decentralization of computation in dense P2P networks and the maintenance of a secure and publicly distributed ledger that gives complete transparency over the entire blockchain. The P2P protocol makes sure that every node holds the latest state of the blockchain.

The need for decentralization is the key motivation behind the blockchain technology, and decentralization is achieved by distributing the computation tasks to all the nodes of the blockchain network. Decentralization solves several problems of traditional systems; the single point of failure is one such problem. For example, in a centralized system such as a bank, the user would always communicate with the same third-party bank to fetch their account details. Although this transaction may be possible almost every time, 100% uptime is not guaranteed, as this server is centralized and has just a few backup servers for load balancing. There could well be a situation where all the servers could be flooded with requests, resulting in crashes and server shutdown. This downtime is something that's inevitable, even in perfectly architected servers. If the same scenario was faced in a decentralized network, it wouldn't be an issue, because all the transaction data would be distributed across all the nodes, meaning that each node can act as a backup node in case of failure, maintaining the integrity of the data (another key benefit of blockchain-based solutions). This is something that's achieved by maintaining a distributed ledger of blockchain data. Blockchain immutability, which is a key factor in trusting the integrity of the blockchain, ensures the integrity of the ledger, which is publicly accessible to all nodes.

Characteristics of blockchain

A blockchain, put simply, is a chain of blocks that are secured to each other via cryptography. Cryptography hash pointers are used as references to link each block in the blockchain of the public ledger. Although this sounds very secure since no intruder would be able to break the blockchain and insert their own versions of the blocks, it's not *completely* secure. Since the ledger is entirely transparent and public, any node could insert their block to reproduce the entire blockchain and create their own version of it. Eventually, they could later propagate the block to every node in the network and prove that their blockchain is the legitimate one. This shows that immutability cannot be achieved just by connecting all the blocks and forming a secure ledger. Achieving immutability needs to be assisted by some kind of decentralized economic mechanism that gives a fair chance to each and every node in the network to vote on block creation, and also makes it harder to reconstruct blocks once they are appended.

Satoshi Nakamoto's proposed solution to this problem is the only reason that Bitcoin is implementable in a decentralized environment. The PoW consensus algorithm used in Bitcoin was the first – and is still the best known – solution. It promises a high degree of immutability to the public ledger and secures it, even in a trustless network. In terms of cryptocurrency, the nodes that perform PoW are called **mining nodes**. As the name suggests, mining is the act of forging new blocks to be appended to the blockchain. The amount of work that it takes to mine ensures that the blockchain is immutable and that tampering with any past transactions is nearly impossible.

This is because of the fact that any node that wants to tamper with past data should be able to reconstruct all the blocks by providing PoW and competing with all the other mining nodes. This is nearly impossible unless the node in question owns the majority of the computing power of the network, in which case, the attacker would stand a chance of beating all the nodes. This is why Bitcoin's consensus algorithm is widely used in public blockchain applications to achieve higher immutability of records.

However, immutability is not the only characteristic exhibited by blockchain technology. Due to the decentralized nature of the blockchain, every single transaction in the blockchain is replicated across all the nodes of a network. The replication of information provides greater **robustness** to the blockchain. Replicated transactions must be validated by every node to achieve consensus. This ensures that the transactions are publicly visible and all the blockchain data is **transparent** to the network. The transparency provided by the blockchain can be a boon for some use cases and a curse for others. This is why variants of blockchain were created, as described in a later section of this chapter.

All these characteristics of the blockchain make it a perfect public ledger, or an effective instance of **distributed ledger technology** (**DLT**). Bitcoin's blockchain, along with its consensus mechanism, is the most resilient DLT to date.

Background of DLT

Ever since the invention of networking, there has been debate about the centralization and decentralization of computing architecture. We have seen interest between these two computing architecture models fluctuate over time. Mainframe architectures were used in enterprises to house great amounts of computing power, memory, and storage. They were largely centralized, and terminals without much computing power were used to connect to these machines in order to perform required operations. Then, personal computers were introduced for household usage, with enough computation power, memory, and storage to perform basic operations. This gave rise to the client-server architecture, in which clients communicate with the server to perform computation. The server usually performs heavy computing in a distributed system and syncs the result with the client.

The cloud computing architecture provides easy access to the server from any computing device, since the architecture itself is globally accessible. However, a cloud computing architecture is centralized, and its hardware resources are distributed and not transparent to the client. There is still a lack of trust between cloud vendors and end users. This is the reason why we are witnessing a transition from other computing models to decentralization. DLT is the key to achieving this milestone and ushering in the age of decentralization.

A distributed ledger is, at its core, a replicated and shared digital database that is spread across geographical regions. A P2P network and a consensus algorithm are required to ensure an effective distributed ledger. Blockchain technology is one of the techniques used to achieve a distributed ledger, but it is not the only data structure of DLT:

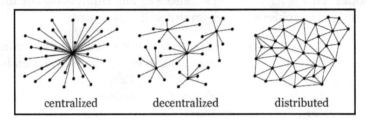

centralized   decentralized   distributed

Figure 1.2: The evolution of computer architectures, up to the birth of DLT (source: https://en.wikipedia.org)

Background: The earliest thing that could be compared to DLT dates back to 500 AD when the Pacific island of Yap depended upon a currency called Rai, which were stones that could weigh more than 200 kilograms. Since the stones were incredibly heavy to carry, ownership of Rai was memorized by every adult of the island. The oral ownership record made sure that there was no need for a single party to maintain records of who had Rai.

The different types of blockchain

The growing number of use cases for blockchain, as well as an increasing awareness of its limitations, has given rise to a variety of successful blockchain implementations. In this section, we'll be trying to grasp the essence of each one of them.

Public blockchain (permissionless)

The blockchain concept has been widely used and adapted due to its transparency and how every node participates in contributing to the growth of the blockchain. The early blockchain model, the product of Bitcoin, is completely open and permissionless and is popularly known as a public blockchain. Public blockchains are popular due to the impartial way in which the nodes are treated.

Public blockchains work seamlessly in trustless networks due to the immutable nature of the records. Bitcoin, Ethereum, and several other projects that have inherited PoW-like consensus algorithms ensure that recorded transactions are non-editable.

Public blockchains are ideal for cryptocurrency projects where recorded transactions should not be modified. However, public blockchains often face scalability issues at some point if the necessary changes aren't implemented. One of the most visible issues of Bitcoin is its mining approach (PoW), which is very expensive in terms of the electricity required for miners to solve the puzzle. The average time for block creation is 10 minutes. Therefore, the difficulty level of mining has been adjusted to maintain this time. This has resulted in a very expensive PoW environment due to competition among miners. We'll not be able to predict the future of Bitcoin or any other public blockchain due to these complex attributes, and only the natural evolution of the technology can decide its fate.

Due to these pros and cons, the permissionless or public blockchain is well suited for transparent applications, where the blockchain should inherently secure the system since the network is trustless.

Private blockchain (permissioned)

Private blockchains were introduced mostly to widen the scope of blockchain technology. The permissioned blockchain, as the name suggests, uses the opposite approach to that of the public blockchain. Private blockchains came about mainly to solve some of the issues we saw in public blockchains and to make blockchain technology scalable.

Permissioned blockchains introduce access control to provide specific access to the participants in a network. Each permissioned blockchain will have an administrator who assigns roles for the participants in the network. Permissioned blockchains ensure that bad actors are not a part of the validation or block-creation processes and thus eliminate any potential attacks on the blockchain. A network involving a permissioned blockchain is mostly a trusted network.

Private blockchains are suitable for organizations where a ledger only needs to be shared internally. Permissioned blockchains are often mutable or not strictly immutable, and their transactions can be modified with some effort; this is in stark contrast to public blockchains, where this is nearly impossible. Permissioned blockchains are still decentralized ledgers, but they will have some nodes with limited capability within the organization, whereas nodes in public blockchains are treated impartially.

 Note: Private blockchains do not use Bitcoin's PoW consensus algorithm as their consensus algorithm. In fact, private blockchains were created to eliminate the costly consensus approach of public blockchains, to make blockchain technology applicable in trusted environments.

Consortium blockchain

The consortium blockchain is a hybrid blockchain that is semi-decentralized. It combines the best features of both permissionless and permissioned blockchains. Instead of assigning most tasks to a single organization, a consortium blockchain assigns the same tasks to nodes maintained by multiple organizations. Instead of having a single validator node, there can be multiple nodes. Although a consortium blockchain is permissioned, it's more decentralized than a private blockchain.

Overview of blocks

Now that we have a fair understanding of blockchain, we're going to give an overview of blocks, which are responsible for building a blockchain.

Block attributes

If we consider a blockchain as a data structure, then the blocks are aggregated sets of data that are used for formation of the blockchain. Blockchain formation is similar to linked list formation, where each node has a reference to the next node in the sequence. In the case of blockchain, each block has a reference to the previous node, thus forming a link all the way to the initial block (known as the **genesis block**) of the chain. As we mentioned earlier, a blockchain can be stored in either flat file or database format. Bitcoin uses `LevelDB` to store metadata about all the blocks that are downloaded to the disk.

Just like a linked list node, each block has a pointer, which is the identifier of the block. These are just hashed values of the block's header data. More detail about hashing will be covered in `Chapter 2`, *A Bit of Cryptography*. We can consider the hash as a unique identifier of a fixed size that represents each block; no two blocks will have the same identifier. Since all the blocks are linked together by this hash value, each block will have the identifier of the previous block. The previous block is referred to as the parent block, and each block can have only one parent.

Each block could also be referenced by the height of the blockchain. This height is nothing but the distance of the block, or the block count, from the genesis block. Height is an important attribute of the blockchain, as it's easier to refer to a block with a plain number rather than a lengthy hash value. The block hash is not a hash value of the entire block, but rather the hash value of the block header, which consists only of metadata. In Bitcoin, a SHA256 hashing algorithm is used to hash the block header and to create a unique identifier for the block.

Structure of the block

Although all blockchains consist of linking blocks together to form an immutable ledger, different block structures can be adopted depending on the application. Permissioned and permissionless blockchains, for instance, have slight variations in their block structure. We'

We'll be using Bitcoin's permissionless block structure as a reference to try and identify its characteristics:

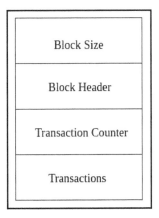

Figure 1.3: Structure of a block

A block consists of the components mentioned in *Figure 1.3*. **Block Header** and **Transactions** are the most important parts of the block, as they are responsible for the hash value, which is the identity of the block. The **Block Size** is the size of the entire block. The **Block Header** contains all the metadata of the block, and the **Transaction Counter** has the count of transactions. Finally, all the **Transactions** are stored in the block.

As mentioned before, a blockchain starts with an initial block called the genesis block. If the chain is traversed backward from any given block, it will end up at the genesis block, proving that the entire chain is legitimate and valid. The genesis block is often statically coded in a public or permissionless blockchain, but it's created by the first participant in the case of the permissioned blockchain.

Block header

The block header, as stated before, consists of the metadata of the block. This holds the information that's needed to link the blocks in the blockchain:

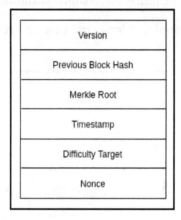

Figure 1.4: Structure of a block header

Each block header will have the components outlined in *Figure 1.4*. These are the minimum fields required in a permissionless blockchain, such as Bitcoin, to efficiently create a block that can be appended to an immutable blockchain. The **Previous Block Hash** field is a reference to the last block created. The **Merkle Root** is the value of the Merkle hash tree; it summarizes all the transactions in the block. **Timestamp**, **Difficulty Target**, and **Nonce** are used by the PoW consensus algorithm to solve the hash puzzle. We'll be revisiting these concepts in more depth throughout the book.

 Note: Unlike in a permissionless blockchain, where consensus algorithms are used to generate blocks, permissioned blockchains use the signature of the block creator to represent the block identity. However, blocks in permissioned blockchains maintain previous block identifiers, just as permissionless blockchains do.

Linking blocks

As we know, blocks are linked in a blockchain using references, just like in a linked list, but here the blocks are linked by referencing the hash value (identifier) of the previous block. Each full node in a blockchain network will maintain a complete blockchain and append a new block whenever it has one to append. Due to the decentralized nature of the blockchain, each node will verify the block before linking it to the local blockchain record.

The computed hash value of each block is the combination of the hash of the previous block and its own block data. This results in a dependency between neighboring blocks and nearly unbreakable links:

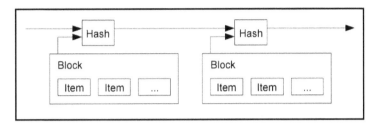

Figure 1.5: Linking blocks using hashes, from Bitcoin: A Peer-to-Peer Electronic Cash System, S. Nakamoto

Satoshi explained how the concept of timestamping should be used. All the items are hashed and the block is timestamped, meaning that the subsequent block will include this timestamp, creating an ordered chain of blocks.

Each node in the blockchain network follows a simple process for appending new blocks to its existing local blockchain. Whenever a node receives a block from the network, it checks for the previous block hash. If the hash value matches with the hash value of the last block on the node's local blockchain, then the node accepts this block and appends it to the current blockchain. As long as this is the longest known blockchain, the blocks would be considered valid by all the peers in the network in a PoW-based blockchain.

Influence of Moore's law on blockchain technology

Gordon Moore, the co-founder of Fairchild Semiconductor and Intel, observed that the number of components per electrical integrated circuit would grow by at least a factor of two for every year. Back in 1965, he also projected that this rate of growth would continue for at least another decade. Over the years, he revised the forecast to doubling every two years. This observation was geared toward the number of transistors in a dense integrated circuit and has been used in the semiconductor industry to set targets for research and development. But it isn't only limited to the chip-manufacturing field; it has also been used to make observations about technological and social change, as well as productivity and economic growth.

Moore's law has been adapted and applied to approximate the rate of change in network capacity, pixels in images, storage device size, and much more. Blockchain is a technology of the future that might have to overcome multiple limitations in order to achieve healthy long-term development. Moore's law would help in deciding the complexity required for any blockchain application so that the application doesn't have to struggle with future scalability issues.

Since every node in the network maintains the complete blockchain ledger, blockchain data keeps increasing in size as time goes on. This raises some concerns regarding scalability, as each node needs to maintain the blockchain locally (such is the nature of the distributed network). Satoshi Nakamoto had mentioned that the growth of the block header size would be around 4.2 MB per year, and Moore's law would guarantee growth of at least 1.2 GB RAM (in 2008) per year, which should not pose any problems for block storage even if they are maintained in node memory.

Public blockchains, such as Bitcoin, have to deal with the hash rate of the hardware for their consensus algorithms. Bitcoin-mining hardware has been able to keep up with Moore's law, providing the required hash rate in accordance with the growing difficulty rate. However, the future of Bitcoin mining relies on Moore's law and the hardware being able to keep up with the difficulty without causing much loss to the miners:

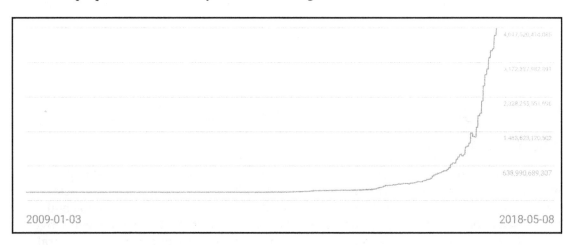

Figure 1.6: The exponential growth of Bitcoin's difficulty target (source: blockchain.info)

Summary

This chapter has introduced us to everything we need to fuel the study of blockchain in the coming chapters. Having got to know the background of blockchain technology, including its purposes and how it works, we should now fully understand the potential of this technology and how it can solve problems in some of our current systems.

Now that we have a fair understanding of the technology, in the next chapter, Chapter 2, *A Bit of Cryptography*, we will walk through the concepts surrounding the backbone of blockchain technology. In that chapter, we'll be exploring the building blocks for an understanding of blockchain.

A Bit of Cryptography

2

This chapter will cover all the basics of cryptography that are required for you to understand the vital role it plays in blockchain technology. We will delve deeply into all the aspects of cryptography that blockchain relies on. We will explain a few concepts in practical terms so that we can implement them with ease in later chapters. These include the following:

- Cryptography in blockchain
- Classical cryptography
- Cryptographic primitives
- Merkle trees
- Encoding schemes

Modern cryptography is the study of private or secure communication. The fundamental objective of cryptography is to enable two people to communicate over an unsecure medium. This is achieved by encrypting a plaintext from the sender to form a ciphertext that can only be decrypted by the receiver, with whom the sender shares a secret. However, third parties can access the channel by which the ciphertext is transported, but the text doesn't have any meaning to it, so it doesn't matter whether the channel is secure or not. Cryptography has evolved and can now be applied in a wide variety of fields, including blockchain. We will start our overview of cryptography with an underlying and fundamental cipher implementation, and then we will move on to advanced and modern cryptography topics.

Cryptography is crucial for information security services such as authentication, confidentiality, and integrity. In the 19th century, **Auguste Kerckhoffs** outlined what has come to be known as Kerckhoffs's principle: A cryptosystem should be secure even if everything about the system, except the key, is public knowledge. The key is the only asset in cryptography that has to be kept secret and protected from intruder attacks.

Cryptography in blockchain

Although we have mentioned that cryptography is crucial to the success of blockchain technology, we haven't explored any topic in particular. Most cryptographic primitives have some role or other in the creation of a decentralized blockchain application. We will study all the primitives that contribute to blockchain in this chapter.

Hashing is used in most blockchain applications to create links between blocks. It is also used in consensus algorithms such as proof-of-work, which basically exploits the hashing power of the computing systems that form the blockchain network. Digital signatures are used to sign and verify events such as transactions. Asymmetric key cryptography is a core concept in blockchain applications that gives identity to the participants of the network or can prove the ownership of assets.

Hence, cryptography is an excellent tool for accomplishing some of the tasks required to replace trusted third parties and create a trustless environment in a decentralized network.

Classical cryptography

In this section, we'll look at a number of cryptographical techniques that have been used in historical ciphers. These ad hoc ciphers are not secure enough to be used in modern applications, but because of their simplicity, they can encourage us to learn more about cryptography. Exploring the weaknesses of classical cryptography also helps us to learn more about some of the principles of cryptography. Take a look at the following diagram:

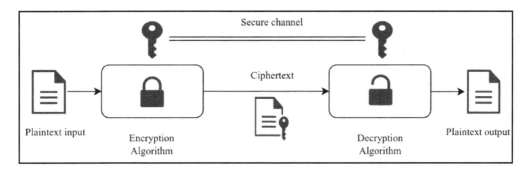

Figure 2.1: Model of conventional encryption

Figure 2.1 shows the conventional encryption model used to encrypt a plaintext using a secret key that is shared with the other user over a secure channel. The user who wants to read the text will decrypt the ciphertext using the secret key, which will return the original plaintext. The key is private, and the encryption and decryption algorithms are made public because it is impossible to decrypt the ciphertext without the key.

Two types of operation are used to transform plaintext to ciphertext: substitution and transposition. Both of these techniques ensure that the operation is reversible, and therefore they could be used in encryption algorithms.

A substitution cipher is an encryption method in which the characters in plaintext are replaced by other characters in a fixed manner. The simplest example of a substitution cipher is Caesar's cipher, where plaintext letters are substituted by shifting the alphabet by three places: the letter A is replaced with D, B with E, and so on. The obvious problem with this cipher is that the method is fixed and that there is no key involved. A variant of Caesar's cipher, called the Shift cipher, was introduced, where the amount of shift from the plaintext to the ciphertext varies, and this amount of shift can act as a key. Although this solved the immediate problem, it wasn't practical enough as the key could be guessed with a brute-force or an exhaustive search attack. The polyalphabetic cipher was the next stage in the evolution of ciphers. This cipher introduced a number of substitutions at different positions in the message.

A transposition cipher is an encryption method where the positions of plaintext letters are shifted according to a known system. Only the order of plaintext is altered. All the letters of the plaintext remain the same. The Rail Fence cipher and the Route cipher are two well-known transposition ciphers. This kind of cipher technique could be decrypted by finding the transposition patterns using anagramming.

Cryptographic primitives

Cryptographic primitives are low-level cryptographic algorithms that are used to construct cryptographic protocols used by applications. These are the building blocks of designing a cryptographic system. A designer planning to implement a cryptographic protocol in a system doesn't have to worry about the low-level abstraction of the primitives and can concentrate entirely on building the application:

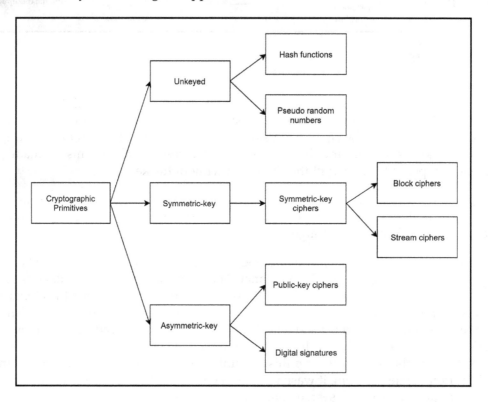

Figure 2.2: Taxonomy of cryptographic primitives

Figure 2.2 shows a detailed classification of cryptographic primitives. Blockchain technology makes use of most of these cryptographic primitives to achieve basic blockchain functionalities and secure data on the decentralized network: asymmetric cryptography for managing keys; digital signatures for transactions; and, most importantly, hashing, which is the backbone of the blockchain, are some of the most commonly used primitives of cryptography. We will cover all of these primitives, along with some others, to get a clear insight into them.

Symmetric key cryptography

The symmetric key is a key-based cryptography whose algorithms use the same keys to perform encryption of plaintext and decryption of the ciphertext. These keys are shared between two parties over a secure channel. Any participant owning the shared key can perform both encryption and decryption operations on the data. A symmetric key cipher can either be stream encrypted or block encrypted.

Symmetric key cryptography doesn't play any significant role in blockchain-based applications. However, it will provide a better insight into key-based cryptography before we look into asymmetric cryptography.

Stream cipher

The stream cipher uses symmetric key cryptography. Each plaintext character is encrypted one at a time, like a stream, to create the ciphertext. A keystream, or stream of characters, is used to encrypt the plaintext characters. A pseudorandom string is used, which acts as a keystream. This pseudorandom string is generated from a random seed value using digital shift registers (generator) as shown in *Figure 2.3*. The seed used is the secret key, which is also used to decrypt the created ciphertext.

For a stream cipher to be secure, its pseudorandom generator should be unpredictable, and its seed value used to generate the keystream should never be reused to reduce the possible attacks. Stream ciphers are generally faster than block ciphers and have low hardware requirements, as demonstrated in the following diagram:

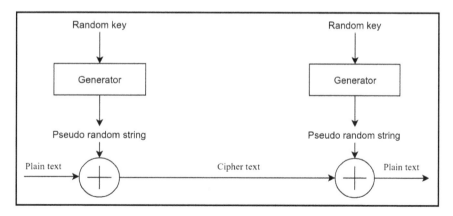

Figure 2.3: Flow diagram of the stream cipher

Block cipher

A block cipher is a cipher in which encryption is performed on a fixed-length block of characters from the plaintext. This cipher technique is widely used to implement encryption on bulk data. The usual block sizes are 64 bits, 128 bits, and 256 bits. For example, a 64-bit block cipher will take 64-bit plaintext as input and give out 64-bit ciphertext. The plaintext will pad some of the blocks in case some of the plaintext falls short of filling a block. Because the keys used in block ciphers are considerably long, they are robust against brute-force attacks. These ciphers are also the building blocks of other cryptographic protocols, such as hash functions and random number generators. **Data Encryption Standard (DES)**, **Advanced Encryption Standard (AES)**, **International Data Encryption Algorithm (IDEA)**, and **Blowfish** are some popular block cipher algorithms.

Data Encryption Standard

DES used to be the most widely used block cipher, and it was used as an industrial standard as well. It's still popular, but it has been replaced by other advanced block ciphers in many applications. DES uses 64-bit blocks with a 64-bit key. 8 bits in the key are used as parity bits for error detection, so the key size is technically 56 bits. It's been proven to be vulnerable to brute-force attacks and some cryptanalysis attacks, which is due to its limited key size. 3DES was introduced to overcome this problem by running DES three times with different 56-bit keys. But 3DES proved to be slower than other block ciphers, such as AES.

DES uses 8 bits of the key as parity bits for error detection while transmitting or storing the keys. The bits in the 8th, 16th, 24th, ..., 64th positions are used to calculate odd parity, that is, the number of 1s in each byte of the key is odd.

Advanced Encryption Standard

AES is one of the most widely used block ciphers in modern applications. The Rijndael algorithm was selected as the AES after a 5-year public competition to choose a replacement for DES. It has a fixed block size of 128 bits and varying key sizes of 128, 192, or 256 bits. AES is an iterated cipher: the number of rounds of iteration depends on the key length.

AES is secure against all known attacks. There appear to be no ways to attack AES that are faster than exhaustive search. The best ways to attack AES only apply to variants of the cipher that have the fewest iterations.

An example implementation of AES

Let's implement the AES cipher technique using a Python cryptographic library called `PyCryptodome`. We will be using the `PyCryptodome` library throughout this chapter to implement other ciphers and hashing algorithms.

PyCryptodome is a self-contained Python package of low-level cryptographic primitives. PyCryptodome is a forked project of the `PyCrypto` library and is an active project with extended primitive support. So, it is an almost drop-in replacement for the old `PyCrypto` library.

We will use the AES module from `Crypto.Cipher` package and we will also import a module from `Crypto.Random` package to generate a random key for AES, as follows:

```
from Crypto.Cipher import AES
from Crypto.Random import get_random_bytes
```

The encrypting end will create the ciphertext by using a randomly selected symmetric key. Once we have imported the required modules, a 16-byte key is generated using the `Crypto.Random` package. This is written to a file, which needs to be kept secret:

```
with open("aes.key", "wb") as file_out:
    key = get_random_bytes(16)
    file_out.write(key)
```

The AES cipher object is created by passing the key. Cipher mode EAX is used in the code. This object is used to encrypt the data. Nonce, tag, and ciphertext are stored and transmitted to the decryption end:

```
data = "plaintext for AES"
cipher = AES.new(key, AES.MODE_EAX)
cipher_text, tag = cipher.encrypt_and_digest(data.encode())
with open("encrypted.bin", "wb") as file_out:
    [file_out.write(x) for x in (cipher.nonce, tag, cipher_text)]
print("Data is encrypted and stored in a file")
```

The decryption part of AES uses the same 16-byte symmetric key generated during encryption. Ideally, this key has to be transferred over a secure channel to the recipient. The received encrypted binary file is read to get the nonce, tag, and the ciphertext itself. The AES cipher object is created using the same key and nonce value. Finally, decryption is performed using the `decrypt_and_verify` method by providing `cipher_text` and `tag`. The tag is provided to perform verification; it checks for any modifications in the ciphertext:

```
with open("aes.key", "rb") as file_in:
    key = file_in.read(16)
with open("encrypted.bin", "rb") as file_in:
    nonce, tag, cipher_text = [file_in.read(x) for x in (16, 16, -1)]

cipher = AES.new(key, AES.MODE_EAX, nonce)
data = cipher.decrypt_and_verify(cipher_text, tag)
print("Decrypted data is : \"{}\"".format(data.decode()))
```

A successful execution of both the encryption and decryption operations will produce the following output:

```
Data is encrypted and stored in a file
Decrypted data is : "plaintext for AES"
```

When the encryption and decryption parts of the AES program are run, we get the original data back after decryption. Any modification to the ciphertext would result in a MAC check error, and Python would throw `ValueError: MAC check failed`.

 A detailed Jupyter Notebook and scripts included in this chapter can be found in the GitHub repository for this book.

Asymmetric key cryptography

Asymmetric key cryptography is a widely used encryption technique in modern cryptography. It has a lot of applications other than encryption. It is also commonly used in several elements of blockchain, so we will cover this cryptography technique in depth, along with its primitives.

Symmetric key cryptography uses a shared key for both encryption and decryption. The biggest problem with this is that the shared key needs to be exchanged between participants over a secure channel, which can be quite hard to achieve. It also defeats the objective of encryption if we have a secure channel for communication in the first place. This is where asymmetric cryptography comes in. It uses a pair of keys called a public/private pair. The public key is constructed from the private key and can be freely broadcasted to other users.

 In 1978, Ronald Rivest, Adi Shamir, and Leonard Adleman created the first public-key algorithm, known as the RSA algorithm.

Public-key algorithms enable the creation of a public key from a randomly generated private key. The created public key could not be used to infer the private key. In other words, the creation of the public key from the private key is a one-way process. This is the concept on which the security of public-key cryptography relies. The public-key algorithm not only performs encryption, but also provides authentication functionality.

The holder of the private key can use this key to authenticate to a system that is aware of the user's public key, as demonstrated in the following diagram:

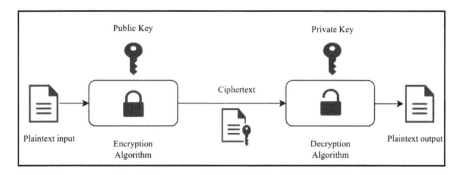

Figure 2.4: Asymmetric key cryptography

As we can see in the diagram, there is no need for a secure channel to share the keys, unlike in symmetric cryptography. The encryption and decryption algorithms are identical, and the constructed key pairs play a vital role in the encryption/decryption process. As discussed earlier, asymmetric key algorithms can also be used to provide authentication. One application of this mechanism is digital signatures: only users with the private key could sign a message, and anyone possessing the public key could verify the authenticity of the message. Digital signatures could be used for non-repudiation as well. Blockchain applications, especially crypto currencies, make use of digital signatures to sign transactions using a private key to prove ownership. Thus, blockchain technology relies mainly on asymmetric cryptographic algorithms. Diffie-Hellman key exchange, DSA, ElGamal, RSA, and **Elliptic-curve cryptography** (**ECC**) are some of the approaches to asymmetric key cryptography.

The strength of a public-key cryptography system depends on how feasible it is to infer the private key from the publicly available information about the key. Although it is infeasible, it is not impossible, and security relies solely on the key size and key generation mechanism. Asymmetric keys are not widely used due to their complexity and the time it takes to encrypt/decrypt large files. They are commonly used in digital signatures or key exchange mechanisms rather than in encryption protocols.

All asymmetric key algorithms are based on a number theory problem that ensures the characteristics required for key generation and the encryption and decryption processes. Based on different ways of solving the mathematical problem in number theory, asymmetrical key generation is broadly characterized in three ways: prime factorization, discrete logarithm, and elliptic-curve. All public-private key algorithms are based on these mathematical problems. All these problems are similar in functionality to trapdoor functions.

 A trapdoor function is a function where it is easy to compute the values in one way but infeasible to find the inverse. This means that it is difficult to find the original input values supplied to the function from the result. This functionality is widely used in asymmetrical cryptography.

Prime factorization

Prime factorization is a concept in number theory regarding the decomposition of a number into the product of two prime numbers. Prime factorization is a subset of integer factorization, in which a composite number is factored into the product of any two integers.

It is challenging to find the factors of semi-primes (numbers that result from the product of two prime numbers) because they have only a single pair of factors, and the complexity of finding the factors increases as the size of the prime number used in the product increases. There is no known efficient factorization algorithm for finding factors when numbers are of a certain size. RSA uses prime factorization, presuming that it's really difficult to find the private key from the exposed product of prime numbers. This presumed difficulty is the reason behind the use of prime factorization in cryptography.

Discrete logarithm

A discrete logarithm is based on the modular arithmetic settings on a discrete logarithm where the solution is infeasible to find. The logarithm $\log_b a$ is a discrete logarithm that has the integer solution x so that $b^x = a$. There is no efficient general method for finding the solution to a discrete logarithm. When modular arithmetic is used with a discrete logarithm, it's known as modular exponentiation, and this problem becomes really difficult. This problem is generally used with the Diffie-Hellman key exchange algorithm.

Let's consider an example of modular exponentiation:

```
3³ mod 5 = 2
```

It is easy to find the result of the preceding function, which is 2, but it is difficult to find the exponent value 3 from the result. The preceding modulo operation can also be represented with a *congruence as $3^3 \cong 2\ (mod\ 5)$.*

 Suppose a and b are two integers, and m is a positive integer. Then the phrase $a \cong b\ (mod\ m)$ is called **congruence** and is read as "a is congruent to b modulo m," which states that m *divides a-b.*

Elliptic-curve

An elliptic curve is a plane real algebraic curve with an equation in the form $y^2 = x^3 + ax + b$. An elliptic curve should be a non-singular curve, meaning no cusps, self-intersections, or isolated points. An elliptic curve on a finite field is used in the cryptography system. ECC is used in Bitcoin to generate private-public key pair, so we will be covering this in depth in a later section of the chapter:

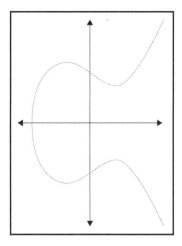

Figure 2.5: An elliptic curve (similar to that used in Bitcoin)

 The public-private key concept in asymmetric cryptography is used in bitcoin and other cryptocurrencies to identify the owner of the asset. Private keys are used to represent the ownership of coins in cryptocurrency.

RSA cryptosystem

RSA is one of the initial implementations of public-private cryptography. It uses the principle of prime factorization to generate a public-private key pair, which acts as a trapdoor function. Encryption is performed using the public key, which is distributed to everyone, and decryption is performed using the secretly kept private key.

 The idea of an asymmetric public-private key cryptosystem is attributed to Whitfield Diffie and Martin Hellman, who published this concept in 1976.

The public and private key pair are computed with the help of two large prime numbers. The public key is published to the user, and the private key is kept secret. The prime numbers are also kept secret. As long as the prime numbers used are large, it is infeasible to compute the private key from the public key. The whole RSA cryptosystem is based on the number theory problem of integer factorization, which ensures that the difficulty of prime factorization is proportional to the size of the prime numbers used.

RSA parameter generation

Before looking at encryption and decryption using RSA, we need to consider the RSA parameter generation process. Here are the steps involved in this process:

1. Select two distinct large prime numbers, p, and q.
2. Compute $n = p*q$ and $\varphi(n) = (p - 1)*(q - 1)$.
3. Choose a random integer e, such that $1 < e < \varphi(n)$ and $gcd\ (e, \varphi(n)) = 1$, that is, integer e and $\varphi(n)$, are coprime.
4. Find $d \equiv e^{-1}\ (mod\ \varphi(n))$, where e^{-1} is the modular multiplicative inverse of e.

 A modular multiplicative inverse of an integer a is an integer x, such that the product ax is congruent to 1 with respect to the modulus m.

More clearly, find d such that $d*e \equiv 1\ (mod\ \varphi(n))$, meaning find a value d such that $d*e$ has a remainder of 1 when divided by $\varphi(n)$.

5. The public key is denoted by (e, n) and the private key by (d, p, q). Here, e is called the public exponent, and d the private exponent.

Encryption and decryption using RSA

Encryption is performed in RSA using the distributed public key. Message *M* is converted to integer *m* such that $0 \le m < n$. Ciphertext *c* is computed using the exposed public exponent, as follows:

$$c \equiv m^e \bmod (n)$$

Anyone who possesses the public exponent can perform encryption on the message and transmit it to whoever possesses the private exponent. Whoever has access to the ciphertext and private exponent can perform decryption as follows:

$$m \equiv c^d \bmod (n)$$

Message *M* could be regenerated from the decrypted integer *m*. This is how RSA makes use of the prime factorization technique to perform encryption and decryption. The process could be performed reasonably quickly for small messages, but it is not the preferred way of encryption for large messages. This is why RSA is widely used in cryptographic primitives, such as digital signatures, rather than encryption.

An example implementation of RSA

The example uses the RSA packages in the Python `PyCryptodome` library. The following packages are imported for RSA key generation and the encryption and decryption operations:

```
from Crypto.PublicKey import RSA
from Crypto.Cipher import PKCS1_OAEP
```

A 2048-bit RSA key is created using the `generate` method from the `RSA` package. The public key is exported from this generated key and made public. The `key` object should be kept secret. A cipher object is created using the public key, and encryption is performed on the message using this object:

```
message = "plaintext for RSA"
key = RSA.generate(2048)
public = key.publickey()

cipher = PKCS1_OAEP.new(public)
cipher_text = cipher.encrypt(message.encode())
print("Data is encrypted")
```

The decryption operation is performed in a similar way to the encryption operation, but the private part of the key pair is used instead of the public part. The ciphertext is given as input to the decrypt method, which decrypts it and gives back the decrypted message:

```
cipher = PKCS1_OAEP.new(key)
message = cipher.decrypt(cipher_text)
print("Decrypted data is : \"{}\"".format(message.decode()))
```

A successful execution of the preceding script will output the following:

```
Data is encrypted
Decrypted data is : "plaintext for RSA"
```

Elliptic-curve cryptography

ECC is a public-private cryptography based on the elliptic curve mentioned earlier. It performs the addition of points on the elliptic curve to compute public-private key pairs. ECC requires smaller key sizes than other asymmetric key cryptosystems, such as RSA. ECC is widely used in key exchange mechanisms and digital signatures and is rarely used in encryption systems.

 ECC provides the same level of security as RSA, but has a smaller key size. A 256-bit ECC key is equivalent to a 3,072-bit RSA key. Similarly, a 384-bit ECC key provides the same level of security as a 7,680-bit RSA key, and so on. We can clearly see the advantage of less computation time due to the smaller key size in ECC.

Due to its key size advantage compared to RSA, ECC is used in *Bitcoin's* addressing system, along with transaction signing operations. It is also popular in other blockchain applications. Other applications of ECC are Tor, iMessages, SSH, and SSL/TLS.

Before diving into the cryptography applications of ECC, let's look at some of its properties:

- An elliptic curve is represented by a cubic equation:

$$y^2 = x^3 + ax + b$$

- An elliptic curve has horizontal symmetry
- A non-vertical line will intersect the curve at a maximum of three points

RSA cryptography uses prime factorization. The factorization of a semi-prime number is really difficult. When used in this domain, it forms a trapdoor (one way) function. Similarly, elliptic-curve-based algorithms can use discrete logarithms. Finding the discrete logarithm of a random element on an elliptic curve with respect to a point on the same curve is a severe problem. We will go through the step-by-step procedure of constructing a public key from a private key and study the one-way nature of the ECC key generation process.

Operations on elliptic curves

Elliptic curves used in cryptography are curves that are constructed in a finite field. They have the following form:

$$y^2 = x^3 + ax + b \ mod \ (p)$$

The modulus operation on p indicates that the curve is over a finite field of prime numbers of the order p. We need to understand some terminology and operations of elliptic curves before moving on to the cryptographic applications.

 A finite field is a field with a finite number of elements defined by parameter p, which is a prime number. Thus, the finite field is $F_p = \{0, \ldots, p\text{-}1\}$. It is represented by modulo p in the equation.

All the elements used in ECC must be agreed upon by the cryptography actors. These elements are called elliptical curve domain parameters. $\{p, a, b, G, n, h\}$ are the parameters used in ECC. These parameters are defined as follows:

- p: The finite field is defined by this prime number.
- a and b: These are the constants used in the equation.
- G: The set of all points in the curve is defined by this generator, also known as the base point.
- n: This represents the order of the base point or generator G, a smallest positive number n such that $nG = \infty$.
- h: This is the cofactor, which is the ratio of the orders of the group and sub group (n), and it must be small ($h <= 4$), usually $h=1$.

Bitcoin's **Elliptical Curve Digital Signature Algorithm**
(**ECDSA**) curve uses a unique set of domain parameters defined in
secp256k1. You can find the technical specifications of the curve used in
secp256k1 in a later section of this chapter.

The operations performed on an elliptical curve are called dot operations, and they are
point addition and point doubling. We will explain both of these operations using a
geometrical approach to facilitate a clear understanding. Python scripts and notebooks
related to these operations can be found in the GitHub repository for this book:

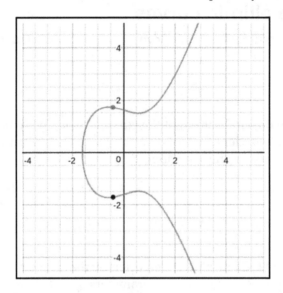

Figure 2.6: An elliptical graph with co-ordinates and grids (created using www.desmos.com)

We will use the elliptical curve in *Figure 2.6* to perform all the operations.

Point addition

Let's assume that P and Q are two points on the elliptic curve. P is not equal to Q; they are two distinct points on the curve. Point addition is explained geometrically as follows:

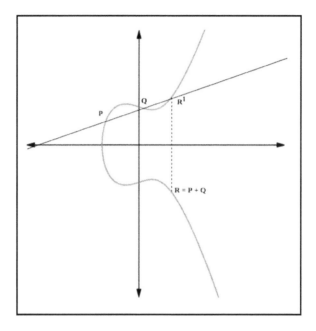

Figure 2.7: Point addition of P and Q

The following steps are performed on the elliptic curve as shown in *Figure 2.7* to add two points.

1. Draw a straight line between points P *(x1, y1)* and Q *(x2, y2)*
2. The line will intersect the elliptic curve at point R^1
3. A reflection of point R^1 about the x axis gives point R *(x3, y3)*, which is the result of the addition of P and Q

Point doubling

Point doubling is a similar operation to point addition, with the exception that point Q is moved to the same location as point P ($P = Q$):

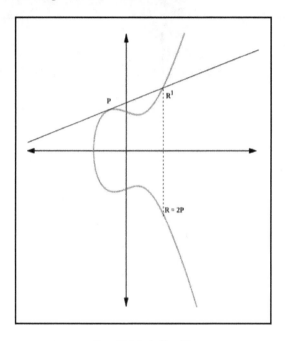

Figure 2.8: Point doubling of P

The following steps are performed on the elliptic curve as shown in *Figure 2.8* to compute point doubling:

1. Draw a tangent (since there is only one point) to the curve at point P
2. This line will intersect the curve at point R^1
3. A reflection of point R^1 about the x axis gives point R, and this is point doubling or a multiple of R ($2R$)

Point doubling is the concept used in ECC to construct the public key from the private key. The following section explains in depth how point doubling is used in the generation of the public key.

Computing the public key

Now that we have defined point doubling, we can calculate a point on the curve that is the multiple of the given point generator, point G (for example, $4G = G + G + G + G$), and this could be computed using point doubling.

Let's use this concept to compute a public-private key pair in an asymmetric cryptography system.

Every curve domain parameter is the same for a given specification. Refer to the technical specifications of the secp256k1 standard in a later section of this chapter that is used in Bitcoin and other blockchain applications' digital signature algorithms. Let's say k is a randomly chosen private key, and K is the public key to be generated. The generator of the curve, G, has a standard value. The public key could be computed by performing the following operation on the curve:

$$K = k*G$$

We can generate the public key using this equation on an elliptic curve using point doubling. Point doubling on an elliptic curve is a one-way operation. It is, therefore, a challenging task to compute the multiplied value k after the required point K has been found:

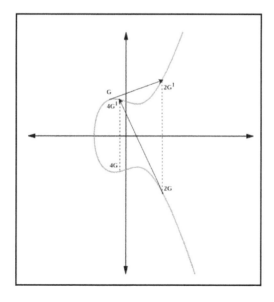

Figure 2.9: Multiplying the generator by an integer using point doubling

Figure 2.9 shows the process of multiplying an integer value by the base point *G*. In this case, points *2G* and *4G* are derived using point doubling of *G* on the given curve. This geometrical method could be used to generate the public key, *K*, by multiplying the generator by the private key *k* times.

Technical details of secp256k1

Bitcoin uses a specific elliptical curve, and the domain parameters used in the curve are defined in the secp256k1 standard. This curve is represented by the following cubic equation in a finite field of prime order *p*:

$$y^2 \bmod (p) = x^3 + 7 \bmod (p)$$

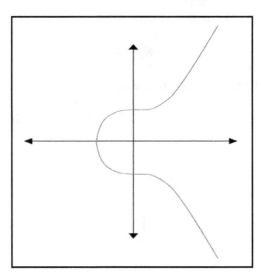

Figure 2.10: secp256k1's elliptic curve over real numbers

As the name suggests, secp256k1 can have a key size of up to 256 bits. The details of the domain parameters used by secp256k1 are represented in hexadecimal strings and are as follows:

- Large prime numbers are used in the finite field.
  - *p = FFFFFFFF FFFFFFFF FFFFFFFF FFFFFFFF FFFFFFFF FFFFFFFF FFFFFFFE FFFFFC2F*

The preceding hexadecimal representation of p will have the following decimal value:

$$p = 2^{256} - 2^{32} - 2^{9} - 2^{8} - 2^{7} - 2^{6} - 2^{4} - 1$$

- Constants of the curve $y^2 = x^3 + 7$ are as follows:
    - a = 00000000 00000000 00000000 00000000 00000000 00000000 00000000 00000000
    - b = 00000000 00000000 00000000 00000000 00000000 00000000 00000000 00000007

- The original representation of base point G has a lengthier hexadecimal string, but it can be represented in a compressed form as follows:
    - G = 02 79BE667E F9DCBBAC 55A06295 CE870B07 029BFCDB 2DCE28D9 59F2815B 16F81798

- The order n of G and the cofactor are as follows:
    - n = FFFFFFFF FFFFFFFF FFFFFFFF FFFFFFFE BAAEDCE6 AF48A03B BFD25E8C D0364141
    - h = 01

All these values remain the same for any computation in secp256k1. And this specification is strong enough to withstand brute-force attempts to compute the private key from the public key.

Digital signatures

So far, we have covered various different methods of encryption in the categories of symmetric and asymmetric cryptography. We also had a look at a few of the advantages of symmetric encryption techniques compared to asymmetric techniques. Thus, asymmetric cryptography is a rarely used encryption methodology. But the distinct design of asymmetrical keys makes it a suitable technique for applications other than encryption, and digital signature is one of them.

A digital signature is a method of providing proof of ownership of digital documents. Public-private key cryptography is widely used in the field of digital signatures due to their asymmetric key property. The owner can use the private key to sign a message or document, and the verifier can verify their ownership using the public key, which is distributed to everyone.

The process is similar to the handwritten signatures used in the real world, where an owner of an asset can use their signature to perform any action on that asset and anyone can verify the signature by comparing it with a signature that was used previously. The digital signature is more secure than the hand-written signature since it is infeasible to forge a signature without owning the private key:

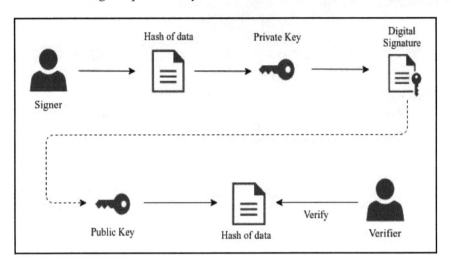

Figure 2.11: Design diagram of a digital signature

Digital signatures could be used as a mechanism for ensuring the authenticity, non-repudiation, and integrity of an action. We can take an example of a software company distributing updates to its clients. How do these clients ensure that they can trust these software updates? This is where the digital signature helps to provide authenticity and integrity for those updates by allowing clients to verify them with the distributed public keys. Only the owners of the software can sign the software updates because they possess the private key.

How does it work?

As shown in *Figure 2.11*, the digital signature process consists of two parts: signing, and verification. Unlike with encryption, the digital signature performs the first operation, signing using the private key. Verification uses the public key distributed by the signer.

A hashing algorithm generates a unique fixed length value that is used during the construction and verification of a digital signature. Refer to the next section for a detailed explanation of cryptographic hashing.

Signing process

The signing operation is performed by the owner of the message using the private key to prove their authenticity. Let's say Alice is the owner of a document that has a message *m*, and wants to distribute it to others in the network. Now, Alice will initially hash the message and use her private key to sign the document. The signature is created as follows, where F_s is the signature function, F_h is the hashing function, *m* is the message, and *dA* is Alice's private key:

$$S = F_s \left(F_h \left(m \right), dA \right)$$

Alice will now distribute her signature, along with the message, to everyone in the network.

Verification process

Verification is a process performed by anyone who possesses information that is made public by the owner. Public information usually has a public key, a message, and the signature of the message. Let's assume that Bob possesses all the public information and wishes to verify the message to check its authenticity. Bob uses a signature verification algorithm, which requires a hash of the message, the public key, and the signature. The algorithm will verify that the message hasn't been tampered with by anyone. An implemented example of both the signing and verification processes can be found later in the chapter.

Elliptical Curve Digital Signature Algorithm (ECDSA)

ECDSA is a digital signature algorithm that makes use of ECC to create the key pairs used in the signing and verification process of the digital signature. Because of the advantages of ECC compared to other public-key algorithms, it is commonly used in blockchain applications to sign transactions or events.

ECDSA makes use of temporary key pairs to calculate a signature pair, *R* and *S*. A temporary private key *k* is chosen randomly on the elliptical curve, and the corresponding public key is calculated as $P = k*G$. The signature is calculated as follows:

$$S = k^{-1} \left(Hash(m) + dA * R \right) mod \left(p \right)$$

Variables used in the signing operation are defined as follows:

- k is the temporary private key
- R is the x coordinate of the temporary public key
- dA is the private key
- m is the message
- p is the prime order of the elliptic curve

Verification is performed in ECDSA using the R, S pair and the public key. The point P is derived as follows:

$$P = S^{-1}*Hash(m)*G + S^{-1}*R*Qa$$

Variables used in the verification operation are defined as follows:

- Qa is the public key of the signer
- m is the message
- G is the generator point of the elliptical curve

 An ECDSA digital signature algorithm is used in Bitcoin to sign transactions created by the owner by using their own private key.

ECDSA example to create and verify a digital signature

The following packages are used to perform hashing, ECC key creation, and signature creation and verification:

```
from Crypto.Hash import SHA256
from Crypto.PublicKey import ECC
from Crypto.Signature import DSS
```

The key is generated on the secp256k1 elliptical curve using the ECC.generate method, and both public and private keys are exported:

```
key = ECC.generate(curve='P-256')
with open('ecc.pub', 'wt') as f:
    f.write(key.public_key().export_key(format='PEM'))
with open('ecc.pem', 'wt') as f:
    f.write(key.export_key(format='PEM'))
```

Messages that need to be signed are hashed using the SHA256 algorithm, and then a signer object is created using the DSS package by providing a private key. The hashed message is then signed by the owner:

```
message = b'ECDSA message for signature'
key = ECC.import_key(open('ecc.pem').read())
h = SHA256.new(message)
signer = DSS.new(key, 'fips-186-3')
signature = signer.sign(h)
```

Signature verification in the following code is similar to that of signing. The received message is hashed initially since the hashing was performed at the sender side as well. The distributed public key is imported and used to create a new DSS object for verification. The hashed message and the received signature are used for verification. The verify function throws a ValueError if the message or signature was tampered with:

```
h = SHA256.new(message)
key = ECC.import_key(open('ecc.pub').read())
verifier = DSS.new(key, 'fips-186-3')
try:
    verifier.verify(h, signature)
    print("The message is authentic.")
except ValueError:
    print("The message is not authentic.")
```

Cryptographic hashing

A cryptographic hash function is a type of function that maps arbitrary sized data to a fixed size string called a hash. Hash functions possess certain properties that make them ideal for use in cryptography.

Hash functions are widely used in hash table data structures. A hash table stores the data in a key-value pair. Hash tables are used when large keys need to be converted into smaller keys using a hash function, and then the values are mapped to these smaller keys. This makes the mapping of key to value quite easy, and this could be achieved in O(1) time complexity. This is due to the fact that hash functions have a constant time complexity.

We have repeatedly mentioned that hashing is the backbone of blockchain architecture, and it has several properties that make it really valuable and ideal for blockchain implementation.

Every hash function has the following properties:

- Pre-image resistance: Given a computed hash $h = hash\ (m)$, where m is the message, it should be infeasible to find the message from the given hash value.
- Second pre-image resistance: Given a message $m1$, it should be infeasible to find another message $m2$ such that $hash\ (m1) = hash\ (m2)$.
- Collision resistance: A hash is said to have collided when there are at least two messages that produce the same hash value. It should be infeasible to find two messages $m1$ and $m2$ where $hash\ (m1) = hash\ (m2)$, that is, it should be challenging to find two messages that have the same hash value. This is similar to the second pre-image resistance, but any two messages can be chosen here. So, this property implies second pre-image resistance.

Although every hash function has these properties, a good hash function is expected to possess additional properties in order to provide strong security:

- A hash function should take a constant time for any input.
- Any bit changed in the message should result in a completely new hash value compared to the hash of the previous message. It should be very difficult to analyze the hash value created by the hash function.

 Hashing is used in blockchain to create a unique identity string for each block by computing its hash value. Each block will maintain the hash value of the previous block and thus form a chain of blocks. Hashing provides integrity to the blocks of the blockchain ledger.

Hashing algorithms

Hashing algorithms are categorized based on their implementation, resulting digest size, and many other things. Some of the classifications include Message Digest, **Secure Hashing Algorithms (SHA)**, and **RACE Integrity Primitives Evaluation Message Digest (RIPEMD)**.

Message Digest

This is one of the popular hashing algorithm groups used during the early 1990s. They are 128-bit hash functions, and md4 and md5 are its variants. Many vulnerabilities have been detected in the function since its adoption. Still, these functions are used to create file digests to ensure their integrity.

Secure Hash Algorithms (SHA)

SHA-0 is the first version of the SHA algorithm. In 2004, several weaknesses were exposed in this algorithm, resulting in the creation of a stronger version of SHA-0 called SHA-1. In 2005, an attack on SHA-1 reported that it would find a collision in fewer hashing operations.

SHA-2 was created to overcome SHA-1's vulnerabilities, and it could be implemented with a digest size of 224, 256, 384, and 512 bits. SHA-2 is a widely used standard in modern cryptographic applications. Bitcoin uses the SHA-256 variant as a hashing algorithm to solve proof-of-work puzzles.

SHA-3 is the latest family of functions with 224-, 256-, 384-, and 512-bit variants.

Hashing example using an SHA-256 algorithm

The following example script uses the SHA-256 hashing algorithm to compute a digest of the message:

```
from Crypto.Hash import SHA256

hash_object = SHA256.new(data=b'First')
print(hash_object.hexdigest())

hash_object.update(b'd')
print(hash_object.hexdigest())
```

Let's consider the output of the preceding script and make a few observations:

```
a151ceb1711aad529a7704248f03333990022ebbfa07a7f04c004d70c167919f
18902d9ed3b47effdb6faf90ea69b2ef08ef3d25c60a13454ccaef7e60d1cfe1
```

As we can see, both the hash values in the output have 64 hexadecimal digits (256 bits) irrespective of the size of the message. The first hash value has a message "First," and the second one has "Firstd" (the update function appends the new message to the previous one). Although there is a difference of one character at the end, the entire SHA-256 hash value looks completely different. This property of SHA-256 makes sure that it is pre-image resistant, and thus very difficult to break.

Merkle hash trees

A Merkle tree is a binary tree where all the leaf nodes represent hashes of the data blocks. Each parent node has the hashed value of the hashes of its children. Hashing continues until the root node of the tree. Merkle trees are used to summarize bulk sets of data and create a fingerprint for each set.

A tree is a data structure in computer science that consists of a root node and a subtree of parent and children nodes and is represented by positioning a root node at the top. A binary tree is a tree where each parent has at most two nodes. Merkle trees are used in Bitcoin, Ethereum, and other blockchain applications to summarize all the transactions included in each block. SHA-256 is used as a hash function in bitcoin's Merkle tree, as can be seen in the following diagram:

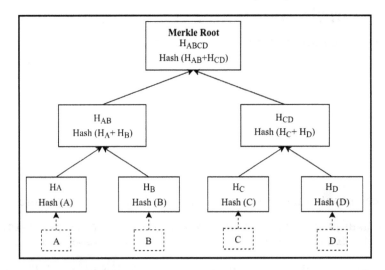

Figure 2.12: Merkle tree that summarizes all the leaves

A Merkle tree is constructed from the bottom up from the leaf nodes. In *Figure 2.12*, leaf nodes will consist only of hashed values of data blocks A, B, C, and D represented by H_A, H_B, H_C, and H_D respectively. Each parent node will construct its hash by concatenating the hash values of the child nodes and hashing them again:

$$H_{AB} = Hash \ (H_A + H_B)$$

This process is continued until the root node hash value H_{ABCD} is calculated.

 Since each Merkle tree node (other than leaf nodes) calculates its hash based on its child nodes, it has to maintain a balanced tree, that is, each node (other than leaf nodes) should have two child nodes. This could be achieved by duplicating existing single child nodes.

Merkle trees not only provide a way of summarizing an entire data block, but they can also efficiently verify whether a data block exists. Verification could be achieved in just $log_2(n)$ complexity.

Encoding schemes

Encoding schemes are generally used in data storage or the transmission of textual data over a medium. You can often observe the conversion of binary to text-encoding schemes in primitive cryptographic implementations.

Encoding schemes provide a compact way of representing long sequences of characters using a base. For example, a decimal system uses base 10, which uses characters from 0-9, and a hexadecimal system uses additional characters from A-F, along with the numbers from the decimal system. The bigger the base of a system, the smaller the size of the encoded string.

Base64 is an encoding scheme that is widely used to store and transmit large files such as an image. It uses 26 lowercase letters, 26 uppercase letters, 10 numerical characters, and 2 special characters ("+" and "/").

Base58 is an encoding scheme developed for Bitcoin and used in several blockchain applications. Base58 is actually a subset of Base64 and was created with the intention of providing better readability. The characters in Base64 that are omitted in Base58 are 0 (zero), O (uppercase o), l (lowercase L), I (uppercase i), and the special characters "+" and "/."

Bitcoin's 34-character Base58-encoded wallet address is as follows:

16RhN7MhhTRMDdrS3szys5pEpmS2YGTMsk

Summary

This chapter covered all the essential cryptography topics, from classic cipher techniques to advanced cryptographic primitives. We began the chapter by discussing the classical cipher techniques. We explored both symmetric and asymmetric cryptography, along with a few examples. Cryptographic primitives, such as hashing and digital signatures, were covered in greater detail as they will act as the foundation for the blockchain concepts covered throughout this book.

Since we have covered some of the essential concepts in cryptography and looked at their respective applications, in the next chapter, we will try to implement some of the cryptography concepts that are applicable to the blockchain protocol by looking at a simple blockchain example.

Cryptography in Blockchain

3

In the previous chapters, we introduced cryptography that are relevant to blockchain. Although we have a clear understanding of some of these cryptographic primitives, we haven't explored their applications in a real blockchain application. In this chapter, we will cover some of the applications of cryptographic primitives, which will include hash functions and digital signatures. We will cover them in-depth by actually implementing them in a basic blockchain application.

In this chapter, we'll cover the following topics:

- Hashing in blockchain
- Digital signatures in blockchain

One thing to note is that each cryptographic primitive that is used with blockchain technology has a distinct role. Hash functions and digital signatures are two concepts of cryptography that are extensively used with blockchain.

We can mainly observe three layers in the blockchain technology. These are a *peer-to-peer network layer*, a *consensus layer*, which deals with the block creation and validation mechanism, and an *application layer*, which utilizes underlying blockchain in order to build an application. Cryptography is mainly used in the consensus and application layers of the blockchain. A hashing algorithm is mainly used to create block identity, ensure the integrity of the blockchain, and also acts as a key ingredient of consensus algorithms, such as Bitcoin's Proof of Work. The digital signature, on the other hand, deals with the application layer, where it is used to validate events by embedding them in transactions.

Since hashing and digital signatures contribute to the blockchain at different layers, we will cover the significance of these concepts throughout different sections of this chapter.

Hashing in blockchain

Hashing is an important concept in blockchain and has a huge role in the functioning of a blockchain application. The applications of hash functions range from minor blockchain implementations, such as creating a digest for a large amount of data, to major implementations, such as maintaining the integrity of the blocks in the chain. Hash functions are also used in Proof of Work consensus algorithms to solve the Byzantine failure problem, which we'll cover in depth, later in the chapter. To begin with, we'll explore some concepts of blockchain that make use of hash functions.

Linking blocks in a blockchain

As defined in the introductory chapter, a blockchain is a continuously growing collection of blocks that are chained together to form an open ledger by using cryptography as a key ingredient. Each block in the blockchain is given an identity to mark that block as unique, and this is achieved by using the hash functions that will generate a digest for that block. The collision resistance property of the cryptographic hash function, as mentioned in the previous chapter, Chapter 2, *A Bit of Cryptography*, ensures that it is infeasible to find two blocks that will result in the same hash value. As a result, the hash function guarantees the uniqueness of the identity created for the block.

When a new block is created, it will backreference the previous block using the digest of the previous block, thus linking that block to the blockchain. Modifying any of the blocks would change the identity of that block due to the new hash value. As a result, this would break the chain, as one of the block references will be invalid due to the newly generated hash value. Therefore, it's infeasible to modify a block such that it generates the same hash value as before. This is due to the pre-image resistance property of the cryptographic hash function, which ensures that the data of the blocks cannot be predicted even if we possess the hash value. This is why, once a chain of blocks is created, the integrity of the chain is ensured as each block references the previous block. The only way to modify the data of a block is by modifying all the subsequent blocks by updating its reference to the previous block:

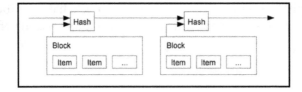

Figure 3.1: Linking blocks using hashes from *A Peer-to-Peer Electronic Cash System*, S. Nakamoto

The preceding *Figure 3.1* shows the design of blockchain from the original paper, *Bitcoin: A Peer-to-Peer Electronic Cash System*, by *Satoshi Nakamoto*, the creator of the original reference implementation of Bitcoin. It shows that each block's hash value is affected by the value of the previous block's hash value, thereby linking each block in the blockchain. Anyone who holds a copy of the blockchain ledger will be able to verify whether all of the blocks in the blockchain are valid just by verifying each block's hash with the next block.

Linking blocks using an SHA256 hashing algorithm

Blocks in the blockchain are chained together by referencing the hash values of previous blocks. SHA256 is the most popular hashing algorithm used in the blockchain platform since it was used in the Bitcoin implementation. Firstly, we will define the structure and functionality of the blocks, before finally constructing the blockchain with the help of the hashing algorithm.

Block structure

Let's consider a simple block whose header and data are combined to create a data structure called **Block**. Each Block will contain the following: an index, the previous hash, a timestamp, data, and its own hash value:

```python
class Block(object):
    """A class representing the block for the blockchain"""

    def __init__(self, index, previous_hash, timestamp, data, hash):
        self.index = index
        self.previous_hash = previous_hash
        self.timestamp = timestamp
        self.data = data
        self.hash = hash
```

The preceding code snippet defines a Python class called `Block` that has all the basic attributes of a blockchain block. Usually, a block will contain both a header and a body, with the header containing metadata about the block. However, the preceding example doesn't distinguish between the header and the body. A typical blockchain application, such as Bitcoin, will have a huge set of data that could be in the form of transactions, but in the example, we will consider the data to be of a `string` type.

A typical block will also contain a nonce and a difficulty target in the header. This information is used in consensus algorithms, such as Proof of Work. Since our intention is just to describe a blockchain, these fields are outside the scope of this section.

Blockchain functionality

The block linking process consists of several elements, such as creating a structure from the information, calculating the hash of the block, and appending it to the blockchain.

Let's break down each of these functionalities into blockchain methods:

```
class Blockchain(object):
    """A class representing list of blocks"""

    def __init__(self):

        self._chain = [self.get_genesis_block()]
        self.timestamp = int(datetime.now().timestamp()
```

The preceding class is a collection of class methods that create a valid blockchain using a hash function. The constructor of the `Blockchain` will initialize a chain by appending a genesis block, which is the first block of the blockchain, and doesn't have any reference to a previous block:

```
def get_genesis_block(self):
    """creates first block of the chain"""

    return Block(0, "0", 1465154705, "my genesis block!!",
"816534932c2b7154836da6afc367695e6337db8a921823784c14378abed4f7d7"
 )
```

A genesis block is a hardcoded block that is appended to the beginning of the blockchain. It is created with static contents. The preceding genesis block has a hardcoded hash value that is created using SHA-256, as follows:

```
SHA256.new(data=(str(0) + "0"+ str(1465154705) +"my genesis
 block!!").encode()).hexdigest()

def calculate_hash(self, index, previous_hash, timestamp, data):
    """calculates SHA256 hash value"""

    hash_object = SHA256.new(data=(str(index) + previous_hash +
 str(timestamp) + data).encode())
    return hash_object.hexdigest()
```

`calculate_hash` is a crucial method in the blockchain because this method creates a hash value that binds all the blocks together. An SHA-256 hash value is created using the PyCryptodome package, as shown in the previous chapter. This method concatenates the block index, the hash value of the previous block, the timestamp, and the data required to create a string that needs to be hashed. The SHA256 hash function generates a digest that is the hash value of that block.

We need to find the hash value of the previous block during the creation of the next block. The following function identifies the last block appended to the chain:

```
def get_latest_block(self):
    """gets the last block from the blockchain"""

    try:
        return self._chain[-1]
    except IndexError as e:
        return None
```

The following function will build a block by constructing all the attributes that are required to create a `Block` object. It will also calculate the hash value for the current block. A new `Block` object consisting of the block structure will finally be created:

```
def create_block(self, block_data):
    """creates a new block with the given block data"""

    previous_block = self.get_latest_block()
    next_index = previous_block.index + 1
    next_timestamp = self.timestamp
    next_hash = self.calculate_hash(next_index,
previous_block.hash, next_timestamp, block_data)
    return Block(next_index, previous_block.hash, next_timestamp,
block_data, next_hash)
```

 Note: We have created `next_timestamp` based on a static timestamp value that is created when the blockchain object is created. Although this is not true in an actual blockchain, we have done this intentionally to explain a particular case that will be explained during the code execution.

The following functions are used to add, reset, and read the blocks of the blockchain. The `add_block` method and the `chain` attribute are the only class members that need to be exposed to the user:

```
def add_block(self, data):
    """appends a new block to the blockchain"""

    self._chain.append(self.create_block(data))
```

```
    @property
    def chain(self):
        """created a dict containing list of block objects to view"""

        return self.dict(self._chain)

    def dict(self, chain):
        """converts list of block objects to dictionary"""

        return json.loads(json.dumps(chain, default=lambda o:
    o.__dict__))

    def reset(self):
        """resets the blockchain blocks except genesis block"""

        self._chain = [self._chain[0]]
```

Creating a blockchain

Now that we have defined all the required functionalities of a simple blockchain linker, we'll emulate one by creating both a few blocks and a blockchain:

```
new_chain = Blockchain()
new_chain.add_block(data="first block data")
new_chain.add_block(data="second block data")
new_chain.add_block(data="third block data")

print(json.dumps(new_chain.chain))

new_chain.reset()

new_chain.add_block(data="first block data")
new_chain.add_block(data="second block data")
new_chain.add_block(data="third block data")

print(json.dumps(new_chain.chain))
```

The preceding code snippet creates a `Blockchain` object and adds three blocks to it, along with an existing genesis block. This operation is performed again after resetting the blockchain. An important observation here is that both outputs of `new_chain.chain` will produce a list of blocks containing the block hashes shown in the following output. This is due to the fact that all the attributes contributing to the creation of the hash value are the same during execution. The hash function always produces the same hash value if fed with the same input.

The timestamp is hardcoded in the genesis block and is intentionally kept constant for all the blocks to show that hash values computed with the similar data will generate the same value every time:

```
[
    {
        "index": 0,
        "data": "my genesis block!!",
        "hash":
"816534932c2b7154836da6afc367695e6337db8a921823784c14378abed4f7d7",
        "previous_hash": "0",
        "timestamp": 1465154705
    },
    {
        "index": 1,
        "data": "first block data",
        "hash":
"c8028a8a867a639fec693243f88a4e04f0ab5872f6913da53210316bd97d6ebb",
        "previous_hash":
"816534932c2b7154836da6afc367695e6337db8a921823784c14378abed4f7d7",
        "timestamp": "1521059029"
    },
    {
        "index": 2,
        "data": "second block data",
        "hash":
"aba71ef94fdc7d70bd39e5aa3eeef6fd53ac8e7fc102c2f638126c8a74d5cefe",
        "previous_hash":
"c8028a8a867a639fec693243f88a4e04f0ab5872f6913da53210316bd97d6ebb",
        "timestamp": "1521059029"
    },
    {
        "index": 3,
        "data": "third block data",
        "hash":
"f208c8375036ad785c9226d09585bd50a2b3993300f75e041dc3f2f0b6cfdd2b",
        "previous_hash":
"aba71ef94fdc7d70bd39e5aa3eeef6fd53ac8e7fc102c2f638126c8a74d5cefe",
        "timestamp": "1521059029"
    }
]
```

The preceding output will be generated two times during the actual execution. The output shows how the blocks in our blockchain are linked using cryptographic hashes. Each block in the blockchain has a `previous_hash` value that matches the hash value of the previous block. Index 0 is the hardcoded genesis block with no `previous_hash`, and index 1 has a `previous_hash` value that matches the genesis block's hash. All the other blocks are linked in the same manner.

Let's try to alter the data in a block and insert the rest of the blocks in the chain:

```
new_chain.reset()
new_chain.add_block(data="modified first block data")
new_chain.add_block(data="second block data")
new_chain.add_block(data="third block data")

print(json.dumps(new_chain.chain))
```

This would produce the following list of blocks in the blockchain:

```
[
  {
    "hash":
"816534932c2b7154836da6afc367695e6337db8a921823784c14378abed4f7d7",
    "data": "my genesis block!!",
    "index": 0,
    "timestamp": 1465154705,
    "previous_hash": "0"
  },
  {
    "hash":
"06045fb547175c5cd32b3ba326ce9768c22771c3e128f801bbec19ea1eb20052",
    "data": "modified first block data",
    "index": 1,
    "timestamp": "1521086845",
    "previous_hash":
"816534932c2b7154836da6afc367695e6337db8a921823784c14378abed4f7d7"
  },
  {
    "hash":
"40c54c31afda040d037dae637ab1ec6e5eb9b132c761b9eadda21e68c0897a65",
    "data": "second block data",
    "index": 2,
    "timestamp": "1521086845",
    "previous_hash":
"06045fb547175c5cd32b3ba326ce9768c22771c3e128f801bbec19ea1eb20052"
  },
  {
    "hash":
```

```
"466083f34143e7f99196de01cd7777c52b0763624acd2895f0d28047c670eb41",
    "data": "third block data",
    "index": 3,
    "timestamp": "1521086845",
    "previous_hash":
"40c54c31afda040d037dae637ab1ec6e5eb9b132c761b9eadda21e68c0897a65"
  }
]
```

The preceding list of blocks shows similar block link properties to the earlier blockchain, but an interesting observation is that although only the block data of index 1 has been modified, the hash values of all the other blocks are different to the previous block output. This is due to the chaining or ripple effect. Because each block stores the hash value of the previous block, each block is affected by this modification. This leads to the creation of a new blockchain. This is the reason why blockchains are secure: A single block cannot be modified without affecting the other blocks in the ledger.

 The complete script of the preceding sample blockchain application can be found in the GitHub repository of the book (`https://github.com/PacktPublishing/Foundations-of-Blockchain`), along with Python packaging.

Byzantine failure problem in blockchain

In the previous section, we saw how the blocks are appended to form a blockchain. We also looked at how the cryptographic hash function plays a vital role to ensure the integrity of the blockchain. Although the blockchain maintains integrity, it doesn't ensure that a single version of blockchain can be maintained in the decentralized network. Every node in the network is capable of maintaining their own version of blockchain since the block creation is not a difficult task. This is a well-known distributed system problem called the Byzantine Generals' Problem, or Byzantine failure.

Byzantine failure is a fault that presents different symptoms to different observers. It occurs when there is a loss of a service in a system that needs to achieve a consensus. This kind of failure is witnessed in distributed systems, where it is difficult to gather information about the status of components, and the presence of bad actors makes it more difficult to reach a consensus.

The term Byzantine failure is derived from the Byzantine Generals' Problem, which is an agreement problem in which a group of generals representing the Byzantine army are planning to attack a city. Some of the generals might decide to attack, whereas others retreat. They should come to an agreement about whether to attack or retreat so that the mission would be a success. Communicating the generals' votes to each other is a difficult task because they are distant from each other and there was no convenient way of communication. Due to this, there would be a delay or miscommunication among the generals. The problem is further elevated by the presence of unreliable generals as they might try to cheat while casting a vote so that the mission fails. If such a system fails to achieve an agreement with the majority of votes, it would result in a failed mission because the army that decided to attack might not have enough support from the rest of the generals. This is a classic agreement problem for which there is no one single solution. The solution to the Byzantine General's Problem is to find a majority vote among the honest generals.

A system that displays a **Byzantine fault tolerance** (**BFT**) is one that can overcome the Byzantine failure problem. In a digital system, cryptographic primitives such as digital signatures can provide fault tolerance for security-critical systems by creating unforgeable message signatures. Achieving data integrity can provide some resistance to the Byzantine failure problem, but it would not be a complete solution.

Now that we understand the Byzantine problem, we can notice that the problem is applicable to any distributed system. The problem also exists in the blockchain network, where participants are spread across a decentralized peer-to-peer network. Maintaining a single truth in a decentralized network is a difficult task, and the involvement of bad actors in the network makes it even more difficult. The decentralized network of a blockchain must agree on a single state to make the blockchain consistent among all the blockchain nodes. The occurrence of the Byzantine problem in a blockchain network is inevitable because blockchain networks exist in a decentralized trustless environment. The nodes of the network should reach a consensus on how to attain a universal blockchain state. Miners, in particular, should reach a consensus because they are the ones that contribute to the growth of the blockchain.

 A blockchain miner is a node that not only validates the data of the blockchain, but also contributes resources to create a new block in the blockchain ledger.

Bitcoin was the first decentralized application that solved the Byzantine problem. It achieved this by using a consensus algorithm called Proof of Work, which was inspired by the Hashcash system proposed in 1997 by Adam Back, a British cryptographer. Hashcash was developed to validate legitimate users and reduce email spam by creating a stamp that requires some amount of computation. The Hashcash stamp was created using a hashing algorithm. Although the stamp creation was time consuming, verification could be performed instantly. Similarly, Bitcoin's Proof of Work also uses a cryptographic hash function to achieve consensus in the network.

 There are several consensus algorithms that achieve a common global view in a blockchain. Proof of Stack, Proof of Activity, Proof of Capacity, and Proof of Elapsed Time are just a few examples. Even the popular Ethereum blockchain framework currently uses the Proof of Work consensus, but there have been active development efforts to include Proof of Stake in the future release of Ethereum.

How does Proof of Work ensure Byzantine fault tolerance?

Proof of Work is a consensus algorithm designed to make sure that each participant node in the network that creates a block must prove that it has done a certain amount of work on the block before it is inserted in the public blockchain ledger.

Bitcoin's Proof of Work consensus algorithm was designed to make sure that blockchain data is immutable and cannot easily be altered by bad actors. Majority decisions in a blockchain network are represented by the longest chain; this is because it has proof of having done the most work. Whilst this system would achieve a consensus in a decentralized network, what if a bad actor tries to create an alternate blockchain with some fraudulent transactions? This isn't easy when Proof of Work is being used. Whenever a bad actor makes a modification to a block that was created earlier, all the successive blocks would be recreated, all of which would redo the work. Recreating all the blocks would take a very long time as the process requires a lot of computation power. However, you'll find that often, the work of a bad actor will be rejected by the majority of the network because it was not able to keep up with the work done by the honest nodes.

Thus, Proof of Work helps to achieve a BFT system, even in the presence of dishonest nodes.

Although Proof of Work provides a practical solution to the Byzantine failure problem, an attack called 51% could theoretically result in Byzantine failure. In a 51% attack, the majority of the computation power in the blockchain network is controlled by a dishonest entity. This implies that the Bitcoin can have 50% faulty nodes and still function without failing. This is the fault tolerance of Bitcoin's consensus mechanism. The 51% attack is covered in more detail in `Chapter 10`, *Blockchain Security*.

How does Proof of Work use cryptography?

Proof of Work is a consensus algorithm that uses a cryptographic hashing puzzle to make sure that a certain amount of work has been done before a block is created. Bitcoin's Proof of Work uses the SHA-256 hash function to create a hashing puzzle.

Blocks in a blockchain network are created by a special type of validator node called a miner. These miner nodes compete with each other to solve the hashing puzzle in order to produce a block to be appended to the ledger.

Blockchain miners will start to solve the hashing puzzle whenever they have data (often, a set of transactions) that needs to be included in a block. The following *Figure 3.2* shows the basic structure of a block header used in a Proof of Work-based blockchain application. A puzzle solver will create a hash value of the header, generally using the SHA256 hash function. The puzzle here is to find a hash value for the header so that the hash begins with a known number of zero bits:

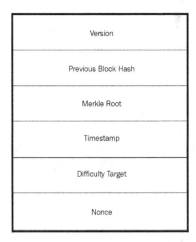

Figure 3.2: The basic structure of a block header

We have mentioned previously the characteristics of a hash function; that is, the hash value cannot be predicted because the creation of a hash value is a one-way process. As a result, it's difficult to predict the contents of the header, which would result in the hash value beginning with a certain number of zero bits. The only way to achieve this is by repeatedly trying out different header values and computing the hash value using the hash function. A different header is created by altering a variable field called **nonce** in the header. A random nonce is assigned to create a different header for the hash function. Once the miner finds a nonce that will produce a hash value with the required number of zero bits, the puzzle is solved, and the nonce is recorded in the block header.

Using a hash function to perform Proof of Work turns out to be a good approach because it is difficult to fraudulently compute a hash value due to its cryptographic characteristics. Hash functions make sure that a certain amount of CPU effort has been used to compute hash values, and that the hash rate of the computer is the Proof of Work during this process.

An example implementation of Proof of Work

In the previous section, we covered how Proof of Work used a hashing algorithm. We also looked at computing a target hash to solve the hashing puzzle. We're now going to implement a Proof of Work algorithm using the SHA-256 algorithm in order to analyze how hashing and probability contribute to this consensus algorithm.

Since the main intention of the Proof of Work algorithm is to find a nonce that, when attached to the blockchain header, results in the required target hash value, the task here is to randomly guess a nonce value and establish the digest value of the block. Thanks to the properties of hash functions, which make guessing the nonce really hard and non-deterministic, the only way to find the nonce is to actually try out each nonce using the hash function and find a nonce that will satisfy the target hash value. Although the solution is non-deterministic, due to the properties of hash functions, Proof of Work is affected by probability. Although finding the solution depends on luck, the puzzle is often solved by the miner node that has done the most work. This is due to the fact that the probability of finding the nonce increases with the amount of work done.

Each puzzle solved in the Proof of Work has a difficulty level that decides the target hash value to be created. The difficulty level is decided by the number of zero bits required at the beginning of the resulting hash value. The puzzle's difficulty level is increased by increasing the required number of 0 bits in the hash values. This is again due to the fact that the probability of finding a small hash value is lower than the probability of finding any hash values including the large hash values due to the smaller sample space.

This example implementation of Proof of Work will illustrate the role of probability in this consensus algorithm:

```python
from Crypto.Hash import SHA256

text = "I am Satoshi Nakamoto"


for nonce in range(20):

    input_data = text + str(nonce)

    hash_data = SHA256.new(input_data.encode()).hexdigest()

    print(input_data, '=>', hash_data)
```

 The code to demonstrate nonce is inspired by the code snippet from *Mastering Bitcoin – First Edition* by *Andreas M. Antonopoulos*.

The preceding code snippet is a simple example of generating hashes to solve the Proof of Work hashing puzzle. The nonce is created in an incremental fashion and appended to the input data. The hash value is computed using the SHA-256 algorithm, and this is repeated for all the nonce values.

The program will generate the following hashes for the nonce-appended data:

```
I am Satoshi
 Nakamoto0=>a80a81401765c8eddee25df36728d732acb6d135...
I am Satoshi
 Nakamoto1=>f7bc9a6304a4647bb41241a677b5345fe3cd30db...
I am Satoshi
 Nakamoto2=>ea758a8134b115298a1583ffb80ae62939a2d086...
I am Satoshi
 Nakamoto3=>bfa9779618ff072c903d773de30c99bd6e2fd70b...
I am Satoshi
 Nakamoto4=>bce8564de9a83c18c31944a66bde992ff1a77513...
I am Satoshi
 Nakamoto5=>eb362c3cf3479be0a97a20163589038e4dbead49...
I am Satoshi
 Nakamoto6=>4a2fd48e3be420d0d28e202360cfbaba410bedde...
I am Satoshi
 Nakamoto7=>790b5a1349a5f2b909bf74d0d166b17a333c7fd8...
I am Satoshi
 Nakamoto8=>702c45e5b15aa54b625d68dd947f1597b1fa571d...
I am Satoshi
```

```
 Nakamoto9=>7007cf7dd40f5e933cd89fff5b791ff0614d9c60...
I am Satoshi
 Nakamoto10=>c2f38c81992f4614206a21537bd634af7178964...
I am Satoshi
 Nakamoto11=>7045da6ed8a914690f087690e1e8d662cf9e56f...
I am Satoshi
 Nakamoto12=>60f01db30c1a0d4cbce2b4b22e88b9b93f58f10...
I am Satoshi
 Nakamoto13=>0ebc56d59a34f5082aaef3d66b37a661696c2b6...
I am Satoshi
 Nakamoto14=>27ead1ca85da66981fd9da01a8c6816f54cfa0d...
I am Satoshi
 Nakamoto15=>394809fb809c5f83ce97ab554a2812cd901d3b1...
I am Satoshi
 Nakamoto16=>8fa4992219df33f50834465d30474298a7d5ec7...
I am Satoshi
 Nakamoto17=>dca9b8b4f8d8e1521fa4eaa46f4f0cdf9ae0e69...
I am Satoshi
 Nakamoto18=>9989a401b2a3a318b01e9ca9a22b0f39d82e48b...
I am Satoshi
 Nakamoto19=>cda56022ecb5b67b2bc93a2d764e75fc6ec6e6e...
```

Although each input for the preceding hash values differs by only the last two digits, the hash output values are completely different due to the properties of hash functions. This is why it is infeasible to detect a nonce that would produce the target hash value and therefore solve the puzzle.

Example of finding a nonce to solve Proof of Work

The following example will illustrate how to find a nonce by brute force, with the help of the SHA-256 algorithm, in order to find a hash value that will satisfy the target hash. The target hash value is determined by setting the difficulty bits in the Proof of Work algorithm. We will modify the blockchain linker that we created earlier on to include the Proof of Work algorithm while creating a new block. Firstly, let's modify a few functions of the blockchain example to include the consensus algorithm.

The `Block` class used to create a new block to be added to blockchain is modified to take two extra members, called `difficulty_bits` and `nonce`. We'll also include `difficulty_bits` in the header of any Proof of Work-based blockchain application:

```
from Crypto.Hash import SHA256
from datetime import datetime

class Block(object):
    """A class representing the block for the blockchain"""
```

```
        def __init__(self, index, previous_hash, timestamp, data,
    difficulty_bits, nonce, hash):
            self.index = index
            self.previous_hash = previous_hash
            self.timestamp = timestamp
            self.data = data
            self.difficulty_bits = difficulty_bits
            self.nonce = nonce
            self.hash = hash
```

`self.difficulty_bits` is also included in the `Blockchain` class to use as a parameter while a miner is performing the Proof of Work algorithm:

```
    class Blockchain(object):
        """A class representing list of blocks"""

        def __init__(self):

            self._chain = [self.get_genesis_block()]
            self.timestamp = int(datetime.now().timestamp())
            self.difficulty_bits = 0
```

The `create_block` function will add both `nonce` and `difficulty_bits`, which are both set by the user while mining a new block. This information is included in the block to verify the block later once it is broadcast to every node in the network:

```
    def create_block(self, block_data):
        """creates a new block with the given block data"""

        previous_block = self.get_latest_block()
        next_index = previous_block.index + 1
        next_timestamp = self.timestamp
        next_hash, next_nonce = self.calculate_hash(next_index,
    previous_block.hash, next_timestamp, block_data)
        return Block(next_index, previous_block.hash, next_timestamp,
    block_data, self.difficulty_bits, next_nonce, next_hash)
```

The `calculate_hash` method is then modified to compute a header and call the function to perform Proof of Work by computing the nonce:

```
    def calculate_hash(self, index, previous_hash, timestamp, data):
        """calculates SHA256 hash value by solving hash puzzle"""

        header = str(index) + previous_hash + str(timestamp) + data +
    str(self.difficulty_bits)

        hash_value, nonce = self.proof_of_work(header)
        return hash_value, nonce
```

The `proof_of_work` method performs a search on each nonce by incrementing its value in order to find a hash value that is less than the target value. The target value is computed by using the `difficulty_bits` value provided.

Each time a hash value is calculated using the SHA256 hash function, the resulting hexadecimal digest is converted to a decimal value and compared with the target decimal value. If the computed hash value is less than the target value, it signifies that the hash value starts with a value that is greater than or equal to the `difficulty_bits`, so the nonce and the hash value is returned:

```
def proof_of_work(self, header):

    target = 2 ** (256 - difficulty_bits)

    for nonce in range(max_nonce):
        hash_result = SHA256.new(data=(str(header) +
    str(nonce)).encode()).hexdigest()

        if int(hash_result, 16) < target:
            print("Success with nonce %d" % nonce)
            print("Hash is %s" % hash_result)
            return (hash_result, nonce)

    print("Failed after %d (max_nonce) tries" % nonce)
    return nonce
```

The following Python main method will create a new Blockchain object class that will create a new chain with a genesis block. The `for` loop will create a new block, each time increasing `difficulty_bits` by 1. The `proof_of_work` function will be invoked each time a block is created:

```
max_nonce = 2 ** 32  # 4 billion

if __name__ == '__main__':

    new_chain = Blockchain()

    for difficulty_bits in range(32):
        difficulty = 2 ** difficulty_bits
        new_chain.difficulty_bits = difficulty_bits
        print("Difficulty: %ld (%d bits)" % (difficulty,
    difficulty_bits))
        print("Starting search...")

        start_time = datetime.now()
```

```
        new_block_data = 'test block with transactions'
        new_chain.add_block(data=new_block_data)

        end_time = datetime.now()

        elapsed_time = (end_time - start_time).total_seconds()
        print("Elapsed Time: %.4f seconds" % elapsed_time)

        if elapsed_time > 0:

            hash_power = float(int(new_chain.chain[-
1].get("nonce")) / elapsed_time)
            print("Hashing Power: %ld hashes per second" %
hash_power)
```

We'll find the output of the proof of work example as follows. It prints out the hashing power of the system used, the nonce, and the time elapsed during the creation of the block:

```
Difficulty: 1 (0 bits)
Starting search...
Success with nonce 0
Hash is
 365190b63a9ae8443e9dfb7463bcac6c207c29cdd0e8a5f251285d4d5ddbacb3
Elapsed Time: 0.0029 seconds
Hashing Power: 0 hashes per second
Difficulty: 2 (1 bits)
Starting search...
Success with nonce 0
Hash is
 67aad7ed255c1f7f3b6427cb75c60b6a9520c1ed19747d4f62b701691958f3b7
Elapsed Time: 0.0001 seconds
Hashing Power: 0 hashes per second

[...]

Difficulty: 64 (6 bits)
Starting search...
Success with nonce 4
Hash is
 0061db8a0100345e7a1675d39f8c5dae34c89712365d9761e30546c0dbb17e6d
Elapsed Time: 0.0002 seconds
Hashing Power: 17316 hashes per second
Difficulty: 128 (7 bits)
Starting search...
Success with nonce 22
Hash is
 0129f5f8dfae6063b09da9b6655848e4797c0ac22e1dba97dca6d9e6bfdbf6cb
Elapsed Time: 0.0009 seconds
```

```
Hashing Power: 23732 hashes per second

[...]

Difficulty: 33554432 (25 bits)
Starting search...
Success with nonce 3819559
Hash is
  0000001085152816d24bf7f32625295a0617a719b72f4f868e06003329975a9d
Elapsed Time: 122.2431 seconds
Hashing Power: 31245 hashes per second
Difficulty: 67108864 (26 bits)
Starting search...
Success with nonce 12980169
Hash is
  0000003435ba522e2c2d52fc7ad31b144103a99694299621a2a0573fb6f6be9c
Elapsed Time: 410.8903 seconds
Hashing Power: 31590 hashes per second
Difficulty: 134217728 (27 bits)
Starting search...
```

It is quite evident from this example output that the time taken to compute the solution is directly proportional to the number of difficulty bits used. To be precise, for every bit increase in the difficulty level, the probability of finding the nonce decreases by half because the target space decreases by half. Although occasionally luck might help us solve some puzzles, probability theory holds for the majority of cases with the proof of work consensus algorithm.

Digital signatures in blockchain

Digital signatures are a product of asymmetric key cryptography, and they are a great way of establishing trust between parties in a trustless environment. As mentioned at the beginning of this chapter, digital signatures are used in the application layer of the blockchain. They are mostly used to validate the events in transactions that are inserted in the blocks. They are used to validate the transactions, since verification can be performed by anyone who possesses the public key of the generated public-private key pair.

The asymmetric key cryptography provides a way to identify an entity. Anyone can prove the identity by owning the private key. Creating an identity for the participants allows them to perform operations such as asset management. We will explore digital identity and asset management in depth in this section in order to understand the role of digital signatures in blockchain.

Creating an identity

As we have covered digital signatures and the public-private key in the previous chapter, we are already aware of the properties and security of digital signatures. To recap, they provide a way for a node that possesses the private key to sign a message to prove their identity. This can then be verified by anyone who has access to the distributed public key.

An identity is created by generating a public-private key pair. This is similar to creating an account in the blockchain network. The following code shows how a public-private key pair is generated by the `ecdsa` Python package using an elliptic curve:

```python
import binascii
from ecdsa import SigningKey, VerifyingKey, SECP256k1, keys

class Wallet:
    def __init__(self):

        self.private_key = None
        self.public_key = None

    def generate_key_pair(self):

        sk = SigningKey.generate(curve=SECP256k1)
        self.private_key = binascii.b2a_hex(sk.to_string()).decode()
        self.public_key =
binascii.b2a_hex(sk.get_verifying_key().to_string()).decode()
```

The key pair is generated using a special elliptic curve, secp256k1, which is also used in Bitcoin's digital signature generation. The following lines of code will create a public-private key pair:

```python
account = Wallet()
account.generate_key_pair()
print("Generated public key: %s" % account.public_key)
print("Generated private key: %s" % account.private_key)
```

A 64-character (256-bit) private key and a 128-character public key are generated in hexadecimal format as follows:

```
Generated public key:
  b7f5edffe6d3532ed743e07c4de5551c2d7476a4053221999ce40edec2607bb4ef
  7ecb9fc6ecf735fd3802fada56c42e18474f8bad269a965f95863f9fc38158
Generated private key:
  6eb9035be1dabd01fadcb6a9f92946decc868046184c7810a43806eb6cc46237
```

The private key is always kept secret, and the public key is used to generate the public address of the user and is then embedded in the transaction.

Signatures in transaction

Digital signatures are used in transactions due to their properties that ensure the integrity of the transaction contents and non-repudiation of any events in the transaction. A transaction embedded into the block will contain a certain action that is being signed by someone who possesses the private key. Owning the private key thus proves the identity of the signer.

The following code shows a simple transaction with transaction id, signature, and public key. The transaction can only be signed by the owner of the corresponding private key of the public key. The transactions of Bitcoin and other blockchain platforms have several fields in the transaction to perform value transfer, while transactions of cryptocurrency are covered in greater detail in Chapter 5, *Cryptocurrency*:

```
class Transaction:

    def __init__(self, public_key):
        self.id = randint(1, 10**5)
        self.signature = None
        self.public_key = public_key
```

A signature is then created by signing the hashed content of the transaction with the private key of the corresponding public key:

```
def sign(self, private_key):

        data_to_sign = SHA256.new(str(self.id).encode()).digest()

        sk = SigningKey.from_string(bytes.fromhex(private_key),
    curve=SECP256k1)
        self.signature =
    binascii.b2a_hex(sk.sign(data_to_sign)).decode()
```

The transaction is then verified with the help of only the transaction contents, created signature, and the public key. Verification will only fail if the signature or the transaction contents were modified. This operation also verifies the integrity of the transaction:

```
def verify(self):

        vk = VerifyingKey.from_string(bytes.fromhex(self.public_key),
    curve=SECP256k1)

        try:
            vk.verify(bytes.fromhex(self.signature),
    SHA256.new(str(self.id).encode()).digest())
```

```
    except keys.BadSignatureError:
        print('invalid transaction signature')
        return False

    return True
```

A transaction can be successfully verified every time as long as the signature or data is not altered. The following code generates a signature and successfully verifies it:

```
tx = Transaction(account.public_key)
tx.sign(account.private_key)
print("Generated signature: %s" % tx.signature)
tx.verify()

Generated signature:
 943ed91d7ceb2a57d4e972845acda7ea818b994a840d3101d192ebe33a7c1f4d68
 55e50ed7b882cd4d372d540187f52f2d5b3a6144a58fc20098095f1726849f
```

When the transaction contents are modified or, in this case, the transaction ID is, then the verification fails:

```
tx.id = '1234'
tx.verify()
```

The transaction constructed in this section demonstrates the basic signing and verification process. An actual transaction can be used to transfer value from one user to other. In the next section, we'll cover the basic asset management that can be performed using the transactions.

Asset ownership in blockchain

A blockchain network is a decentralized peer-to-peer network, where nodes communicate with each other to create, exchange, and validate blocks. Most of the users in the blockchain network are interested in the application layer of the blockchain where operations can be performed by creating transactions. An identity can easily be created in the network, as we saw in the previous section of this chapter. Nodes can perform operations such as asset creation or asset transfer. Each operation that deals with assets is valid if they are approved by the asset owner. The asset owners prove their identity by signing the transactions using their private key.

Asset management operations, such as transferring the asset, can only be performed by the owner, but it can be verified by anyone in the network. All the operation details are embedded in transactions, and digital signatures are used by the asset owners to sign those transactions. They then broadcast these transactions to every node in the blockchain so that they are included in the next block to be appended to the blockchain ledger.

Transferring an asset

The ownership of an asset can be proven by possession of the private key for an address (public key) to which the asset belongs. Whenever the ownership of an asset needs to be transferred, users use their private key to sign the transaction, firstly proving their ownership, and from there transferring the ownership to the desired user.

We're now going to look at a detailed example to better explain asset ownership. Alice is a user who claims to own an asset in the blockchain network. She wishes to transfer this asset to her friend, Bob. She has access to her private key, and she uses it to create a transaction with a digital signature, which will prove that she owns the asset. The signing process is performed using the digital signature that is similar to what we used earlier in this chapter when ECDSA was used as a signing algorithm, which also made use of an ECC key pair. The following *Figure 3.3* shows how Alice creates a signature by signing the transaction contents that contain asset transfer information:

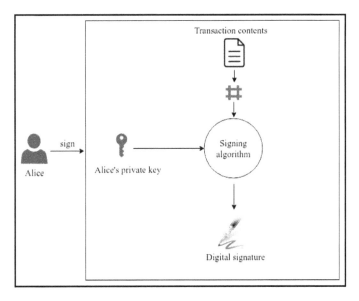

Figure 3.3: Alice signing a transaction to transfer an asset

All the information provided in this example of creating a transaction is from a high level and is not an accurate representation of transactions in practical blockchain applications. A detailed explanation of transactions is outside the scope of this chapter, but it will be covered in `Chapter 5,` *Cryptocurrency*.

Transmitting the transaction

Once the asset transfer information has been signed by the user, other information, such as the user's public key for verification, the destination public address, and other information that is necessary for verification, is provided. This information is broadcast to all the nodes so that it can be included in the blockchain:

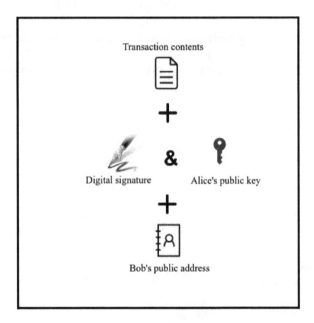

Figure 3.4: Information in a transaction

As shown in the preceding *Figure 3.4*, Alice will include information such as her public key and Bob's address in the transaction. The information provided in the transaction should suffice for Bob to claim that the asset belongs to him once the transaction has been included in any of the blocks in the blockchain.

The public address of the node acts as an identifier for the node and is constructed from the public key by performing hashing and encoding. `Chapter 5`, *Cryptocurrency*, will cover this in detail.

Claiming the asset

When an asset is transferred and transmitted with the information required in the transaction, the blockchain network will ensure that it is included in the blockchain after validating the transaction and the block in which it was included. When the transaction is included in the blockchain, everyone will be able to see this transaction, but only the owner to whom it was addressed will be able to claim the asset:

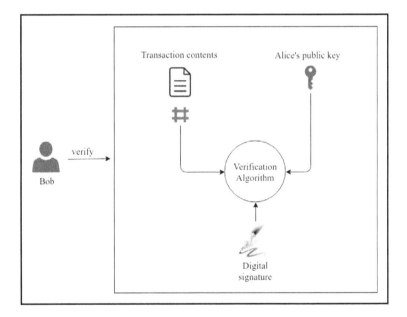

Figure 3.5: Bob verifying the transaction by means of public information

The level of security provided by the asymmetric key cryptography used in the digital signature will make sure that only the node that owns the private key corresponding to the public address will be able to claim the asset that was transferred to that address.

The preceding *Figure 3.5* shows that when Bob's node recognizes that a transaction has taken place in which an asset has been transferred to his address, he tries to verify the transaction with the public information provided in the transaction. Once he verifies that Alice has created a valid transaction, he can perform any action on the asset by providing his private key and thus proving that the asset belongs to him. This is how digital signatures ensure that an asset can easily be transferred by creating transactions, and the blockchain ensures the distribution of the transaction throughout the decentralized network.

Blockchain wallets

A blockchain wallet is a piece of software that holds all the private keys owned by a particular user. While physical wallets hold hard cash, blockchain wallets hold all the private keys a user possesses, which will help the user claim assets that belong to them.

 Wallets are a famous concept in cryptocurrency. A user holding the private key will be able to view their account balance when a transaction is recorded in the blockchain. Wallet nodes used in Bitcoin are called **Simplified Payment Verification (SPV)** nodes.

A single wallet can store any number of keys, which means a node can have multiple destination addresses. These keys are created in two distinct ways: deterministically and non-deterministically.

A **non-deterministic wallet** is a collection of randomly created private keys that bear no relation to each other. Private keys created with these wallets are difficult to maintain because it is difficult to reconstruct the keys in the event that they are lost. So, every key in the wallet has to be backed up to prevent any loss that could take place in the event of a wallet failure.

A **deterministic wallet** is also called a seed wallet because all the keys in this wallet are derived from a single seed. All the keys can easily be reproduced just by accessing the seed. All the keys in a simple deterministic wallet are created by hashing a string and an incremental nonce. In the case of wallet failure, seed information alone is sufficient to recover the private keys, so there is no need to back up all the keys in the wallet.

Summary

In this chapter, we've covered foundations of the facets of cryptography in blockchain by identifying its application in the basic blockchain architecture. This will serve as a foundation for the more advanced blockchain topics that we'll cover in later chapters.

Now that we have been introduced to the basic blockchain architecture, with cryptography as its backbone, it's time to move on to the counterpart of blockchain technology – decentralized networking. This will be covered in the next chapter and will help us to understand the use of blockchain within a trustless network.

4
Networking in Blockchain

In the previous chapters, we covered the cryptography concepts that are essential for blockchain to function in a trustless network. But we haven't discussed what a trustless network is. A decentralized network facilitates a trustless environment. In this chapter, we will explore how blockchain achieves decentralization with **peer-to-peer** (**P2P**) networking.

In this chapter, we will cover the following topics:

- P2P networking
- Network discovery
- Block synchronization
- Building a simple blockchain in a P2P network

We know that blockchain was created to remove the trust in a single central authority by building a trustless network that decentralizes all the tasks that are otherwise centralized in a single entity. P2P networking is an architecture style used to achieve this decentralization in blockchain applications. We'll begin this chapter by exploring the definition, history, and architecture of P2P networking.

Peer-to-peer (P2P) networking

The basic definition of a P2P network is a network where groups of independent computers called nodes are interconnected, sharing data without the assistance of any centralized servers. It is an architecture on top of the internet. Participants or nodes in this type of network are called peers because they are all equal and have equal responsibility within the network. Since there are no special nodes in a P2P network, each peer is both a service provider and a consumer.

History of P2P network

The early vision of the World Wide Web was aligned with the concept of P2P networking, where each user would be an active editor of and contributor to the network. USENET, first developed in 1979, enforced a decentralized model in which USENET servers communicated with each other to share news articles.

Although the P2P model was used in the early days of the internet, its most common use came about when it was implemented in file-sharing services. P2P in filesharing was popularized by the music-sharing application Napster. However, a number of music services followed that had a similar P2P filesharing model. Although Napster was the pioneer, filesharing in P2P has gained a lot of attention due to the BitTorrent protocol, which allows the filesharing of any digital media.

P2P networking architecture

P2P networking is an architecture where each peer acts as a server and a client simultaneously. Since a blockchain network is often implemented on a public network, it is difficult to create a physical topology that is suitable for P2P networking. To create this kind of architecture, a virtual or logical network overlay has to be constructed over the actual physical network topology. A logical network is created to achieve a convenient index of resources and peer discovery in a public network. Although an overlay is formed, data will be exchanged over the TCP/IP network.

Although the underlying physical network could follow any networking topology, the logical network in a P2P architecture will form a mesh-like topology in order to achieve better communication between the peers:

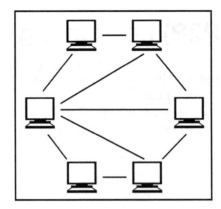

Figure 4.1: Partial physical mesh topology

In a physical mesh topology, each node can establish communication with any other peer, either directly or through some intermediate nodes. Each node will be able to communicate directly if the topology is a full mesh, where each node is linked to all the peers in the network. A partial mesh configuration is always preferable because constructing a full-mesh topology is expensive.

There are two main classifications of a P2P network, based on how the nodes are linked: **unstructured** and **structured P2P networks**.

In an unstructured network, the peers aren't linked to each other in an organized way. Each node is randomly connected to the peers, forming a logical mesh. It is easy to build unstructured networks, and they are very robust due to the redundant distribution of nodes. However, these networks have drawbacks, such as the possibility of request flooding, an effect caused by a lack of knowledge about the distribution of resources.

A structured P2P network overlay is formed by following a specific network topology to make sure that nodes can efficiently perform activities on the network. Creating a structured network ensures that a resource can be fetched from somewhere on the network in a certain time. A **distributed hash table** (**DHT**) is a widely used structured network implementation that provides decentralized lookup service. Resource information in a DHT can be retrieved from hash tables using the key of a key/value pair stored in the table. The value associated with the key provides information about the peer that owns the resource. DHTs are also used in the BitTorrent filesharing protocol as a substitute for centralized lookup services, such as trackers.

 DHT is a lookup service that is maintained in a distributed system. Nodes in a distributed system are responsible for maintaining the mapping from the keys to the values, which provide resource information.

Now that we have an overview of the P2P networking architecture, let's dive into some of the concepts of blockchain technology that are used in P2P networks to form a decentralized blockchain network.

Network discovery

Network discovery in a P2P network is crucial. No network is defined when a new node boots up. The new node must detect at least one blockchain node to be a part of the network. There are several ways in which a node can identify peers and thus discover a network.

Different blockchain frameworks use their own protocols to perform peer discovery and efficient routing. We're going to start by exploring basic P2P network discovery by taking a look at Bitcoin's original implementation.

The simplest way to find the list of peers to connect to is by hardcoding a few of the well-known peers. Using a central server that maintains a list of peers is another approach. Bitcoin holds information about DNS seeds, which provide a high level of reliability when a node is initially set up, and will respond with a list of the IP addresses of the Bitcoin nodes. Once a seed node is detected, the node will establish a TCP connection to perform a handshake with that node. The handshake validates the node by sending the version, the address, local blockchain information, and any other relevant information.

Once a connection is set up between peers that have been discovered by the node, the node can query for information about other nodes that are connected to its peer. Similarly, the node can broadcast its own address information to the connected peers to improve its reachability. Each node also makes sure to maintain a threshold for the number of active connections in order to avoid unnecessary bandwidth usage.

Some blockchain platforms, such as Ethereum, use a cryptographic P2P networking protocol suite called RLPx, which provides a general-purpose transport and interface for applications to communicate via a P2P network. RLPx utilizes a Kademlia-like routing to ensure uniform network formation. After the initial node handshake, packets are encapsulated as frames, which are then encrypted.

Block synchronization

Each node that joins the blockchain network needs to update its local copy of the blockchain to synchronize its state with the global state of the rest of the network. This is achieved by block synchronization. A node that needs to update its blockchain sends a message consisting of blockchain height information. Any peer that has a longer blockchain sends an inventory consisting of metadata about the fixed number of blocks that needs to be added to the host node. Now the node makes a request to all its peers to fetch individual blocks by referring to the inventory it received. The node should make sure not to flood the network with block requests by maintaining a cap on the number of block requests it sends.

Block synchronization is a long process for a newly-joined node. However, once all the blocks are up to date, it can verify the information in the block, such as the transactions on assets. The block synchronization process can be reinitialized whenever the node comes online after being inactive.

Building a simple blockchain in a P2P network

In `Chapter 3`, *Cryptography in Blockchain,* we explored how a consensus can be achieved in a decentralized network with the help of algorithms such as proof-of-work. Since consensus algorithms ensure that the Byzantine failure problem can be solved, a global truth can be maintained in a decentralized network in which there is no trust between the peers. Although consensus algorithms provide a convenient way to maintain a public ledger, each node has to perform a set of operations to maintain the ledger in a distributed network.

We have already created a simple blockchain application that can continuously enlarge its records whenever we have new data to be inserted. Because our blockchain application was deployed and the blocks were created in a single system, we have not yet added any mechanisms to validate the blocks. But when we deploy the blockchain as a public ledger, blocks need to be verified at each node whenever they arrive from the node's peers.

Each node has to perform the following processes in order to achieve a consensus in the network:

- Validate each incoming block for integrity so that it can be appended to the local blockchain
- Select the longest valid chain published by a peer in the decentralized network
- Create a valid block whenever there is some data that needs to be inserted into the public ledger

We're going to build a simple blockchain application that deploys the blockchain in a P2P network. This application is a reference implementation that will help us to understand the decentralization of the blockchain network. Although this application performs network discovery, block synchronization, and block validation, it doesn't follow all the required protocols for simplicity.

Let's now explore a few of the design considerations we need to think about in order to build the application before we dive into its implementation. The following sections cover validation, block synchronization, and the basic interface design used in this application.

Validating a new block

Although blocks are created by a miner node after validating all the previous blocks in the chain, it is the responsibility of each node in the network to perform a block validation to ensure that the block can be appended to the local copy of the blockchain. Block validation is a simple process of checking whether the latest block has a pointer or hash reference pointing to the previous block. When a block includes complex data, such as a set of transactions, independent transactions have to be verified to validate the block. Since we will not be dealing with any complex data inside the block, verifying transactions is beyond the scope of this chapter.

Selecting the longest chain

Finding a global truth in the decentralized network is a strenuous task, and a variety of consensus algorithms help to achieve it. The proof-of-work algorithm, discussed in the previous chapter, is the first and one of the best solutions. It ensures that the longest chain created has the most work contributed to it by legitimate nodes in the network. No consensus algorithm will be included in this application for the sake of simplicity.

Conflict resolution

Although selecting a block may seem an obvious task, there will be situations when two or more nodes create a block at the same time that has different identities due to the different content included in its block. When a node receives different versions of a block of the same height, it will add one of them to the blockchain based on the order of arrival and either rejects the other or keeps it in a memory pool. Due to this, nodes in the network might end up with different versions of the blockchain. This is called a temporary fork or a soft fork.

A soft fork is a type of fork in a blockchain where two or more different versions of the blockchain are created due to simultaneous block creation, or some malfunction. This fork is temporary and is rectified as soon as a longer blockchain propagates through the network.

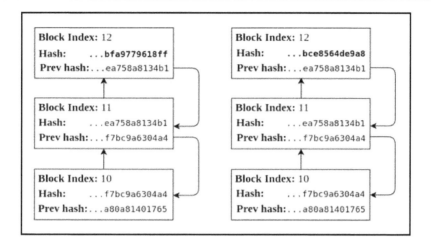

Figure 4.2: A block conflict caused by simultaneous block creation

Figure 4.2 shows how two blockchains have been created due to the simultaneous creation of blocks of the same height. Both the blockchains have the same height and the same blocks, up to index **11**. But there are two different versions of block **12**. As we can see in the figure, one of the blocks has a hash that ends with **...bfa9779618ff**, and the other hash ends with **...bce8564de9a8**. Both blocks are valid because their previous hash value matches with the previous block's hash, **...ea758a8134b1**. At this stage, one of the blocks will be inserted into the main chain, and the other will be rejected.

Although the conflict has been resolved on one node, there will be no global truth of the blockchain throughout the network because other nodes may have decided to accept a different block. This will create a temporary fork in the blockchain, because some nodes have one version of the blockchain, and some have the other version.

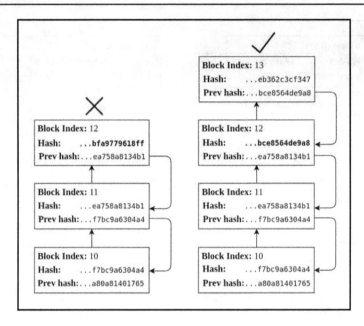

Figure 4.3: Resolving the conflict by accepting the longer chain

This temporary fork will not survive for a long time. As soon as a longer blockchain is created, and when a new block is appended to one of the chains, every node will reject the smaller blockchain and replace their blockchain with the longer one. *Figure 4.3* shows how the blockchain with the hash value **...bce8564de9a8** at index **12** will be accepted as it has increased its blockchain with an additional block, thus forming a longer chain.

Block exchange between peers

Block exchange in this application is performed using both broadcasting query messages and blocks. A newly-joined node goes through an initial block synchronization process to update its local copy of the blockchain.

Initial block synchronization

When a new node joins a network, it connects to one of the available peers in the network; it then tries to exchange its block information with the peer, and updates the local blockchain, if required.

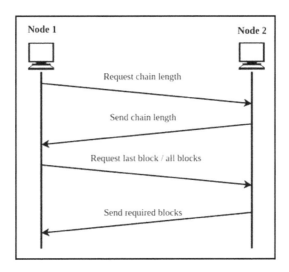

Figure 4.4: Initial block synchronization

The node sends a chain length or last block query message after connecting to the peer. Requesting the chain length is equivalent to requesting the last block to identify its index. If the received block cannot be appended to the local blockchain due the hash mismatch, then the node sends a message to its peer asking it to send all the blocks. The node can also broadcast a message requesting all the blocks to ensure that it receives the longest chain.

Broadcasting scenarios

Nodes communicate with each other in a P2P network by setting up multiple one-to-one connections, because there is no single peer that is completely trustable. Maintaining multiple connections forces each node to broadcast any information to its connected peers in order to distribute data to the entire network and maintain the global truth.

In our application, we will be broadcasting information for several scenarios, as shown in the state transition diagram depicted in *Figure 4.5*:

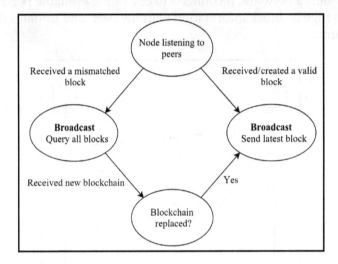

Figure 4.5: State transition diagram for broadcasting

A node in the network performs broadcasting in the following scenarios:

- When a node creates a new block, it has to broadcast it to all its connected peers in order to spread the block's information
- When a node receives a new block from its peer, it has to broadcast it in order to propagate the block in the P2P network
- When a node receives a block that doesn't fit with the current blockchain, it sends a query message to all its peers in order to find the longest chain

Application interfaces

The application provides two user interfaces: an HTTP API interface to access and manipulate blockchain information, and a WebSocket interface at all the nodes to achieve bidirectional communication by creating a long-lived channel:

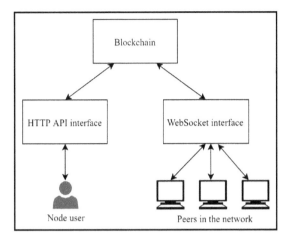

Figure 4.6: Interfaces of the application

Diving into the code

There are three different classes that form three separate parts of the application. The first one is `Server`, which will be dealing with the P2P communication on the blockchain network. The other two classes are `Blockchain` and `Block`, which were covered in the previous chapter and perform basic blockchain operations. The `Blockchain` class also performs enhanced functions in order to validate the blocks received from the peers, as discussed in the application architecture.

The server interface

The server interface is created using a Python web server framework called `Sanic`, which helps to code the web server logic in an asynchronous way:

 Background: Sanic is a lightweight web server framework that can be used to build a high-speed web server. It supports asynchronous programming by supporting Shiny async request handlers. It makes use of an event loop called `uvloop` to achieve better performance.

```
class Server(object):

    def __init__(self):

        self.app = Sanic()
```

```
self.blockchain = Blockchain()
self.sockets = []
self.app.add_route(self.blocks, '/blocks', methods=['GET'])
self.app.add_route(self.mine_block, '/mineBlock', methods=['POST'])
self.app.add_route(self.peers, '/peers', methods=['GET'])
self.app.add_route(self.add_peer, '/addPeer', methods=['POST'])
self.app.add_websocket_route(self.p2p_handler, '/')
```

The preceding code snippet of the `Server` class creates four REST API interfaces for displaying the blocks, mining (creating) a new block, displaying the node's current peers, and adding a new peer. We will be using endpoints created using the `add_route` methods to interact with our node.

We will be using the WebSocket protocol to perform P2P communication between the nodes because it allows bidirectional communication between the connected nodes and maintains an active connection without creating too much load on the web server.

 WebSocket is a communication protocol on top of TCP that provides a bidirectional communication channel, unlike HTTP. It can be used in P2P communication because both ends can send and receive messages simultaneously.

All the API interfaces defined in the preceding snippet invoke the following methods:

```
async def mine_block(self, request):
    try:
        newBlock =
self.blockchain.generate_next_block(request.json["data"])
    except KeyError as e:
        return json({"status": False, "message": "pass value in data
key"})
    self.blockchain.add_block(newBlock)
    await self.broadcast(self.response_latest_msg())
    return json(newBlock)
```

The preceding method implements the functionality required to generate a new block to append. Since it is an HTTP POST method, it accepts a parameter called `data`, which was sent in the HTTP request body. This data is used to create the new block. This method will broadcast the newly created block, as mentioned earlier in the application design section.

Blocks present in the local blockchain are formatted and returned by this method:

```
async def blocks(self, request):
    return json(self.blockchain.blocks)
```

Whenever the user wants to add a peer explicitly, they will use the following interface:

```
async def add_peer(self, request):
    asyncio.ensure_future(self.connect_to_peers
([request.json["peer"]]),
    loop=asyncio.get_event_loop())
    return json({"status": True})
```

This method adds an asynchronous `connect_to_peers` task to the event loop of the web server. All the socket information of the connected peers are maintained for future broadcasting.

The following implementation fetches address and port information from socket objects from all the peers that are maintained by the node after the initial connection:

```
async def peers(self, request):
    peers = map(lambda x: "{}:{}".format(x.remote_address[0],
x.remote_address[1]), self.sockets)
    return json(peers)]

async def connect_to_peers(self, newPeers):
    for peer in newPeers:
        logger.info(peer)
        try:
            ws = await websockets.connect(peer)

            await self.init_connection(ws)
        except Exception as e:
            logger.info(str(e))
```

The `connect_to_peers` method initializes WebSocket connections with all known peers. This method is also invoked when a new peer is added using the HTTP interface. Initial block synchronization is performed using the `init_connection` function. p2p-handler is a WebSocket handler that listens to the connection. It creates a socket and performs block synchronization using `init_connection`:

```
async def p2p_handler(self, request, ws):
    logger.info('listening websocket p2p port on: %d' % port)
    try:
        await self.init_connection(ws)
    except (ConnectionClosed):
        await self.connection_closed(ws)
```

Socket information is removed when a peer gets disconnected:

```
async def connection_closed(self, ws):
```

```
        logger.critical("connection failed to peer")
        self.sockets.remove(ws)
```

Block synchronization is performed by the `init_connection` method by sending a query message requesting the last block of the peer's blockchain. It also adds a message handler that continuously listens to the messages from its peers:

```
async def init_connection(self, ws):

    self.sockets.append(ws)
    await ws.send(JSON.dumps(self.query_chain_length_msg()))

    while True:
        await self.init_message_handler(ws)
```

The message handler on each node listens for three types of message. Two of them are query messages to which the node responds by querying the local blockchain. The `RESPONSE_BLOCKCHAIN` message is a response received from the query made by the local node. This message will be further processed by `handle_blockchain_response`:

```
async def init_message_handler(self, ws):
    data = await ws.recv()
    message = JSON.loads(data)
    logger.info('Received message: {}'.format(data))

    await {
        QUERY_LATEST: self.send_latest_msg,
        QUERY_ALL: self.send_chain_msg,
        RESPONSE_BLOCKCHAIN: self.handle_blockchain_response
    }[message["type"]](ws, message)
```

The following methods serialize the response data to be sent to the peer for its query message requests:

```
async def send_latest_msg(self, ws, *args):
    await ws.send(JSON.dumps(self.response_latest_msg()))

async def send_chain_msg(self, ws, *args):

    await ws.send(JSON.dumps(self.response_chain_msg()))
```

The entire blockchain is sent to the connected peer when it queries the blockchain:

```
def response_chain_msg(self):
    return {
        'type': RESPONSE_BLOCKCHAIN,
        'data': JSON.dumps([block.dict() for block in
self.blockchain.blocks])}
```

The following code snippet fetches the last block from the blockchain and formats it into JSON so it can be sent via the socket channel:

```
def response_latest_msg(self):

    return {
        'type': RESPONSE_BLOCKCHAIN,
        'data': JSON.dumps([self.blockchain.get_latest_block().dict()])
    }
```

The following code snippets are the query request messages used to query connected peers for the blockchain:

```
def query_chain_length_msg(self):

    return {'type': QUERY_LATEST}

def query_all_msg(self):

    return {'type': QUERY_ALL}
```

The following method is invoked in the message handler that is continuously listening to the peer's requests and responses. This method is invoked to process the blockchain information sent by the peers:

```
async def handle_blockchain_response(self, ws, message):
    received_blocks = sorted(JSON.loads(message["data"]), key=lambda k:
k['index'])
    latest_block_received = received_blocks[-1]
    latest_block_held = self.blockchain.get_latest_block()

    if latest_block_received["index"] > latest_block_held.index:
        logger.info('blockchain possibly behind. We got: ' +
str(latest_block_held.index)
            + ' Peer got: ' + str(latest_block_received["index"]))
```

If the last index of the block is not greater than the local blockchain's last index, it will be rejected because the node is only interested in the longest chain:

```
        if latest_block_held.hash ==
latest_block_received["previous_hash"]:
            logger.info("We can append the received block to our
chain")
            self.blockchain.blocks.append
(Block(**latest_block_received))
            await self.broadcast(self.response_latest_msg())
```

The last block received is appended to the local blockchain if it satisfies the hash conditions. If it is satisfied, then it's broadcasted to all the peers:

```
elif len(received_blocks) == 1:
    logger.info("We have to query the chain from our peer")
    await self.broadcast(self.query_all_msg())
else:
    logger.info("Received blockchain is longer than current
blockchain")
    await self.replace_chain(received_blocks)
```

If the last block doesn't satisfy the hash condition, then the local blockchain may be behind by more than one block. The local copy will then be replaced with the received blockchain if it is a full chain. Otherwise, a message is broadcasted to query the entire blockchain.

When a node receives a blockchain that is longer than the current local copy, it will validate the entire blockchain and then replace the entire local blockchain:

```
async def replace_chain(self, newBlocks):

    try:
        if self.blockchain.is_valid_chain(newBlocks) and len(newBlocks)
> len(self.blockchain.blocks):
            logger.info('Received blockchain is valid. Replacing
current blockchain with ' 'received blockchain')
            self.blockchain.blocks = [Block(**block) for block in
newBlocks]
            await self.broadcast(self.response_latest_msg())
        else:
            logger.info('Received blockchain invalid')
    except Exception as e:
        logger.info("Error in replace chain" + str(e))
```

The `broadcast` method then sends all the requests and responses to every peer connected to the node through the established socket connection:

```
async def broadcast(self, message):

    for socket in self.sockets:
        await socket.send(JSON.dumps(message))
```

Block and blockchain interface

The `Block` and `Blockchain` class methods are similar to those used in the previous chapter to build a simple blockchain, with the only enhancement being the validation methods used to validate the received blocks.

The following method is invoked to verify that every block is linked to its previous block:

```
def is_valid_new_block(self, new_block, previous_block):
```

The following condition validates the index of the new block:

```
if previous_block.index + 1 != new_block.index:
    logger.warning('invalid index')
    return False
```

This condition performs hash validation by comparing the hash values of the blocks:

```
if previous_block.hash != new_block.previous_hash:
    logger.warning('invalid previous hash')
    return False
```

This condition checks the integrity of the newly added block by calculating its digest:

```
if self.calculate_hash_for_block(new_block) != new_block.hash:
    logger.info(type(new_block.hash) + ' ' +
type(self.calculate_hash_for_block(new_block)))
    logger.warning('invalid hash: ' +
self.calculate_hash_for_block(new_block) + ' ' + new_block.hash)
    return False
return True
```

The following method is used to validate the entire blockchain when the node wants to replace the local blockchain with the one retrieved from its peer:

```
def is_valid_chain(self, blockchain_to_validate):
    if
self.calculate_hash_for_block(Block(**blockchain_to_validate[0])) !=
self.get_genesis_block().hash:
        return False
```

This condition validates the hardcoded genesis block:

```
temp_blocks = [Block(**blockchain_to_validate[0])]
for currentBlock in blockchain_to_validate[1:]:
    if self.is_valid_new_block(Block(**currentBlock),
temp_blocks[-1]):
        temp_blocks.append(Block(**currentBlock))
```

```
        else:
            return False
    return True
```

Every block of the received blockchain is validated iteratively by invoking `is_valid_new_block`.

Running the blockchain nodes

Although each node has two handlers, one each for the HTTP and WebSocket interfaces. A single web server application instance is sufficient to serve both of them. *Sanic* uses `uvloop` as a scheduler. It asynchronously handles the requests:

```
if __name__ == '__main__':

    server = Server()
    server.app.add_task(server.connect_to_peers(initialPeers))
    server.app.run(host='0.0.0.0', port=port, debug=True)
```

The server application is instantiated, and a task is created to connect the node to `initialPeers`, which is hardcoded by each node. The application will use the default port to create a web server.

Each node will run the server application to join the network. As soon as the node connects to one of the peers, its blockchain syncs with the updated blockchain of the network.

We're now going to run the application by creating three node instances: node1, node2, and node3. Node2 has node1 as its initial peer, and node3 has node2 as its initial peer. When we run all three node instances, they form a ring-like network.

Let's check the peer information of each node by calling the HTTP API endpoint `/peers` for each node:

- **Node1**: ["127.0.0.1:51160"]
- **Node2**: ["127.0.0.1:3001","127.0.0.1:35982"]
- **Node3**: ["127.0.0.1:3002"]

`3001` is the port number assigned to node1. Node2 has port number `3002`, and node3 has port number `3003`. The random port number is the port number of the peer that tried to communicate with the node2. The preceding information clearly shows that node2 has added node1 as its peer and node3 has added node2 as its peer.

All the nodes return the following result when we invoke the `/blocks` HTTP API endpoint:

```
[
  {
    "data": "my genesis block!!",
    "hash":
 "816534932c2b7154836da6afc367695e6337db8a921823784c14378abed4f7d7",
    "index": 0,
    "previous_hash": "0",
    "timestamp": 1465154705
  }
]
```

Let's mine a new block at node2 by using the `/mineBlock` HTTP API endpoint by sending a POST request with the payload `{"data": "created at node2"}`. Since all the nodes are interconnected, forming a mesh, each node will receive the newly broadcasted block and will update its local blockchain ledger. Now, each node reflects the following blockchain:

```
[
  {
    "data": "my genesis block!!",
    "hash":
 "816534932c2b7154836da6afc367695e6337db8a921823784c14378abed4f7d7",
    "index": 0,
    "previous_hash": "0",
    "timestamp": 1465154705
  },
  {
    "data": "created at node2",
    "hash":
 "29630fab36aa1e3abf85b62aee8f84b08438b90e9e19f39d18766cc9208b585c",
    "index": 1,
    "previous_hash":
 "816534932c2b7154836da6afc367695e6337db8a921823784c14378abed4f7d7",
    "timestamp": "1522069707"
  }
]
```

Following this example: The entire P2P blockchain application can be found in the book's GitHub repository. It has a configuration that can be used to set up a Docker cluster using Docker Compose. This will help you to set up any number of blockchain nodes on a single machine.

Summary

This chapter has covered the aspects of P2P networking that are used in blockchain applications by building a simple P2P application with basic functionalities. The basic architectural knowledge that you've gained from this chapter will help you to understand the advanced networking concepts used in some blockchain platforms.

Now that we have a strong background of the blockchain technology after covering several cryptography and networking concepts, we will get introduced to the original and one of the strongest use cases of blockchain technology – Cryptocurrency. In the next chapter, we will apply most of the concepts introduced till now to understand and implement the cryptocurrency use case.

5
Cryptocurrency

In this chapter, we will explore the original and best implementation of blockchain technology—cryptocurrency. Cryptocurrency is much more than just a blockchain application; it makes use of cryptographic primitives such as digital signatures to achieve asset management by using atomic events called transactions. Throughout this chapter, we will be familiarized with all the concepts required to understand how cryptocurrency is different from any of the traditional digital currencies.

In this chapter, we will cover the following topics:

- The basics of Bitcoin
- Keys and addresses
- Transactions
- Mining and consensus
- Blockchain
- Blockchain networks
- The creation of a simple cryptocurrency application

Bitcoin was the first successful cryptocurrency to be deployed in a decentralized network. It is the best-known cryptocurrency to date due to its resilient software and infrastructure, widespread adoption in various fields, and high market capitalization. By the end of 2017, Bitcoin had achieved a market cap of 300 billion USD, which is the highest by any cryptocurrency to date. Most of the cryptocurrencies in the market are inspired by and use similar designs to Bitcoin. We will be using Bitcoin to learn about most of the relevant concepts in cryptocurrency, and later on in this chapter, we will also implement a cryptocurrency similar to Bitcoin.

A cryptocurrency is a digital asset that uses cryptography to secure, spend, and verify its value in the transactions. The cryptocurrency could be transferred from the owner to any recipient without the need for an intermediary to settle the transactions. Although the early adoption of cryptocurrency provided a number of features, such as pseudo anonymity, lower transaction fees, and removing the need for an intermediary, it never achieved true decentralization. There were known issues, such as double-spending. This was when a single asset was transferred to multiple recipients because there was no centralized source to verify these transactions. All of these issues were addressed when a completely decentralized cryptocurrency called Bitcoin was created in 2009. This solved the double-spend issue for the first time in a decentralized network by using immutable blockchain to achieve consensus among the nodes.

Bitcoin basics

Bitcoin is a collection of cryptography and decentralized consensus algorithms that enabled the creation of a complete decentralized digital currency ecosystem.

Bitcoin can be used just like conventional currencies. It can be used to buy and sell goods and services or to just transfer money to people. Bitcoin has several advantages over conventional currencies, such as lower transaction costs and the ability to transfer currency to any part of the world, because it is not controlled by any national authorities. Bitcoin is also entirely virtual, meaning there is no physical form of the currency. The value of Bitcoin is generated by transactions in Bitcoin. Anyone can transfer Bitcoin to a particular Bitcoin address using a transaction. The address of the legitimate recipient of the Bitcoin will be identified by a secret key corresponding to the address. The user can then transfer the Bitcoin to others by constructing a new transaction using the secret key. Generally, a Bitcoin address is created using the public key, and the secret key is the private key counterpart of the public key. The keys are generally stored in a software application called a wallet, but they can also be backed up and stored anywhere if we need better security.

As we know, Bitcoin is the system that paved the way for the invention of blockchain. It utilizes all the concepts we have discussed so far to build a cryptocurrency that functions in a completely decentralized **peer-to-peer** (**P2P**) system. Because of Bitcoin's completely decentralized network, there is no need for a central trusted authority, such as a bank, to act as a moderator and validate the transactions. Instead, everyone in the Bitcoin ecosystem participates in ensuring that valid transactions take place.

Bitcoin software is open source, and anyone can join the Bitcoin network by running this software on a device such as a smartphone or a computer. A lighter version of the Bitcoin software can be used on devices where the computing and storage capacity is limited. There is a special type of node called a miner, which uses processing power to verify transactions and contributes to the creation of blocks by solving a hard-cryptographic puzzle. This is a hash puzzle, more specifically called the Proof of Work consensus algorithm, which was discussed in `Chapter 3`, *Cryptography in Blockchain*. Every 10 minutes, a miner can publish a valid block, which is then propagated and validated by everyone on the Bitcoin network. The miner is rewarded in bitcoin for the computing power spent creating the block. Due to an increase in competition in mining, the difficulty of the puzzle has been adjusted so that the average block creation time remains around 10 minutes.

So, every time the miner creates a new block, new bitcoins are minted, which circulate in the Bitcoin network. There is a limit set on the total number of bitcoins that can circulate in the network, and it is hard-capped to 21 million coins.

To sum up, the following innovations helped Bitcoin to survive in a completely trustless network:

- A decentralized P2P network
- A blockchain (public ledger)
- Decentralized consensus algorithm (Proof of Work)
- Transaction validation rules

Throughout this chapter, we will try to explain how Bitcoin uses these concepts, which made its creation possible.

Getting started with Bitcoin Core

Bitcoin is an experimental digital currency that is maintained by an open source community. Bitcoin Core is the name of open source software that enables the use of this currency. It's the original implementation of the Bitcoin system and whose initial release was created by Satoshi Nakamoto.

 Open source software is software whose source code is made available to the public with the right to read, modify, and redistribute it. Although open source code can be covered by different licenses, most of it is free to use for any purpose. Bitcoin is licensed under the MIT license.

Setting up a Bitcoin full node

A Bitcoin full node can be set up for development purposes, or just to enable a user to be a part of the Bitcoin network in order to validate or explore the transactions. The user has to set up all the tools, libraries, and dependent applications they may need if they want to set up a complete development environment, whereas a Bitcoin node can be set up without much effort just by installing the software.

Installing a Bitcoin full node

As mentioned, installing a Bitcoin full node is much simpler than setting up a development environment. Bitcoin full nodes are ideal for users who want to be a part of the Bitcoin network but don't want to worry about any of its implementations.

Running a Bitcoin full node has certain hardware requirements. It needs dedicated storage because it has to store all the blocks of the public ledger. At the time of writing, Bitcoin blockchain blocks occupy around 180 GB of storage. A Bitcoin full node also needs a decent amount of memory and processing power in order to validate the transactions of every block. Bitcoin can be installed on Linux, macOS, and Windows platforms quite easily.

 We will not be providing details about the installation here because it varies from platform to platform. You can find installation details for different platforms in the GitHub repository of the book (`https://github.com/PacktPublishing/Foundations-of-Blockchain`). Moreover, you can find the installation instructions for all the platforms at `https://bitcoin.org/en/full-node`.

Compiling from source code

A Bitcoin development environment is set up by compiling the source code obtained from the Bitcoin repository. The source code of Bitcoin Core is hosted in a GitHub repository under the MIT license. You can either clone and fetch all the branches or download the ZIP file of a specific release.

You can clone the Bitcoin Core project from the `https://github.com/bitcoin/bitcoin.git` repository using the Git tool. Once the project has been cloned, you can either use the latest master code or checkout to any of the release using the Git tag.

The build process might take up to an hour depending on the system's hardware configuration. Compiling the source code involves only a few steps, but they are time-consuming:

1. As the first step, Bitcoin Core needs you to run a script called `autogen.sh`, which creates a set of automatic configuration scripts that examine the system and ensure that your system has all the libraries to compile the code. The shell script is executed as follows:

```
$ ./autogen.sh
```

2. The next step is to use the configure script to customize the build process by enabling or disabling certain features. We can build Bitcoin Core with the default features because most of Bitcoin Core's features are required to set up a node. The configuration script is executed as follows:

```
$ ./configure
```

3. Finally, the source code is compiled to create executables and install the created executables. This is achieved using the following commands:

```
$ make
$ make install
```

The installation of will create a binary called `bitcoind`, which creates the Bitcoin daemon process, and a command-line tool called `bitcoin-cli`, which is used to invoke Bitcoin APIs to communicate with the local Bitcoin node.

Running the Bitcoin node

The Bitcoin daemon process is created when `bitcoind` is executed by creating a configuration file. The basic configuration file consists of a username and password for the JSON-RPC interface. There are several options that can be specified while running to Bitcoin node to alter its behavior. These options can also be specified in the configuration file. Execute `bitcoind --help` to list out the available options. `bitcoind` can be executed after the configuration file is created:

```
$ bitcoind -daemon
```

This will start Bitcoin Core as a background process. It may take several minutes to load the block index and verify the blocks. The `bitcoin-cli` tool can then be used to check the status once the `bitcoind` process has been created.

The following command shows some basic information about Bitcoin Core as well as some local blockchain information. The API was invoked on a `mainnet` chain that had mined 519,993 blocks at the time:

```
$ bitcoin-cli getblockchaininfo
{
    "chain": "main",
    "blocks": 519993,
    "headers": 519993,
    "bestblockhash":
"000000000000000000d4715ff499c5ce23c4b355634d4b59a2fe3823387dd12",
    "difficulty": 3839316899029.672,
    "mediantime": 1524733692,
    "verificationprogress": 0.999994783377989,
    "chainwork":
"000000000000000000000000000000000000000019897317fc702c4837762b2",
    "pruned": false,
    ...
}
```

Bitcoin has several blockchain networks formed by the bitcoin nodes. Each of these networks maintains different blockchain. Bitcoin's main network is called `mainnet` and it has a test network called `testnet`. More information on this topic is covered in the *Blockchain and networks* section of the chapter.

Communicating with the Bitcoin node

Bitcoin Core provides an API through the JSON-RPC interface to facilitate communication with the Bitcoin node. Most of the consensus, wallet, and P2P Bitcoin operations can be performed on the node using this interface. Bitcoin uses `8332` as the default JSON-RPC server port for mainnet. Users should make sure not to allow arbitrary machines to access the JSON-RPC port. Exposing this interface would allow external machines to access private information, which could lead to theft.

Bitcoin has a command-line interface tool, `bitcoin-cli`, that can be used to access all the JSON-RPC APIs.

Any transaction details can be fetched using the `getrawtransaction` RPC command by specifying the transaction ID:

```
$ bitcoin-cli getrawtransaction
4289bf1e7a4295e75fcff0644c44bd1c114511b7ec5407afea64de2d280bddb802000000010
e1bd74a37fa90e5e8de8e4c20ec42a26c70ef40330b5361c560d03f3c8ba7e9000000006a47
304402201a62b24dcbeba9ec65478be8a12ccd31c3c984
9813782d1ca0bcab657a88762402204897f9c9e5e99de969fd5d076d80aebbaef19493f5e27
```

```
3663d4727864a67295b012102b21f43b03f57e029ea43f2cec448d4ff43740af4a68607507f
34fd93be97bc30fefffffff02809698000000000000197
6a914523f63d0e9f8cb9519482fc6a8476689e57555e688ac590657010000000001976a91469
cac07f09af880832eedbcbc7e0dea94fb68e2688acb1bb1300
```

The output is a serialized transaction in hexadecimal format. This data can then be decoded using the `decoderawtransaction` API:

```
$ bitcoin-cli decoderawtransaction
02000000010e1bd74a37fa90e5e8de8e4c20ec42a26c70ef40330b5361c560d03f3c8ba7e90
00000006a47304402201a62b24dcbeba9ec65478be8a12ccd31c3c9849813782d1ca0bcab65
7a88762402204897f9c9e5e99de969fd5d076d80aebbaef19493f5e273663d4727864a67295
b012102b21f43b03f57e029ea43f2cec448d4ff43740af4a68607507f34fd93be97bc30feff
ffff02809698000000000001976a914523f63d0e9f8cb9519482fc6a8476689e57555e688ac5
90657010000000001976a91469cac07f09af880832eedbcbc7e0dea94fb68e2688acb1bb1300
```

This generates a decoded transaction in a human-readable JSON format. We will discuss the decoded transactions in the *Transactions* section of the chapter.

Communicating using scripting language through the JSON-RPC implementation

Any programming language's JSON-RPC implementation can be used to communicate with a Bitcoin node. Let's execute an API using the Python JSON-RPC implementation, which will automatically generate all the Python methods for RPC calls. Python has several libraries with support for JSON-RPC, but we will be using `python-bitcoinlib`, which not only provides a JSON-RPC implementation but can also interface with Bitcoin data structures and protocols. The following Python script accepts a transaction ID in hexadecimal format and converts it into raw bytes using the `lx()` function. An RPC object, `proxy_connection`, which can be used to invoke any API, is created. The `gettransaction` API will fetch the decoded transaction of the transaction ID that was provided:

```
import bitcoin.rpc
from bitcoin.core import lx

bitcoin.SelectParams('testnet')

proxy_connection = bitcoin.rpc.Proxy()
tx_id = lx(input())
print(proxy_connection.gettransaction(tx_id))
```

Keys and addresses

We have covered all the concepts of cryptography that will be required in order to understand the keys, addresses, and wallets used in cryptocurrency. In this section, we will get a thorough grounding of how keys and addresses are used to control the ownership of funds through cryptographic primitives.

We have covered how asymmetric cryptography is used to create public/private keys, which identify the user accounts in the blockchain network. Bitcoin generates public/private key pairs that identify users and help them to claim ownership of funds through digital signatures. The private key is also called the secret key in cryptocurrency because it is kept secret from the public. Digital signatures are a prevalent concept in cryptography that allows the owner of the secret key to create a signature for a transaction and allow anyone to verify a transaction. Secret key owners manage all their keys using lightweight software called a wallet. Keys are independent of the blockchain protocol and are created and managed by the wallet.

Bitcoin uses addresses to identify the Bitcoin user. These addresses are the encoded version of the public key derived from the user's secret key. Let's consider a banking example: Alice transfers the money to Bob by signing a check addressed to Bob. Bitcoin uses a similar approach by signing a transaction using the secret key and providing the recipient's account number, which is the Bitcoin public address. The only public information is the account number, which is similar in concept to making the Bitcoin address public.

Public and private keys

Public and private keys are generated using asymmetric cryptography. Private keys are kept secret in the users' wallets, whereas public keys are made public in the form of a Bitcoin address. Bitcoin uses elliptic curve cryptography to generate the public/private key pair. The private key is selected at random, and elliptic curve multiplication is performed to generate the public key. Elliptic curve multiplication is a one-way cryptographic function that makes it impossible to derive the private key from the exposed public key. You can explore the mathematical explanation and analysis of elliptical curve cryptography in Chapter 2, *A Bit of Cryptography*.

Bitcoin's private key is a randomly selected 256-bit character string or 64-character hexadecimal string. This means that the private key can be any number between 1 and 2^{256}. So, it is impossible to find the corresponding private key of the public key just by brute-forcing 2^{256} combinations. The randomly generated private key is isolated from the Bitcoin network and maintained secretly in the Bitcoin wallet.

Bitcoin's command-line interface can be used to generate secret keys. Bitcoin has a set of APIs that deal with keys and addresses. The following commands are performed on the local wallet. `dumprivkey` fetches the already existing private key, which was generated from the public key:

```
$ bitcoin-cli getnewaddress
1JK1yCXbP2WkwgzbAUqpWTeo9rQkA9seNg

$ bitcoin-cli dumpprivkey 1JK1yCXbP2WkwgzbAUqpWTeo9rQkA9seNg
L2NAKvQsbkeQZyhfPRWw1juQ19ohxGCFbdr8izQSHEmKWYFtVjXK
```

Bitcoin public addresses

Public addresses in Bitcoin are produced from public keys, which consist of digits beginning with 1, or 3 for mainnet. Most Bitcoin addresses are 33 or 34 characters long and use Base58-encoding. Bitcoin public key addresses always represent the owner of the secret key and are used in the recipient field of transactions. However, addresses can also have different uses, such as representing the payment script used in **Pay-to-Script-Hash** (**P2SH**) transactions, which will be covered in the *Transaction* section of this chapter.

Bitcoin addresses are derived from the public key by constructing an encoded string called Base58Check. Base58Check is a Base58 encoded string along with fixed characters that acts as error-checking code. The Base58Check encoded string that represents Bitcoin address has three parts – a prefixed version byte, a payload derived from the public key, and the checksum. The version byte represents the type of Bitcoin address. *Table 5.1* shows a variety of prefixes found in the Bitcoin addresses:

Prefix (Base58)	Use
1	Bitcoin pubkey hash (P2PKH address)
3	Bitcoin script hash (P2SH address)
5	Private key (WIF)
m or n	Bitcoin testnet pubkey hash
2	Bitcoin testnet script hash

Table 5.1: Prefixes used as version bytes (Source: https://en.bitcoin.it)

The second part of the Bitcoin public address is derived from the public key by hashing it using the `SHA256` and `RIPEMD160` hashing algorithms. As we already know, hashing functions are one-way functions, which makes it infeasible to derive the public key from the computed Bitcoin address.

In the following function, K is the public key derived from the private key, and H is the Bitcoin public key hash:

```
H = RIPEMD160(SHA256(K))
```

After constructing the hash value H using the hash functions, the third part of the address, a checksum, is computed from the resultant value. Finally, all the three parts are concatenated and encoded using Base58 encoding, which uses 58 characters (please refer to Chapter 2, *A Bit of Cryptography*, for more details regarding Base58 encoding) to create the Bitcoin public address in the Base58Check format as mentioned earlier:

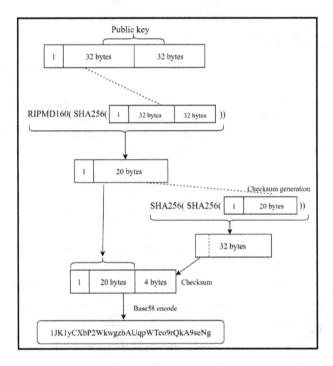

Figure 5.1: Generation of a Bitcoin public address from the public key

Figure 5.1 shows how a 64-byte public key along with the 1-byte version is hashed initially to produce a 20-byte digest. This is the payload, which is then encoded to generate the Bitcoin address. But the final address also consists of checksum bits, which are used to protect against errors. This 4-byte checksum is calculated by hashing the payload twice using the SHA256 hash function and extracting the initial 4 bytes from the resulting 32-byte digest.

This checksum is concatenated with the payload and version byte. Finally, the resulting string is encoded using the Base58 encoding system to generate the Bitcoin address, which will identify the user who is holding the corresponding secret key.

As we know, it is impossible for anyone to generate the private key from the publicly available Bitcoin address. This is due to the functions used to derive the public key. A public key is created using elliptical curve multiplication, which is a one-way function. Similarly, a Bitcoin address is derived from the public key by applying hash functions, which are one-way functions by nature. This prevents anyone from generating the public key from the Bitcoin public address as well:

Figure 5.2: The one-way functionality of Bitcoin address generation

Figure 5.2 depicts the one-way functions used in the generation of the Bitcoin address. Although the Bitcoin address, which represents the identity of the entity holding the private key, is known to the public, the private key cannot be retrieved due to the one-way nature of these functions.

Transactions

We have already covered many of the concepts used in Bitcoin that aid in the creation of a cryptocurrency in a decentralized network. Although every concept has a significant role in Bitcoin, transactions play a central role. Everything else in Bitcoin is designed to ensure that valid transactions are safely included in the blockchain and are propagated to the entire network of nodes.

Unlike traditional bookkeeping, in which an account-based ledger is used, Bitcoin maintains a transaction-based ledger. Every transaction entered into Bitcoin has to be validated before it is included in the blockchain. Bitcoin nodes refer to the transactions included in the other blocks or transaction mempool to validate every transaction. In this section, we will dig deep into concepts such as transaction creation, verification, and the components of transactions.

A transaction mempool is a collection of unconfirmed transactions maintained by each Bitcoin node. The transactions in the mempool will be eventually included in the blockchain. A real-time view of the Bitcoin mempool can be observed at
`https://www.blockchain.com/btc/unconfirmed-transactions.`

Transactions at a high level

Before diving into the low-level details of transactions and their components, let's look at an example that illustrates a simple Bitcoin transaction from the user's point of view. Let's say Alice sends 0.1 bitcoin from her Bitcoin wallet to Bob's wallet. Since she already has more than 0.1 bitcoin in her wallet, a valid transaction will be created and propagated to the network. *Figure 5.3* shows the transaction details in a block explorer application:

Transaction View information about a bitcoin transaction

4289bf1e7a4295e75fc80644c44bd1c11451tb7ec5407a6a64de2d280hddb8

mhqGzwrf7SSjEeBTB5qb1MnodFSafUpJ8n (0.325 BTC - Output) → mo1qeC6G2cLZqeBiSeLgKL2z1QcvsG9Mu3 - (Spent) 0.1 BTC
mqALBeXgSE7tHGF9fdYrhYnwMFW3nnNyH9z - (Unspent) 0.22480473 BTC

2 Confirmations 0.32480473 BTC

Summary		Inputs and Outputs	
Size	225 (bytes)	Total Input	0.325 BTC
Weight	900	Total Output	0.32480473 BTC
Received Time	2018-04-17 05:55:09	Fees	0.00019527 BTC
Lock Time	Block: 1293233	Fee per byte	86.787 sat/B
Included in Blocks	1293234 (2018-04-17 06:04:21 + 9 minutes)	Fee per weight unit	21.697 sat/WU
Confirmations	2 Confirmations	Estimated BTC Transacted	0.1 BTC

Figure 5.3: Bitcoin transaction from Alice to Bob

All the transaction details shown in this section are created using Bitcoin's `testnet` blockchain. You can check the transaction details by switching the Bitcoin node to the testnet blockchain. The block explorer application also runs in the testnet blockchain. You can verify the transactions at `https://testnet.blockexplorer.com.`

Transactions are visible to everyone who has access to the blockchain. A hex editor must be used to read transactions because they are not stored in a human-readable form. Bitcoin Core's command-line interface can read raw transactions and decode them:

```
{ "txid":
"4289bf1e7a4295e75fcff0644c44bd1c114511b7ec5407afea64de2d280bddb8", "hash":
"4289bf1e7a4295e75fcff0644c44bd1c114511b7ec5407afea64de2d280bddb8",
"version": 2, "size": 225, "vsize": 225,
  "locktime": 1293233,
  "vin": [
    {
      "txid":
"e9a78b3c3fd060c561530b3340ef706ca242ec204c8edee8e590fa374ad71b0e",
      "vout": 0,
      "scriptSig": {
        "asm":
"304402201a62b24dcbeba9ec65478be8a12ccd31c3c9849813782d1ca0bcab657a88762402
204897f9c9e5e99de969fd5d076d80aebbaef19493f5e273663d4727864a67295b[ALL]
02b21f43b03f57e029ea43f2cec448d4ff43740af4a68607507f34fd93be97bc30",
        "hex": "47304402201a62b24dcbeba9ec65478be8a12ccd31c3c
9849813782d1ca0bcab657a88762402204897f9c9e5e99de969fd5d076d80aebbaef19493f5
e273663d4727864a67295b012102b21f43b03f57e029ea43f2cec448d4ff43740af4a686075
07f34fd93be97bc30"
      },
      "sequence": 4294967294
    }
  ],
  "vout": [
    {
      "value": 0.10000000,
      "n": 0,
      "scriptPubKey": {
        "asm": "OP_DUP OP_HASH160 523f63d0e9f8cb9519482fc6a8476689e57555e6
OP_EQUALVERIFY OP_CHECKSIG",
        "hex": "76a914523f63d0e9f8cb9519482fc6a8476689e57555e688ac",
        "reqSigs": 1,
        "type": "pubkeyhash",
        "addresses": [
          "mo1qeC6G2cLZqeBiSeLgKL2z1QcvsG9Mu3"
        ]
      }
    },
    {
      "value": 0.22480473,
      "n": 1,
      "scriptPubKey": {
        "asm": "OP_DUP OP_HASH160 69cac07f09af880832eedbcbc7e0dea94fb68e26
OP_EQUALVERIFY OP_CHECKSIG",
        "hex": "76a91469cac07f09af880832eedbcbc7e0dea94fb68e2688ac",
        "reqSigs": 1,
        "type": "pubkeyhash",
        "addresses": [
```

```
            "mqAL8eXgSE7tHGF9fdYhYnwMFW3nnNyH9z"
        ]
      }
    }
  ]
}
```

 The getrawtransaction API is used to retrieve the encoded transaction. It can be decoded using decoderawtransaction. These commands can be invoked using Bitcoin's command-line interface or using any RPC client.

The readable version of the raw transaction has many fields and can be overwhelming at first glance. We will cover some of the components of the transaction in the following section, in order to make sense of the raw transaction.

Transaction input and output

Transactions are primarily constructed with input and output. Each transaction can have multiple inputs and outputs. Unlike account-based bookkeeping, Bitcoin needs to keep track of the output of every transaction. A node needs to have all the transaction output information in order to know the spendable balance of an account. The output can later be referenced in a transaction's input whenever a user wants to spend their cryptocurrency. This output consists of indivisible chunks of currency and can only be broken down after they are consumed in a transaction. The output that is not referenced in any of the transaction's input is referred to as **unspent transaction output** or **UTXO**.

Whenever a user wants to spend the UTXO, it has to be spent entirely. After spending a UTXO, any excess is returned as one more UTXO to the user. This is similar to real-world currency, where coins cannot be broken down into lower values, and change is received for the excess amount paid. Let's consider our previous example, where Alice sends 0.1 bitcoin to Bob. As we can see in *Figure 5.3*, Alice doesn't have a UTXO of value 0.1. So, Alice spends a transaction output of 0.325, which is greater than 0.1. After sending 0.1 bitcoin to Bob, the rest of the amount is sent back to Alice, creating a new UTXO. As we can see from the transaction, Alice gets back slightly less than 0.225 bitcoin to her account.

This is due to the transaction fees levied when inserting the transaction into the blockchain. This fee will be given to the miner for performing Proof of Work. This transaction created two output values, 0.1 and ~0.225. These two output values have to be consumed in their entirety by other input.

Transaction output

As mentioned in the previous section, every transaction creates output that can be consumed later by a transaction input. Each full node client keeps track of all the UTXO so that each transaction input can be easily verified by checking the UTXO pool.

Let's investigate the output of the earlier transaction between Alice and Bob. Transaction outputs are referenced with the vout key:

```
"vout": [
  {
    "value": 0.1,
    "n": 0,
    "scriptPubKey": {
      "asm": "OP_DUP OP_HASH160 523f63d0e9f8cb9519482fc6a8476689e57555e6
OP_EQUALVERIFY OP_CHECKSIG",
      "hex": "76a914523f63d0e9f8cb9519482fc6a8476689e57555e688ac",
      "reqSigs": 1,
      "type": "pubkeyhash",
      "addresses": [
        "mo1qeC6G2cLZqeBiSeLgKL2z1QcvsG9Mu3"
      ]
    }
  }
]
```

The preceding vout is one of the outputs of the transaction. Each output has two major components, **value** and **cryptographic condition**, which explain who owns the transaction. In the preceding transaction, the output value indicates the bitcoin amount transferred to Bob, and scriptPubKey is the cryptographic condition (or the locking script), which ensures that the output amount can only be spent by Bob. scriptPubKey has several fields containing a locking script in serialized (hex) and deserialized (asm) format. It also provides some additional information, such as required signatures (reqSigs), type, and the public addresses of the recipient. Although the transaction output has several fields, only the locking script is of interest for a transaction, and other fields can be derived from it. Most of the locking script is a simple representation of the user's public address. We will look into locking scripts later in this chapter.

Transaction input

A transaction input references UTXOs whenever a user wishes to make a Bitcoin transaction. The transaction input uses an unlocking script to claim the UTXO. A valid transaction input proves the ownership of the UTXO with the help of this unlocking script.

A transaction input can have multiple inputs pointing to multiple UTXOs. The transaction input makes sure that there are enough UTXOs to enable the transaction to take place. In the earlier example, the transaction input had a single input pointing to a UTXO:

```
"vin": [
    {
        "txid":
"e9a78b3c3fd060c561530b3340ef706ca242ec204c8edee8e590fa374ad71b0e",
        "vout": 0,
        "scriptSig": {
          "asm":
"304402201a62b24dcbeba9ec65478be8a12ccd31c3c9849813782d1ca0bcab657a88762402
204897f9c9e5e99de969fd5d076d80aebbaef19493f5e273663d4727864a67295b[ALL]
02b21f43b03f57e029ea43f2cec448d4ff43740af4a68607507f34fd93be97bc30",
          "hex": "47304402201a62b24dcbeba9ec65478be8a12
ccd31c3c9849813782d1ca0bcab657a88762402204897f9c9e5e99de969fd5d076d80aebbae
f19493f5e273663d4727864a67295b012102b21f43b03f57e029ea43f2cec448d4ff43740af
4a68607507f34fd93be97bc30"
        },
        "sequence": 4294967294
    }
],
```

A single UTXO was sufficient to fulfill the transaction. *Figure 5.3* shows that this single UTXO had a value of 0.325, which was enough to send a value of 0.1 to Bob. The transaction input points to the UTXO by using the transaction ID (`txid`) and the sequence number of the transaction that created this UTXO. Like a transaction output, a transaction input contains an unlocking script that proves the user's claim on the UTXO and ensures that the transaction is valid. The spender initially retrieves the UTXO and references it using the transaction ID. An unlocking script is created with the secret information required to unlock the funds. A simple unlocking script will have a digital signature signed with a private key and the corresponding public key. However, the representation could be complex, but it's something we will cover in much more detail in the next section.

In the example, Alice uses `txid` to point to the spendable UTXO in the transaction. Alice then creates an unlocking script and places it in the `scriptSig` field of the transaction. Everyone who gets this transaction will validate it by checking the locking script in the UTXO.

As mentioned earlier, there is a transaction fee that Alice has to pay on top of the 0.1 bitcoin she intends to transfer to Bob. However, there is no transaction fee field in the raw transaction structure. It is calculated by checking the value of all referenced UTXOs and then subtracting this from the transaction input values in the transaction. This additional value, which is not tracked in the transaction output, forms the transaction fee. Each miner will calculate the fee for every transaction and rewards the combined value to themselves in a special coinbase transaction. We will cover more about the coinbase transaction in the *Mining and consensus* section of this chapter.

Transaction verification

Verification of the transaction is performed using an unlocking script and a locking script. Bitcoin uses a simple custom scripting language called Script, which is similar to the stack-based execution language Forth. To validate the transaction, the unlocking script in the input is executed alongside its corresponding locking script. The stack-based execution should return a true value and successfully execute the unlocking script.

In the example, the input's `scriptSig` and the referenced output's `scriptPubKey` are evaluated (in that order), with `scriptPubKey` using the values left on the stack by `scriptSig`. The input is authorized if `scriptPubKey` returns true.

Script

We need to understand the basic execution of the Script language before trying to make sense of the locking and unlocking scripts. Script is simple, a stack-based language that is processed from left to right. It is intentionally not Turing-complete. It doesn't have a complex control flow, such as loops, other than conditions. This makes sure that the program is executed in a predictable time. This was done intentionally to avoid denial-of-service attacks, which create infinite execution loops. The simplicity of the Script language ensures that Bitcoin is not vulnerable to any attacks of this nature.

Script is also stateless, meaning that there is no information stored prior to or after execution. This ensures that execution is not affected by any other aspects of the system and that scripts could be executed on any system.

Script is a stack-based language because it uses a stack data structure during execution. A stack data structure performs push and pop operations on the data items. Push operations add an item to the top of the stack, and pop operations remove the last inserted item. Script executes the program by processing items from left to right. Data items are pushed to the stack whenever they are encountered.

Operators pop an item from the stack and perform operations on them, and then push the results back to the stack. Script has a huge set of operators, which are represented by opcodes that can be used on the items. Arithmetic opcodes such as OP_ADD perform addition on the top two items, whereas the conditional OP_EQUAL opcode evaluates a condition, producing a Boolean result. Bitcoin transaction scripts mostly consist of a conditional operator whose final result must evaluate to a true value if the transaction is to be considered valid.

Script example

Let's take a simple example to execute the script:

```
2 4 OP_ADD 6 OP_EQUAL
```

Execution of the script starts from the left-hand side. The data constants 2 and 4 are inserted into the stack as soon as the execution begins. Next, the script performs an addition operation, represented by the OP_ADD operator. The addition operation is performed on the top two items of the stack after popping them, so *2 + 4 = 6*. The result is pushed back to the stack. The data constant 6 is pushed to the stack when it is encountered. Finally, the conditional OP_EQUAL operator is performed on the stack items. The last two items are popped from the stack and compared to see if they are equal. Since the last two data items in our stack are 6, the equality condition will return a TRUE value.

Locking and unlocking scripts

Bitcoin uses a similar method of script execution but has a different set of opcodes. Bitcoin transactions use locking and unlocking scripts, which are executed together to verify a transaction. As mentioned earlier, a locking script is a spending condition specified in the transaction output, and an unlocking script satisfies this condition when the two scripts are executed together.

We can create a simple locking and unlocking script by breaking down the previous script example. Part of the script could form a locking script, as shown here:

```
4 OP_ADD 6 OP_EQUAL
```

This could only be satisfied by an unlocking script:

```
2
```

Any node will validate these scripts by combining and executing the locking and unlocking scripts sequentially, as shown in the previous example:

```
2 4 OP_ADD 6 OP_EQUAL
```

But these are basic scripts, and anyone with basic arithmetical skill can create an unlocking script in order to spend the transaction output. This is why Bitcoin uses a complex condition with a cryptographic puzzle as a locking script. Only a legitimate owner who has the private key will be able to spend the funds by creating proof with an unlocking script.

The locking script in Bitcoin is referred to as `scriptPubKey`, as seen in the earlier transaction example in the *Transactions* section. This is due to the use of a public key hash (the Bitcoin address) in the locking script to transfer a fund to the owner of the corresponding private key. Similarly, an unlocking script can be found in the `scriptSig` field in the transaction input. The unlocking script generally proves the ownership of the private key corresponding to the public key by creating a digital signature. This is why the unlocking script is generally referred to as `scriptSig`.

In a similar way to the example, Bitcoin transaction validators validate transactions by executing the combined locking and unlocking scripts. Validators retrieve the UTXO referenced by the transaction input and place the locking and unlocking script side by side for sequential execution.

Types of transaction script

Bitcoin currently creates two different basic `scriptSig`/`scriptPubKey` pairs. There are complex transaction scripts that are used rarely in Bitcoin transactions. **Pay-to-PubKeyHash (P2PKH)** and **Pay-to-Script-Hash (P2SH)** are the most popular scripts. The majority of the scripts executed in the Bitcoin network use P2PKH as their transaction script.

P2PKH

Bitcoin transactions create an output transaction with a public key hash called P2PKH. The public key hash denotes the Bitcoin public address of the corresponding private key that a user holds. The user creates a locking script with the recipient's public address. No-one other than the holder of the corresponding private key will be able to claim the transaction output.

In our earlier example, Alice creates a transaction input that contains `scriptSig` and transaction output with `scriptPubKey`.

The following script shows the syntax of `scriptPubKey` and `scriptSig`:

```
scriptPubKey: OP_DUP OP_HASH160 <pubKeyHash> OP_EQUALVERIFY
OP_CHECKSIG
scriptSig: <sig> <pubKey>
```

The validator will combine the scripts and execute them sequentially:

```
<sig> <pubKey> OP_DUP OP_HASH160 <pubKeyHash> OP_EQUALVERIFY
OP_CHECKSIG
```

The signature (`sig`) and public key (`pubKey`) recorded by the spender are pushed into the stack. The `OP_DUP` operator duplicates the `pubKey` in the stack. The next operator, `OP_HASH160`, calculates a 160-bit hash value of the public key using the `SHA256` and `RIPEMD160` algorithms:

```
RIPEMD160(SHA256(pubKey))
```

The `pubKeyHash` value in the locking script is pushed into the stack. The `OP_EQUALVERIFY` operator verifies that the public key hash created from the unlocking script and `pubKeyHash` value previously pushed to the stack are equal. It returns a `TRUE` value if the public key hashes of both the locking and unlocking scripts match. Finally, `OP_CHECKSIG` pops `sig` and `pubKey` from the stack, performs digital signature verification, and verifies that the signature is valid. Once the verification is successful, the script returns a `TRUE` value, indicating that unlocking script is valid.

P2SH

P2SH was introduced by one of the early Bitcoin developers, Gavin Andresen. According to Gavin Andresen, P2SH was created with a purpose:

"To move the responsibility for supplying the conditions to redeem a transaction from the sender of the funds to the redeemer."

– Andresen

In P2SH, funds are addressed to the hash of the script instead of the public address. The script is called a redeem script, which houses all the conditions needed to spend the funds. As Gavin Andresen mentioned, the creator of the transaction doesn't have to worry about the conditions to spend the funds, and needs only mention the hash of the script containing the conditions. When the funds need to be spent, the redeemer should provide the script that matches the mentioned script hash and also make sure that the script evaluates to true.

P2SH provides a means for complicated transactions to take place, unlike P2PKH, which has a specific definition for `scriptPubKey` and `scriptSig`. The specification places no limitations on the script, and therefore absolutely any script can be funded using these addresses. The concept of the script is similar to that of the smart contract, which will be covered in `Chapter 7`, *Diving into Blockchain – Proof of Ownership*.

Mining and consensus

Mining in Bitcoin is a crucial concept to achieve a consensus on the state of the blockchain in the decentralized Bitcoin network. Any node in the Bitcoin network can perform mining operations, and these nodes are rewarded with incentives for their contribution to mining. This has led to confusion between mining and incentivizing. Although incentives are part of mining, that is not the only intention of mining. Mining is a mechanism that underpins the decentralization of the Bitcoin network. It helps to achieve a consensus among the nodes in a trustless network by constructing a blockchain that is accepted by everyone.

Like any other Bitcoin node, a miner also validates new transactions and stores them locally in a memory pool. In addition to performing validation, a miner creates a block of transactions and solves a hash puzzle to include the created block in the global Bitcoin ledger. The miner will be rewarded with two types of incentive once the created block is included in the blockchain: the transaction fees of each transaction and the newly created bitcoins in each block. Transaction fees are the fees charged for the processing of each transaction, and the fee is attached by the creator of the transaction. Each block has a special transaction that creates new bitcoins and awards them to the miner responsible for the creation of the block. This special transaction, called a coinbase transaction, is responsible for the creation of new bitcoins.

Since there is a hard cap on the total number of bitcoins that can be created (21 million), at some point in time in the future, miners will be only rewarded with incentives from the transaction fees. The maximum number of newly created bitcoins that the miner is rewarded halves for every 210,000 blocks created. Since each block's creation time is kept at around 10 minutes, 210,000 blocks are created every four years. The incentive started at 50 bitcoins per block in 2009 when Bitcoin was launched and was later halved in 2012, and again in 2016.

Currently, miners are rewarded with 12.5 newly minted bitcoins for every block they create:

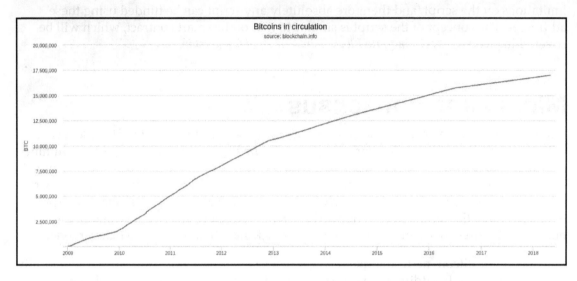

Figure 5.4: The supply of Bitcoin currency over the years till 2018 (Source: www.blockchain.info)

Figure 5.4 shows the supply of Bitcoin over time. The curve is geometrically decreasing due to the halving of the Bitcoin rewards for each block. The Bitcoin network is likely to supply 21 million coins by 2140. The line in the graph will be almost parallel to the x-axis when it nears the year 2040.

Mining a block

Any node in the Bitcoin network can create a block and call itself a miner. A miner has to run a Bitcoin node maintaining the full blockchain. Although mining operations can be performed with minimal hardware requirements, due to high competition among Bitcoin nodes, mining on standalone computing hardware with a minimal hardware configuration is no longer profitable. This is why Bitcoin miners often run specialized computer hardware with higher processing power, such as GPUs.

Due to the increased competition among miners, the mining difficulty of Bitcoin increased. Miners started building specialized integrated circuits designed specifically for mining purposes. These specialized integrated circuits are known as **Application-Specific Integrated Circuits (ASICs)**, and they cannot be used for general-purpose computing. There are several Bitcoin ASIC manufacturers producing ASICs of different capacities. Bitmain's Antminer devices are the most widely used ASICs.

Each miner node will also listen to the Bitcoin network for new transactions and blocks. They perform several tasks before they conclude that they have successfully mined a new block:

- Verification of transactions
- Aggregating transactions into blocks
- Mining the block using the Proof of Work algorithm

Verification of transactions

As we have seen, each valid transaction is created by collecting the UTXOs and unlocking them with appropriate scripts, before using the locking scripts, which will lock the funds for the next owner. The transaction is broadcast to the Bitcoin network so that everyone knows about the updated state of the blockchain. Broadcasting the transaction also makes sure that the transaction reaches a miner node and is included in any blocks that are created.

Although transactions are verified before they are broadcast to the network, a miner node always verifies each and every transaction before including it in the block. A single invalid transaction could result in the entire block being rejected by the Bitcoin network. To prevent unnecessary losses, a miner always ensures that only the valid transactions are included in the block.

Aggregating transactions into a block

Just like any full node in the Bitcoin network, a miner accumulates all the transactions it receives and adds them to the local memory pool. A miner will start constructing a candidate block that could be inserted into the blockchain by including a set of transactions in the block. The node will make sure that any time a new block arrives during the block construction process, all the transactions in the newly-arrived block should be omitted from the candidate block because this would create duplicate transactions.

Once all the metadata of the block and transactions are created for the block, the miner solves the hash puzzle by performing Proof of Work. The block is broadcasted to the Bitcoin network as soon as it successfully creates a Proof of Work for it.

Coinbase transactions

Every block created in the Bitcoin blockchain has a special type of transaction, which is the first transaction of the block. This transaction is created by the miner, which rewards itself with incentives earned from transaction fees and newly created bitcoins, as mentioned earlier.

Here is the coinbase transaction of Bitcoin mainnet block 520,956. Decoding the first transaction of the block will give these details:

```
$ bitcoin-cli getrawtransaction
fc72760e6339eb43111034d76e67ffce69f9f3a4a5aa53f29dfe7299623bbba8
{
  "txid":
"fc72760e6339eb43111034d76e67ffce69f9f3a4a5aa53f29dfe7299623bbba8",
  "hash":
"d06aecb12c942dfd059b0d6ef7fbb76f8310fb2cfd4159984c8dce32d3f94b8f",
  "version": 2,
  "size": 243,
  "vsize": 216,
  "locktime": 0,
  "vin": [
    {
      "coinbase":
"03fcf20704ff5bea5a622f4254432e434f4d2ffabe6d6dcc95de16874f4618351fc3946c85
90509f1c5b0ac2ce802d71786eaef2f0da4301000000000000006e9694143ddc55d50000000
0",
      "sequence": 4294967295
    }
  ],
  "vout": [
    {
      "value": 12.59334356,
      "n": 0,
      "scriptPubKey": {
        "asm": "OP_DUP OP_HASH160
78ce48f88c94df3762da89dc8498205373a8ce6f OP_EQUALVERIFY
OP_CHECKSIG",
        "hex":
"76a91478ce48f88c94df3762da89dc8498205373a8ce6f88ac",
        "reqSigs": 1,
        "type": "pubkeyhash",
```

```
      "addresses": [
        "1C1mCxRukix1KfegAY5zQQJV7samAciZpv"
      ]
    }
  },
  {
    "value": 0.00000000,
    "n": 1,
    "scriptPubKey": {
      "asm": "OP_RETURN
aa21a9edcde65b6fb3a180d2d81bdaab66592c9c2deb778ca3b3464e31d5209737
e67f1b",
      "hex":
"6a24aa21a9edcde65b6fb3a180d2d81bdaab66592c9c2deb778ca3b3464e31d52
09737e67f1b",
      "type": "nulldata"
    }
  }
]
}
```

Coinbase transactions don't have any references to a UTXO in the transaction input because the amount is created from new coins and transaction fees. The address mentioned in the transaction output is the miner's own Bitcoin address, so the entire fund of the coinbase transaction is transferred solely to the miner.

Mining a block using the Proof of Work algorithm

The Proof of Work algorithm is used in Bitcoin to achieve consensus in the Bitcoin network about the blocks that belong to the blockchain. It helps to achieve consistency of data in the ledger among the nodes in the network. The Proof of Work algorithm creates proof that a certain amount of work has been done to create the block.

Bitcoin's Proof of Work is a hash puzzle that uses the SHA256 hash function to find the required hash value and thus solve the puzzle. The Proof of Work algorithm used in Bitcoin is similar to the one explained in Chapter 3, *Cryptography in Blockchain*. You can refer to Chapter 3, *Cryptography in Blockchain*, for more details regarding the implementation and analysis of the Proof of Work algorithm.

Mining pool

We are aware that mining difficulty in Bitcoin is adjusted to maintain an average block creation time of 10 minutes. But due to high competition among miners, the difficulty of solving the hash puzzle has increased over time.

This has forced the miners to upgrade their hardware to achieve higher hash rates. Miners who had limited resources couldn't compete with miners who owned huge computing resources. This was when the mining pool was introduced to pool the resources of individual miners with limited resources.

A mining pool is a pooling of computing resources of miners to share the computing power and attain a higher hash rate to solve the hash puzzle. If the combined hash power of the mining pool solves the hash puzzle for a block, each miner who is part of the mining pool is rewarded based on the amount of hash power contributed. There are a number of mining pools implemented in different languages. A miner can join any of the mining pool servers and start contributing the hash power. Slush Pool is the oldest mining pool and was formerly known as **Bitcoin.cz Mining**.

Mining pools use different protocols to communicate between the miner and the mining pool server. The getblocktemplate, getwork, and stratum protocols are some of the mining protocols used in the mining pools. The stratum mining protocol is a widely used protocol that was designed as a replacement for the getwork protocol.

Each miner connected to the mining pool server has to follow a few steps to successfully contribute to the pool mining:

- A miner has to authorize themselves with the right credentials before working on a job

- They then need to fetch the set of transactions for a job

- Finally, the miner needs to submit the work to the server along with username and job details

There are several ways in which a miner's share can be distributed. Most of the mining pool rewards the miner based on the miner's share for the block that was created by the pool.

The hash rate is the unit used in blockchain mining to determine the computing power or the hashing power of the miner. It is nothing but the number of hashes produced per second.

Blockchain

The blockchain in Bitcoin is a collection of an ordered lists of blocks that connects the previous block with the hash pointer. Bitcoin uses Google's `LevelDB` database to store the blockchain metadata. The identity of each block is created by using the SHA256 hash value of the block header, and this block hash is stored in the block header of the next block in the blockchain in order to form a link.

Block structure

The data structure of a Bitcoin block holds a collection of transactions and metadata information about the block. A block is made up of a header and body, which consists of all the transactions. A block holds more than 500 transactions, on average.

Table 5.2 shows all the fields that are included in a block. The dominant part of the block is the header and transactions, which would occupy variable size. Each field shows the size or the transactions occupied in the block:

Field	Description	Size
Magic no	The value is always 0xD9B4BEF9	4 bytes
Block Size	Number of bytes up to the end of the block	4 bytes
Block Header	Consists of six items	80 bytes
Transaction Counter	Integer count	1 - 9 bytes
Transactions	List of transactions	Variable

Table 5.2: The block structure

Block header

The block header stores the metadata of the block, and its size is 80 bytes, as shown in the previous table. It stores version information with which you can identify the block. `hashPrevBlock` stores a 256-bit hash value of the previous block, which links the blocks and ensures the integrity of the blockchain. `hashMerkleRoot` is the hash digest of the transactions and ensures the integrity of transactions.

The time, difficulty bits, and nonce fields are related to the Proof of Work consensus algorithm:

Field	Purpose	Size
Version	Block version	4 bytes
hashPrevBlock	256-bit hash of the previous block header	32 bytes
hashMerkleRoot	256-bit hash based on all of the transactions in the block	32 bytes
Time	Current timestamp in seconds since 1970-01-01T00:00 UTC	4 bytes
Difficulty Bits	Current target in a compact format (https://en.bitcoin.it/wiki/Target)	4 bytes
Nonce	32-bit number (starts at 0)	4 bytes

Table 5.3: The block header

The genesis block

The genesis block, which is the first block in a blockchain, in Bitcoin was created by Satoshi Nakamoto. It is statically coded so that everyone who runs a Bitcoin core node will only believe one blockchain state.

The genesis block hash can be fetched by fetching the block hash of the 0th index:

```
$ bitcoin-cli getblockhash 0
000000000019d6689c085ae165831e934ff763ae46a2a6c172b3f1b60a8ce26f
```

The following are the block details of the Bitcoin genesis block. This block has a coinbase transaction and no other transactions:

```
$ bitcoin-cli getblock
000000000019d6689c085ae165831e934ff763ae46a2a6c172b3f1b60a8ce26f
{
  "hash":
"000000000019d6689c085ae165831e934ff763ae46a2a6c172b3f1b60a8ce26f",
  "confirmations": 521239,
  "strippedsize": 285,
  "size": 285,
  "weight": 1140,
  "height": 0,
  "version": 1,
  "versionHex": "00000001",
  "merkleroot":
"4a5e1e4baab89f3a32518a88c31bc87f618f76673e2cc77ab2127b7afdeda33b",
```

```
"tx": [
  "4a5e1e4baab89f3a32518a88c31bc87f618f76673e2cc77ab2127b7afdeda33b"
],
"time": 1231006505,
"mediantime": 1231006505,
"nonce": 2083236893,
"bits": "1d00ffff",
"difficulty": 1,
"chainwork":
"0000000000000000000000000000000000000000000000000000000100010001",
"nextblockhash":
"00000000839a8e6886ab5951d76f411475428afc90947ee320161bbf18eb6048"
}
```

The coinbase transaction of the block has the following text, along with the normal data in its transaction input:

```
The Times 03/Jan/2009 Chancellor on brink of second bailout for banks
```

This proves that the first block was mined on or after January 3, 2009. The coinbase transaction also has an output transaction of 50 bitcoins, just like any other coinbase transaction.

Merkle trees

A Bitcoin header has metadata that summarizes all the transactions present in the block. This is achieved by creating a digest using a special type of tree called a Merkle hash tree. As mentioned in `Chapter 2`, *A Bit of Cryptography*, a Merkle hash tree is a binary hash tree that is used to summarize large sets of data. Merkle trees are used to summarize all the transactions in Bitcoin and thus ensure the integrity of the transactions. They provide an efficient way to verify whether a transaction is included in the block.

Merkle trees recursively hash the nodes, starting from the leaves, which are hashes of transactions, until there is only one hash. This hash value summarizes all the transactions in the block and is called the Merkle root. Bitcoin applies the SHA256 hash function twice to create the hash of a transaction.

When there are N transactions in a block, the Merkle tree ensures that it doesn't need more than $2*log2(N)$ calculations to check whether the transaction is included in the block. This makes the Merkle tree implementation a very efficient way to verify whether a transaction is included, as well as to check integrity. Merkle trees are efficient in cases with large numbers of transactions. Even though the number of transactions in a block increases exponentially, the path required to verify a transaction will always be logarithmic due to the binary tree nature of the Merkle tree.

Blockchain networks

The Bitcoin blockchain network is formed of decentralized nodes, and each node communicates with the others using the P2P networking protocol. Each node running the Bitcoin client contributes to the growth of the blockchain and the network. Surprisingly, the Bitcoin network consists of nodes that deal with multiple public blockchains. The main blockchain, which is used to hold transactions with actual value, is called **mainnet**. This is the longest blockchain, with the highest number of participating nodes. Besides mainnet, Bitcoin has several other blockchains for testing purposes. Currently, Bitcoin has the **testnet**, **segnet**, and **regtest** blockchain networks.

Testnet

Testnet is the Bitcoin blockchain version that was created solely for testing purposes. The testnet blockchain works on the same network as mainnet, with features such as wallets, transactions, and mining. The only difference is that the coins circulated in testnet don't have any monetary value. Testnet was created as a test network that can be used by developers to check features and fixes before they are deployed in mainnet. Testing on testnet is crucial because it is impossible to revert the mainnet blockchain due to the decentralization. Testnet is supposed to work with a lightweight configuration by keeping the mining difficulty to a minimum so that even simple hardware can be used for testing. But people tend to use high-configuration hardware in the testing network, which increases the mining difficulty. Every now and then, testnet is recreated by propagating a new genesis block and resetting the difficulty. The current iteration of testnet is called testnet 3.

A testnet blockchain can be created using Bitcoin Core by creating a separate daemon process:

```
$ bitcoind -testnet &
```

This creates a new process, which creates a new testnet blockchain copy. The testnet blockchain is considerably smaller than mainnet. The testnet blockchain syncs all the blocks much more quickly than the mainnet blockchain. Bitcoin's command-line interface is invoked with a similar argument:

```
$ bitcoin-cli -testnet getinfo
```

In 2016, a special-purpose testnet called segnet was created to test the Bitcoin Segregated Witness feature. It is no longer required to run a separate network, however, because the segnet feature has been added to testnet 3.

Regtest

Regtest is a testing blockchain for regression purposes. Unlike testnet, regtest is not a public blockchain. Regtest is a blockchain that can be created by a user for local testing purposes. This is ideal for testing features that don't need to interact very much with the network. You can create your version of the blockchain with a local genesis block. Similar to testnet, a regtest flag is added to the command to launch the process:

```
$ bitcoind -regtest
```

Since the blockchain is a local copy, the user can mine the blocks without worrying about the consensus. The following command mines 500 blocks within a few seconds, and the user will be rewarded with coins in each coinbase transaction:

```
$ bitcoin-cli -regtest generate 500
```

Bitcoin hard forks and altcoins

A hard fork in Bitcoin is an update to the protocol that will not entertain the older protocol, thus requiring everyone to upgrade. Hard fork upgrades often include major changes such as changing the blockchain structure, transaction, or consensus rules. The major difference between a soft fork and hard fork is that the latter is not backward compatible, meaning that the older system will not function in the updated protocol.

There will be two different versions of blockchain after the blockchain hard fork. The multiple versions of blockchain are a result of disagreement among the blockchain nodes to follow a single protocol. Blockchain hard forks often result in protocol upgrades. Bitcoin has had several hard forks, which has resulted in the creation of Bitcoin forked cryptocurrencies. Bitcoin Cash was the first successfully hard-forked cryptocurrency, which was forked at the 478,558[th] block of Bitcoin on 1st August, 2017. Bitcoin Cash was mainly created to increase the block size to 8 MB. Bitcoin Gold and Bitcoin Private were the other two successful hard forks that followed Bitcoin Cash.

Altcoins, or alternative coins are the cryptocurrencies launched after the success of Bitcoin. Altcoins are created on a separate blockchain, unlike Bitcoin's hard forked cryptocurrencies. Most altcoins use the basic framework provided by Bitcoin and try to solve its existing limitations. Few of the coins have tried to increase the transaction speed by using alternative algorithms to Proof of Work, and few others have tried to enhance security by increasing the anonymity of the transactions.

Namecoin was one of the initial well-known altcoins that were based on Bitcoin. Litecoin, Zcash, Dogecoin, and Ethereum are a few of the coins that followed Namecoin. Litecoin is the closest implementation of Bitcoin and has a reputation of being the silver to Bitcoin's gold. Litecoin has a total supply of 84 million coins, which is four times that of Bitcoin. It also increases the transaction speed by reducing the block creation time. Litecoin uses a memory-intensive Proof of Work algorithm called Scrypt.

Thousands of altcoins have been created since the invention of Bitcoin, and the number keeps growing every day. However, Bitcoin is the most widely used cryptocurrency to date.

A simple cryptocurrency application

Creating a cryptocurrency application will allow us to implement all the blockchain concepts we've looked at so far, along with the transaction structure used in Bitcoin, and we can then deploy it in a fully P2P network. We created a blockchain application in a decentralized P2P network in Chapter 4, *Networking in Blockchain*. We will be using the same application to create and propagate the blocks in the network, but also extend the application with the concepts of transactions and wallets to create a completely decentralized cryptocurrency:

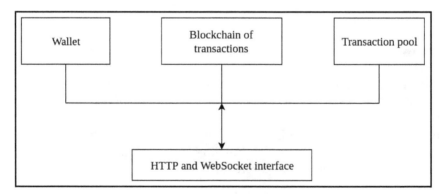

Figure 5.5: A flow diagram connecting all the components of the application

Figure 5.5 shows how the cryptocurrency application can be extended by adding wallet and transaction functionality. We will walk through the implementation of each component in order to understand its functionality.

Transactions

We created an application in which blocks were created with data without verifying the contents of the data. We will extend this functionality by restricting the block to only accepting transaction data. The transaction data is similar to what we have covered in this chapter. It consists of input and output components. The output specifies the recipient of the transaction, and the input makes sure that the user has enough funds for the transaction to take place successfully. The input references an existing unspent output.

Transaction output

Transaction output has a structure that only accepts the recipient's address and the transaction amount. The address is the public key counterpart of the **Elliptic-curve cryptography** (**ECC**) key pair:

```
class TxOut:
    def __init__(self, address, amount):
        self.address = address
        self.amount = amount
```

Transaction input

Transaction input provides information about the funds that will be spent by referencing the spendable transaction output:

```
class TxIn:
    def __init__(self, tx_out_id, tx_out_index, signature):
        self.tx_out_id = tx_out_id
        self.tx_out_index = tx_out_index
        self.signature = signature
```

tx_out_id and tx_out_index are used to reference the transaction output, and the signature provides proof that the spender is the legitimate owner of the fund. Unlike Bitcoin, we have not used a Script-like language to lock and unlock the transactions. Transaction validation will be performed simply by verifying the signature with the help of an **elliptical curve digital signature algorithm** (**ECDSA**).

Transaction structure

A transaction is a collection of valid transaction inputs and outputs, as shown here:

```
class Transaction:
```

```
def __init__(self, tx_ins, tx_outs, tx_id=None):

    self.tx_ins = tx_ins
    self.tx_outs = tx_outs
    self.id = tx_id if tx_id else get_transaction_id(self)
```

A transaction ID is derived from the digest of the entire transaction. The SHA256 hash function is used to calculate the digest of the concatenated transaction input and output contents, as shown here:

```
def get_transaction_id(transaction):

    tx_in_content = reduce(lambda a, b : a + b, map(
        (lambda tx_in: str(tx_in.tx_out_id) + str(tx_in.tx_out_index)),
    transaction.tx_ins), '')

    tx_out_content = reduce(lambda a, b : a + b, map(
        (lambda tx_out: str(tx_out.address) + str(tx_out.amount)),
    transaction.tx_outs), '')

    return SHA256.new((tx_in_content +
tx_out_content).encode()).hexdigest()
```

UTXO

A transaction input will always refer to a UTXO. A list of UTXOs is maintained locally. This list is updated whenever a transaction is processed, and is referred to during transaction validation. Although this list could be generated at any time by traversing the entire blockchain, it is maintained in memory to facilitate speedy transaction validation:

```
class UnspentTxOut:
    def __init__(self, tx_out_id, tx_out_index, address, amount):
        self.tx_out_id = tx_out_id
        self.tx_out_index = tx_out_index
        self.address = address
        self.amount = amount
```

The list of UTXOs is a simple list that is initially created by processing the genesis transaction.

```
self.unspent_tx_outs = process_transactions([self.genesis_transaction], [],
0)
```

Whenever the node creates or receives a transaction, it updates the unspent transaction outputs while processing it. A set of new UTXOs is calculated from the newly added transactions as follows:

```
def update_unspent_tx_outs(a_transactions, a_unspent_tx_outs):

    def find_utxos(t):
        utxos = []
        for index, tx_out in enumerate(t.tx_outs):
            utxos.append(UnspentTxOut(t.id, index, tx_out.address,
tx_out.amount))
        return utxos

    new_utxos = reduce((lambda a, b: a + b), map(lambda t: find_utxos(t),
a_transactions), [])
```

All the UTXOs that are referenced in the transaction input are collected as consumed UTXOs:

```
    consumed_utxos = list(map(lambda txin: UnspentTxOut(txin.tx_out_id,
txin.tx_out_index, '', 0),
        reduce((lambda a, b : a + b), map(lambda t: t.tx_ins,
a_transactions), [])))
```

The updated UTXO list is created by adding the newly created UTXOs and removing all the consumed UTXOs:

```
    resulting_utxos = list(filter(lambda utxo : not
find_unspent_tx_out(utxo.tx_out_id, utxo.tx_out_index, consumed_utxos),
a_unspent_tx_outs)) + new_utxos
    return resulting_utxos
```

Transaction validation

Whenever a node receives a transaction pool or a new block, all the transactions are validated before they store the transaction data in the local blockchain. The structure of each transaction is tested by checking the data structure of each field. Transaction inputs and outputs are also verified so that no invalid input or output is included:

```
def validate_transaction(transaction, a_unspent_tx_outs):

    if not is_valid_transaction_structure(transaction):
        return False
```

The transaction is rejected if the transaction structure is invalid:

```
    if get_transaction_id(transaction) != transaction.id:
        print('invalid tx id: ' + transaction.id)
        return False
```

The transaction ID in this application is calculated using the SHA256 hash function, and this demonstrates the integrity of the transaction. The transaction is considered invalid if the ID is tampered with and doesn't pass the integrity check:

```
has_valid_tx_ins = reduce((lambda a, b: a and b), map(lambda tx_in:
validate_tx_in(tx_in, transaction, a_unspent_tx_outs), transaction.tx_ins),
True)

if not has_valid_tx_ins:
    print('some of the tx_ins are invalid in tx: ' + transaction.id)
    return False
```

Transaction inputs are validated by checking whether they have a reference to a valid UTXO, along with a valid signature signed with the private key of the public key mentioned in the UTXO:

```
total_tx_in_values = reduce((lambda a, b : a + b),
    map(lambda tx_in : get_tx_in_amount(tx_in, a_unspent_tx_outs),
transaction.tx_ins), 0)

total_tx_out_values = reduce((lambda a, b : a + b),
    map(lambda tx_out : tx_out.amount, transaction.tx_outs), 0)

if total_tx_out_values != total_tx_in_values:
    print('total_tx_out_values !== total_tx_in_values in tx: ' +
transaction.id)
        return False
    return True
```

The total transaction output amount is compared with the total transaction input amount by summing the output and input amounts. The transaction is considered invalid if the input amount doesn't match the output amount. In Bitcoin, the transaction output is always lower than the transaction input due to the transaction fee. This amount is included in the coinbase transaction. Since we don't have transaction fees in this application, the input and output amount should always match.

Transaction signing

Transaction signing is a crucial process to unlock the funds so that they can be transferred to a new owner. Every transaction input includes a signature field that contains a signature signed by the owner of the referenced transaction output fund. Each transaction input signs the transaction ID, and this makes sure that none of the transaction inputs can be tampered with because the transaction ID is the digest of the entire transaction. Modifying any of the input will render all the signatures invalid.

We will use packages to perform serialization, signing, and verification of the transaction information:

```
import binascii
from ecdsa import SigningKey, VerifyingKey, SECP256k1
```

 Although we have used `pycryptodome` as the core library for cryptography throughout the book, we will make use of the `ecdsa` package for digital signatures in this application due to its exclusive support for digital signatures.

The referenced UTXO is fetched in order to find the public key to validate whether the signer is the owner of the funds:

```
def sign_tx_in(transaction, tx_in_index, private_key, a_unspent_tx_outs):

    tx_in = transaction.tx_ins[tx_in_index]
    data_to_sign = str(transaction.id)
    referenced_utxo = find_unspent_tx_out(tx_in.tx_out_id,
tx_in.tx_out_index, a_unspent_tx_outs)
    if referenced_utxo is None:
        print('could not find referenced txOut')
        return False
```

The signer's public key is compared with the referenced UTXO public key to check whether the signer is authorized to sign the transaction input:

```
    referenced_address = referenced_utxo.address
    if get_public_key(private_key) != referenced_address:
        print('trying to sign an input with private' + ' key that does not
match the address that is referenced in tx_in')
        return False
```

Finally, the transaction ID is signed using the user's private key. The signature is created using ECDSA with a `secp256k1` curve. Refer to `Chapter 2`, *A Bit of Cryptography*, for more details on ECDSA signing and verification with a secp256k1 curve:

```
    sk = SigningKey.from_string(private_key, curve=SECP256k1)
    signature = binascii.b2a_hex(sk.sign(data_to_sign.encode())).decode()
    return signature
```

Wallet

As we know, a wallet secures the ownership of funds by storing the private keys of the user.

The implementation of a wallet gives us only abstract operations, such as viewing the balance of the user's account and sending funds to another user. The wallet is often considered an end user application for those who don't want or need to understand the internal implementation of transactions.

Key management

We will implement the generation of a key pair and store the keys in plaintext, that is, without applying any encryption. Although wallets can store multiple keys, which can also be generated by a seed phrase, we will use a single key per wallet in this application to keep the wallet implementation as simple as possible. The following method will read the private key and convert the hexadecimal to byte representation:

```
PRIV_KEY_LOC = 'private_key'
from ecdsa import SigningKey

def generate_private_key():
    sk = SigningKey.generate(curve=SECP256k1)
    with open(PRIV_KEY_LOC, 'wt') as file_obj:
        file_obj.write(binascii.b2a_hex(sk.to_string()).decode())
```

Wallet is initialized by creating a private key using the ecdsa package. The SigningKey class has a generate method which is used to create a signing key in ecdsa. This key is then converted to hexadecimal format and then stored in a file.

```
def get_private_from_wallet():
    return binascii.a2b_hex(open(PRIV_KEY_LOC).read())
```

The public key can be generated by using the private key at any time. The following method creates a `SigningKey` object by reading the raw private key. This object can generate a verifying key, which is the public key:

```
def get_public_from_wallet():
    sk = SigningKey.from_string(get_private_from_wallet(),
curve=SECP256k1)
    vk = sk.get_verifying_key()
    return binascii.b2a_hex(vk.to_string()).decode()
```

Wallet balance

Owning funds in cryptocurrency boils down to claiming the transaction outputs that are addressed to the user. The wallet's balance is calculated by collecting all the UTXOs whose addresses match the public key counterpart of the user's private key.

Since our application maintains a single private key per wallet, all the UTXOs of the user will be referenced to a single public address, which isn't the case in implementations where user-owned UTXOs will be addressed to multiple addresses. The following method finds the sum of all the funds amounts specified in the UTXOs whose addresses match the user's public key:

```
def get_balance(address, unspent_tx_outs):
    return sum(map(lambda utxo : utxo.amount, find_unspent_tx_outs(address,
unspent_tx_outs)))
```

The public address in our application is a public key. This isn't the case in other cryptocurrency applications, which may use locking and unlocking scripts, and the public address is generated from the public key by using a hashing function.

Creating transactions

The process of creating a transaction is simply the construction of a transaction object that has a valid set of transaction inputs and outputs that satisfy the transaction request of the user.

Consuming UTXOs

To create a transaction to transfer funds, you need to combine one or more UTXOs, just like gathering coins or cash to pay someone. *Figure 5.6* shows how two UTXOs that have the values 40 and 10 are combined to create a transaction output of 45 to pay to the other user. The remaining output value of 5 is called the change amount, and this will be addressed back to the creator of the transaction in a similar way to receiving change when we pay for something in a shop:

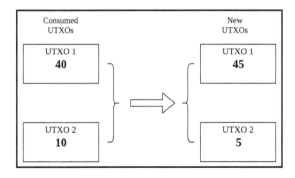

Figure 5.6: The creation of new output transaction outputs from the available UTXOs

The user wallet selects a set of UTXOs that could be used to spend a particular amount. The total value of the selected UTXOs will always be either equal to or greater than the required amount. The following method traverses serially and selects all the transaction outputs that are enough to satisfy the requested amount. The excess amount, which is required to create a new transaction output, is calculated, and this is sent to the transaction creator:

```python
def find_tx_outs_for_amount(amount, my_unspent_tx_outs):
    current_amount = 0
    incl_unspent_tx_outs = []
    for my_unspent_tx_out in my_unspent_tx_outs:
        incl_unspent_tx_outs.append(my_unspent_tx_out)
        current_amount = current_amount + my_unspent_tx_out.amount
        if current_amount >= amount:
            left_over_amount = current_amount - amount
            return incl_unspent_tx_outs, left_over_amount
    e_msg = 'Cannot create transaction from the available unspent
transaction outputs.' \
            ' Required amount:' + str(amount) + '. Available
unspent_tx_outs:' +
            json.dumps(my_unspent_tx_outs)
    print(e_msg)
    return None, None
```

Constructing a transaction

Transactions are created by constructing valid transaction inputs and outputs. Consumable UTXOs are fetched by the `find_tx_outs_for_amount` method, as described in the previous section. Transaction inputs will be created for these UTXOs. The leftover amount is used to create a change transaction:

```python
def create_transaction(receiver_address, amount, private_key,
                       unspent_tx_outs, tx_pool):

    my_address = get_public_key(private_key)

    my_unspent_tx_outs_a = list(filter(lambda utxo: utxo.address ==
my_address, unspent_tx_outs))

    my_unspent_tx_outs = filter_tx_pool_txs(my_unspent_tx_outs_a, tx_pool)
```

User's unspent transactions are filtered and will be referenced in the transaction inputs:

```python
    incl_unspent_tx_outs, left_over_amount =
find_tx_outs_for_amount(amount, my_unspent_tx_outs)
    if not incl_unspent_tx_outs:
        return None
```

Transaction inputs are created using the `TxIn` class by initially keeping the signature field empty:

```
def to_unsigned_tx_in(unspent_tx_out):
    tx_in = TxIn(unspent_tx_out.tx_out_id,
unspent_tx_out.tx_out_index, '')
        return tx_in

    unsigned_tx_ins = list(map(to_unsigned_tx_in,
incl_unspent_tx_outs))
```

The transaction is created with the unsigned transaction input and output values created with the `create_tx_outs` method. This method creates the recipient and change transaction output:

```
tx = Transaction(unsigned_tx_ins,
        create_tx_outs(receiver_address, my_address, amount,
left_over_amount))
```

Finally, the unsigned transaction inputs are signed by the wallet owner using the private key:

```
def sign_transaction(tx, index):
    tx.tx_ins[index].signature = sign_tx_in(tx, index, private_key,
unspent_tx_outs)

    for index, txIn in enumerate(tx.tx_ins):
        sign_transaction(tx, index)
    return tx
```

Transaction management

Once the transactions are created, they should be included in the blockchain in order to update the global transaction state. Transactions that haven't yet been included in the blockchain are called **unconfirmed transactions**. Unconfirmed transactions are always locally stored in a pool called a transaction pool. This is the same as Bitcoin's mempool.

Transaction pool

All the unconfirmed transactions created by the user and other nodes are included in the transaction pool. The transaction pool could be a local file or an in-memory pool. We will maintain all the transactions in a list stored in memory:

```
transaction_pool = []
```

Whenever a transaction is created by a node, it is added to the local transaction pool before broadcasting. The following `send_transaction` method adds the transaction to the pool after creating the transaction:

```
def send_transaction(self, address, amount):
    tx = create_transaction(address, amount, get_private_from_wallet(),
      self.get_unspent_tx_outs(), get_transaction_pool())
    add_to_transaction_pool(tx, self.get_unspent_tx_outs())
    return tx
```

These transactions remain in the pool until they are included in the blockchain. The pool of transactions needs to be updated once the transaction is included in a block. The node updates its pool whenever it receives a new block. The following method removes the transaction from the pool when it fails to find the UTXO referenced by the transaction input:

```
def update_transaction_pool(unspent_tx_outs):
    global transaction_pool
    for tx in transaction_pool[:]:
        for tx_in in tx.tx_ins:
            if not has_tx_in(tx_in, unspent_tx_outs):
                transaction_pool.remove(tx)
                print('removing the following transactions from txPool: %s'
% json.dumps(tx))
                break
```

The missing UTXO signifies that the transaction has been included in the blockchain, and so the transaction can be removed from the pool.

Broadcasting

A user node can mine a block for transactions itself or propagate transactions to the blockchain network so that some other node can mine the transactions. Our blockchain application has only communicated block information so far. Since not all transaction creators want to mine blocks themselves, transactions need to communicate to the nodes. We will add two more message types to the application. Refer to the message types described in `Chapter 4`, *Networking in Blockchain*, for more details.

These are the formats of query and response messages that will be exchanged between the nodes. Similar to the broadcasting of blocks, transactions are broadcast when a new transaction is created by a node and when it receives an unconfirmed transaction from other nodes. The node will broadcast a transaction pool query message when it first connects to another node:

```
QUERY_TRANSACTION_POOL = 3
RESPONSE_TRANSACTION_POOL = 4
def query_transaction_pool_msg(self):
    return {
                'type': QUERY_TRANSACTION_POOL,
                'data': None
    }

def response_transaction_pool_msg(self):
    return {
                'data': JSON.dumps(get_transaction_pool())
    }
```

Blockchain

Although the blockchain part of the application is pretty similar to the application created in Chapter 4, *Networking in Blockchain*, we have added some functionality due to the introduction of the transaction data structure.

Mining a blockchain without transactions is straightforward; it just entails the construction of a block with a header and data. But when the arbitrary data is replaced with transaction data, the node needs to fetch the transactions from the local transaction pool:

```
def construct_next_block(self):
    coinbase_tx = get_coinbase_transaction(get_public_from_wallet(),
self.blocks[-1].index + 1)
    block_data = [coinbase_tx] + get_transaction_pool()
    return self.generate_next_block(block_data)
```

This method constructs and mines a block's data, which contains a coinbase transaction and transactions from the pool. The block will be added to the blockchain once the block header and transactions are validated.

Application endpoints

As mentioned earlier, the application has an HTTP interface that it uses to manage the nodes and a WebSocket interface for P2P communication between the nodes. Here are some of the endpoints that are required to manage the nodes:

- /blocks

- /block/<hash>

- /mineBlock

- /transaction/<id>

- /sendTransaction

The sendTransaction endpoint will basically create the transaction and add it to the pool, as explained in the *Transaction Management* section. Unconfirmed transactions are included in the blockchain by using the /mineBlock endpoint.

The following output shows the state of the blockchain before any other transactions are performed because it contains a genesis block:

```
[
  {
    "data": {
      "id":
"baeece2d8e57aef79ef4e693df0485ca8938ad1f27fa9a0426c8788a3802f02f",
      "tx_ins": [
        {
          "signature": "",
          "tx_out_id": "",
          "tx_out_index": 0
        }
      ],
      "tx_outs": [
        {
          "address":
"0ae66e6adc350ec5c7961cc59cb53372dd421447d4d1b6d11ef8637ac21972068
 8f8019485ac751414049162f1a71c1cc86c4e58bffb836a0d2eea3f324708df",
          "amount": 50
        }
      ]
    },
    "difficulty_bits": 0,
    "hash":
"816534932c2b7154836da6afc367695e6337db8a921823784c14378abed4f7d7",
    "index": 0,
    "nonce": 0,
    "previous_hash": "0",
    "timestamp": 1465154705
  }
]
```

Once a transaction is confirmed by inserting it to the blockchain, it can be viewed by sending an HTTP GET request to the `blocks` or `transaction` endpoint. Here is the transaction result thrown out when hitting the transaction endpoint with the transaction ID:

```
{
  "data": {
    "id":
"ac3d108ebbde3b657a5875ff4237682decf530e6dd6c4b7a77711b89e23a8618",
    "tx_ins": [
      {
        "signature":
"901ea472a28294280fb7468fbc61efa0ddc5a98e375d022b4b7724a4184325c4c
2182c1091b493aec69f7ef81d912648a9e29b7941651c5fd660f72764698383",
        "tx_out_id":
"baeece2d8e57aef79ef4e693df0485ca8938ad1f27fa9a0426c8788a3802f02f",
        "tx_out_index": 0
      }
    ],
    "tx_outs": [
      {
        "address":
"0ae66e6adc350ec5c7961cc59cb53372dd421447d4d1b6d11ef8637ac21972068
8f8019485ac751414049162f1a71c1cc86c4e58bffb836a0d2eea3f324708d2",
        "amount": 20
      },
      {
        "address":
"0ae66e6adc350ec5c7961cc59cb53372dd421447d4d1b6d11ef8637ac21972068
8f8019485ac751414049162f1a71c1cc86c4e58bffb836a0d2eea3f324708df",
        "amount": 30
      }
    ]
  }
}
```

This transaction consumed the transaction output of the genesis block, which had a value of 50. Since a transaction totaling 20 coins was created, the remaining 30 coins were sent back to the owner.

 The entire application's code can be found in the GitHub repository. Since not all the components of the application are described here, refer to the code in the repository in order to understand and execute the implementation. You will also find a block explorer and wallet UI for this application.

Summary

Since the concept of blockchain originated from a cryptocurrency, the best way to understand the true implementation of the blockchain technology is through a cryptocurrency application. In this chapter, we have covered all the concepts of cryptocurrency with the help of Bitcoin in order to understand how cryptocurrency functions in a decentralized network.

We started with the basics of Bitcoin and how they are set up to form a decentralized network. Then we dived into several concepts, such as keys, addresses, and wallets, used in Bitcoin. Bitcoin transactions were explored in depth since those are the events that bring value to the Bitcoin network. We also dived into the essence of blockchain, including mining and consensus of Bitcoin. Finally, we concluded the chapter by creating a simple cryptocurrency application.

This chapter serves as a reference because it elaborates on most of the concepts used to deploy a basic cryptocurrency. Now that we are familiar with the key concepts of a decentralized application, we will dive into blockchain by creating an application using the existing platform in the next chapter.

Diving into Blockchain - Proof of Existence

6

So far in this book, we've looked at the fundamental concepts of blockchain technology, exploring topics such as cryptography and decentralized networking. We've also created a simple blockchain application and made ourselves familiar with the transactions used in the decentralized cryptocurrency application. Although the blockchain applications we created gave us an overview of blockchain technology, we haven't yet looked at any use cases other than those in cryptocurrency that require a decentralized network. By diving into blockchain, we'll introduce and become familiar with the blockchain framework, which will end with us building a blockchain application by constructing the use case featured.

In this chapter, we will cover the following topics:

- The blockchain platform, specifically:
    - Why did we choose to go with MultiChain?
    - An introduction to the basics of MultiChain
    - The functionalities contained within MultiChain
- How to set up the blockchain environment
- The architecture of Proof of Existence
- How to build a Proof of Existence application

Before we look into the varying aspects of the Multichain blockchain platform, it's important to understand the core blockchain platform. Any user who wants to build a decentralized application will not be required to build all the components from scratch.

Instead, you'll find that it's always better to use an existing framework. Why? Because it will help you to build the application with considerably less effort. Existing blockchain platforms provide a framework for app development where you won't have to worry about the underlying blockchain concepts used, and instead offers you the ability to focus more on implementing the blockchain use case. A user wouldn't have to worry much about the scalability of a blockchain network built in this way because the platform has already been tested by thousands of developers and users. Thus the system should be resilient.

Each blockchain platform comes with its own set of characteristics and features beyond the basics of building a decentralized network using the blockchain technology. Some blockchain platforms offer basic functionalities derived from the Bitcoin project, whereas others provide advanced scripting capabilities in order to deploy intelligent applications from within the blockchain network. You'll find that there are a vast number of platforms to choose from in order to both develop and deploy applications, but it is always best to select a framework based on the use case of the application you are creating. Some notable blockchain projects that provide a platform to develop applications are *Ethereum*, *Hyperledger*, *Neo*, *MultiChain*, *Corda*, and *BigchainDB*. The list is huge, and we will look into a few of these platforms in `Chapter 8`, *Blockchain Projects*.

Since we have a large number of options to choose from, it is difficult to find the best platform because most of them can be successfully used for the same use case we are going to use. However, each platform is designed for a specific purpose. We will point out the selection criteria for blockchain platforms in `Chapter 12`, *Blockchain Use Cases*, where we will discuss several blockchain use cases. Throughout this chapter, we will discuss the use case of building a Proof of Existence application using MultiChain. We'll discuss the justification for choosing this platform in the following sections.

MultiChain blockchain platform

MultiChain is one of the many platforms that help enable enterprises to both build and deploy blockchain applications with ease. As we already know, Bitcoin has a resilient public blockchain that can scale its network and handle transactions, which are ideal for public blockchains. This was achieved when the MultiChain project was created by taking inspiration from Bitcoin and creating a private blockchain platform.

A public blockchain maintained in Bitcoin does introduce a few restrictions, such as limited asset distribution, a transaction cost, lower transaction rates, and transparent transactions. Although it is difficult to escape these restrictions in the public blockchain, not all the use cases need to bear these restrictions.

A use case that can be implemented in a private network shouldn't pay for each transaction, achieve a higher transaction speed, or even set access control for operation. MultiChain helps to achieve all of these from within a private network.

Below you'll find some of the features of MultiChain that helped it to overcome the problems in Bitcoin that prevented it from implementing the general use cases in an enterprise as a private blockchain:

- There's no limit on blockchain asset creation. This is because it will be capped by the organization.

- You won't encounter a transaction cost. This is because the internal nodes don't need to be rewarded.

- There's a removal in the delay of transaction confirmation, which is due to the Proof of Work consensus algorithm.

- There's a mitigation of the lack of privacy in blockchain transactions. This is caused by providing access control to blockchain nodes.

Why choose MultiChain?

As we have already mentioned, there are several blockchain platforms to choose from when we implement a blockchain application. The choice of framework mostly depends on the use case of the application that we are going to implement.

There are several reasons for picking the MultiChain platform over other platforms. One of the biggest factors is the simplicity of implementing our Proof of Existence use case within the platform. MultiChain helps us to build our use case without needing to write any complex logic for deployment and execution, making it much more accessible. MultiChain also has a feature called data stream that will be used to store information in the blockchain without needing to alter the data structure. We will achieve this by looking into the stream concept later in this chapter, under the section, *Getting started with MultiChain*. Another factor to consider when selecting the MultiChain is that it's very similar to Bitcoin, which makes it easier for us to understand all its extended functionality.

All these factors influenced us to select MultiChain as a suitable platform to build our first blockchain application. We will cover some of the features of MultiChain in the coming sections.

The basics of MultiChain

MultiChain is a project that was forked from Bitcoin; therefore this makes it compatible with the Bitcoin ecosystem. It's a permissioned-based blockchain that implies that any operation performed on the blockchain is access controlled. Nodes on the network do not necessarily have the same permission on the blockchain. Whilst some nodes could be assigned basic permissions to read the blockchain, others could either be given write permission or even be made admins. MultiChain can also be configured without permissions, making every node in the network equal. The flexible nature of MultiChain makes it easy to implement blockchain use cases without investing many development resources.

MultiChain provides us with complete asset management cycle, which is similar to Bitcoin transactions. Assets provide us with a flexible way to work with their metadata. Since our Proof of Existence use case doesn't deal with identities, we will not be using asset management concepts to create our application. MultiChain also offers data storage and retrieval mechanisms with the help of data streams. In our example, we will be using the streams feature for data storage in the Proof of Existence application.

MultiChain functionalities

As we've explained before, MultiChain inherits most of its functionalities from the Bitcoin project and helps developers to create applications without needing to learn a whole new ecosystem. MultiChain has a set of additional functionalities that makes building and deploying a blockchain application effortless for a developer. In this section, we're going to talk about a few of these functionalities.

Permission management

When a MultiChain blockchain is deployed in an enterprise as a private network, it could be configured so that each node has a different level of access control. When a permission mode is enabled in a blockchain network, each peer has to be given permission explicitly by using their public addresses. Some of the permission levels are connect, send, receive, issue, mine, activate, and admin. Permissions can also be assigned for a specific asset, making the permission management more granular. Access control can also be revoked at any time by the node. Permission management makes sure that none of the unknown peers are allowed inside the private blockchain or set up a hierarchy in the organization by deciding different levels of access control for different nodes. Permission management is an important functionality in a private blockchain.

Asset management

Asset management is a concept derived from Bitcoin transactions. Bitcoin has a single asset that is validated by transactions. Although Bitcoin has the provision to store additional assets in its transaction metadata, they are not validated by the blockchain nodes. MultiChain solves this problem by providing functionality that enables you to create multiple types of asset and still validate all the assets' transactions. MultiChain has a complete asset management life cycle.

Stream management

A stream is a mechanism used to provide data storage in the MultiChain blockchain. It acts as a convenient way to store and retrieve data in key-value pairs. Multiple items can be published to a single data stream. A node has to subscribe to a stream before performing operations on it. Stream items could be indexed by key, signature, and block number, to name just a few.

Setting up a blockchain environment

A blockchain network is a decentralized network, and each node should have similar information about the blockchain ledger. A decentralized network can be set up in an open network by allowing everyone to connect to and perform operations on the blockchain, or equally, it could be maintained in a private network. A public blockchain network is achieved by enabling connect permissions in every node. Enterprises typically prefer to establish a private network as it helps keep the bad actors away. This network configuration can be easily configured in MultiChain at each node.

Running MultiChain nodes

MultiChain can be installed on Linux, Windows, and Mac platforms with 64-bit processors that have at least 512 MB of RAM and 1 GB of storage. The installation involves the extraction of compressed compiled files that can be downloaded from the MultiChain site. MultiChain is an open source project developed in C++. Each node can use the open source code and compile it to gain more control over the program's logic.

Installation instructions for direct installation of MultiChain on machines, as well as building from the source code, can be found in the GitHub repository of the book or on MultiChain's official site: `https://www.multichain.com/download-install`. We'll be using Linux distribution Ubuntu 16.04 for the demonstration in this book.

Each MultiChain node comes with three main binaries, called `multichaind`, `multichain-cli`, and `multichain-util`.

- `multichaind`: This is a process that runs on each node as a daemon. This process is the backbone of the node, and initiates all the tasks required to keep the local blockchain up to date.

- `multichain-cli`: This provides a command-line interface that you can use to perform operations on the blockchain by executing the APIs.

- `multichain-util`: This is a tool that you can use to perform operations such as creating a new blockchain.

Getting started with MultiChain

Now that we are familiar with the MultiChain platform, and equally with the process of setting up a node in the private network, we need to create a blockchain so that the data can be published and shared among the peers in the network. The first step is to introduce all the functionalities before moving on to implementing our use case.

Creating a chain

Once a node has been set up, it can either join an existing network by connecting to a chain, or it can create its own chain. `multichain-util` is used to create a new chain, as follows:

```
$ multichain-util create chain1
```

This creates a new local blockchain. The node then has to start a process by using `multichaind` to connect to the chain created. Multiple chains can be initialized on a single machine by starting multiple `multichaind` daemon processes. A `multichaind` process is created as follows:

```
$ multichaind chain1 -daemon
```

The preceding line instantiates a process and starts the server. The genesis block is then mined by the node for the created chain. This code will yield an address, which can then be used by other nodes to connect to the chain that was just created.

Connecting to an existing chain

If a chain is created in a private network, other nodes can then connect to the created node and perform operations on the same blockchain. Any node can connect to the chain using the following command:

```
$ multichaind chain1@[ip-address]:[port]
```

Any remote node in the network can connect to the chain using the IP address and the MultiChain port. Each MultiChain daemon process assigns a different port number to its server. If the connect permission of the chain configuration is not set to open, then each node in the network has to be explicitly given permission by the admin, as follows:

```
$ multichain-cli chain1 grant [node-address] connect
```

Node-address is the public address, or wallet address, of the node, which is extracted from the public key of the public-private key pair of the wallet. The node can try to connect to the chain by restarting `multichaind` as follows, but only once permission is granted to it:

```
$ multichaind chain1 -daemon
```

Checking the blockchain

A node is completely set up in a private blockchain network after a successful connection to a blockchain is made. The local blockchain will be updated by accepting blocks from nodes in the network. The blockchain's status can be verified by issuing the following command through the command-line interface:

```
$ multichain-cli chain1 getinfo
```

This command provides general information about the node, MultiChain, and several blockchain parameters in a key-value paired document, as follows:

```
{"method":"getinfo","params":[],"id":1,"chain_name":"chain1"}
{
  "version": "1.0.2",
  "nodeversion": 10002901,
  "protocolversion": 10009,
  "chainname": "chain1",
```

```
    "description": "MultiChain chain1",
    "protocol": "multichain",
    "port": 4273,
    "setupblocks": 60,
    "nodeaddress": "chain1@192.168.0.107:4273",
    "burnaddress": "1XXXXXXQrXXXXXXEeXXXXXXXBXXXXXXaDTujx",
    "incomingpaused": false,
    "miningpaused": false,
    "walletversion": 60000,
    "balance": 0,
    "walletdbversion": 2,
    "reindex": false,
    "blocks": 59,
    "timeoffset": 0,
    "connections": 0,
    "proxy": "",
    "difficulty": 6e-8,
    "testnet": false,
    "keypoololdest": 1523352447,
    "keypoolsize": 2,
    "paytxfee": 0,
    "relayfee": 0,
    "errors": ""
}
```

 Note: All the MultiChain commands can be run in an interactive mode by initially launching the shell with a `multichain-cli chain1` command. This opens up an interface where all the commands can be executed with the keyword and the required arguments. The full list of commands can be obtained by typing `help`.

Working with streams

As mentioned earlier, streams are used to store data items as key-value pairs in a blockchain. Streams act as a convenient way to store data. They can be easily created and managed using the command-line interface. All the commands used here are executed after entering an interactive mode by executing the following command:

```
multichain-cli chain1
```

The user can check all the streams in the chain by issuing the `liststreams` command, which returns the details of all the streams along with a default stream called `root`. A new stream can then be created by executing the following command:

```
create stream stream1 false
```

`stream1` is the name of the newly created stream. The stream items can only be created for `stream1` by the admins and nodes with explicit permissions if false is passed as an argument. Permission to publish stream items can be given to a specific node using the `grant` command if the `create` command is set to false initially.

A key-value pair data item can also be published to the created stream using the following `publish` command. The value of the stream item should always be specified as a hexadecimal string:

```
publish stream1 key1 73747265616d2064617461
```

Whenever a node wants to listen to the published stream items, it has to listen to the stream by subscribing to it; this can be effected via the following command:

```
subscribe stream1
liststreamitems stream1
```

Executing that command will result in all the items published to the stream being displayed, along with information such as the publisher address, block creation time, transaction ID, and a number of block confirmations. The published hexadecimal value is stored in the `data` key:

```
[
  {
    "publishers": [
      "1MpkvCWj1Z9ZYfzBQzk4QvR1qih4ZiaHfh9Dd3"
    ],
    "key": "key1",
    "data": "73747265616d2064617461",
    "confirmations": 11,
    "blocktime": 1523373741,
    "txid":
"23ad75620539f9995eef990856090e4c016e4da46bee82905483021b68da616e"
  }
]
```

Now that we have covered the basic functionalities provided by the MultiChain platform, we have all the key ingredients needed to build our own application.

Proof of Existence architecture

Proof of Existence is a mechanism that proves whether a digital document exists at a specific time. A blockchain acts as a good substitute for a notary because it can prove the existence of a document without the need for a third party. Each document is identified by creating its digest using a hashing algorithm, such as SHA-256. The identity of the document is then stored in the blockchain by timestamping the transaction.

 A blockchain implementation of Proof of Existence was created in early 2013 by developers Manuel Araoz and Esteban Ordano. It was released as an open source project. This service used Bitcoin's public network to store information about the document. The information about the document was stored in transaction metadata called OP_RETURN, which allowed the storage of arbitrary information in the transaction.

Proof of Existence architecture has two use cases during its life cycle. Any user who wants to prove the existence of a file performs publishing, and anyone can check this proof by performing verification. The architecture for the application will consist of a user interface, a backend interface to the blockchain node, and the blockchain itself.

Publishing the document

The owner of a document who wants to prove its existence at a specific time can upload the document to the Proof of Existence application. The owner can add additional information that needs to be retained along with the document, such as a document description, size, and user details. The user-facing part of the application will then accept this data along with the document. A digest of the document is then created using a hashing algorithm to uniquely identify the document and represent it in a fixed sized identity. The document information, along with the digest, will be sent to the web interface of the blockchain application.

The web interface of the blockchain application performs a specific operation on the MultiChain blockchain whenever required. When the publishing operation is invoked with all the required data, the application will create an item and request that the MultiChain node publishes it in the blockchain stream. Once the transaction reaches one of the nodes in the network, it will then be exchanged and included in one of the blocks, and finally, it will be embedded into the blockchain ledger.

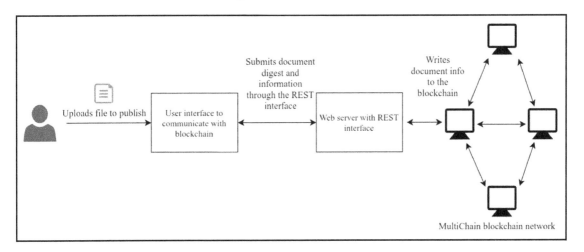

Figure 6.1: The architecture diagram for the publication of the Proof of Existence of a document

Verifying the document

Users who want to verify the existence of a document will follow a similar process to those publishing the document, as seen previously. However, they'll need to have access to the document in order to fetch its existence information. The user who wants to verify the document will perform a similar interaction with the web interface when the verification function is triggered. The verification operation in MultiChain blockchain will then verify whether the operation is invoked. The web interface will accept the digest of the document, and it will use this digest to query the MultiChain blockchain for the document information.

The document information stored in the MultiChain stream can then be retrieved by submitting the digest of the document, as demonstrated in the following diagram:

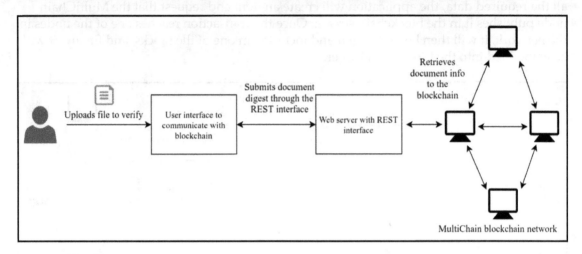

Figure 6.2: The architecture diagram for verifying the Proof of Existence of a document

The blockchain node will be able to find the item in the stream if it's included in one of the blocks. Verification of Proof of Existence is claimed to be successful if the item is found in the blockchain stream and acknowledges the user by providing more information about the document.

Building the Proof of Existence application

As we have discussed in the architecture of the Proof of Existence application, each blockchain node has a web interface through which its user will publish and verify the existence of a document.

We will be creating a web interface that will communicate with the deployed MultiChain node. The user will then communicate with the web interface through the use of REST APIs. In our example, we'll be using the Python Sanic web server used in Chapter 4, *Networking in Blockchain*, to create simple REST APIs. This web interface will then communicate with the MultiChain node's JSON-RPC server, which will allow the node to perform any operation on the MultiChain blockchain. All the functionality provided by the multichain-cli will be available in the JSON-RPC invocation. We will be using a Python driver called Savoir to communicate with the JSON-RPC server of the MultiChain node.

In this section, we'll break down the server-side application into three parts to accommodate the architecture. These parts are as follows:

- MultiChain JSON-RPC driver

- Proof of Existence library

- Proof of Existence web server

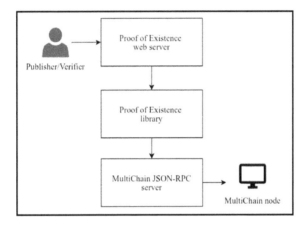

Figure 6.3: The layered architecture of the server-side application

The preceding *Figure 6.3* depicts the layered architecture, by means of which the user communicates with the high-level web server interface, and the application interacts with the MultiChain node through a low-level JSON-RPC driver.

MultiChain JSON-RPC driver

We'll be using a driver to communicate with the MultiChain node. MultiChain provides a JSON-RPC server that can be used to perform any blockchain operations that is needed.

In our use case, we'll be using a Python driver called `Savoir`, which will connect to the JSON-RPC server of the MultiChain node and invoke the requisite functions:

```
from Savoir import Savoir

class MultichainClient(object):

    def __init__(self, **kwargs):
```

```
        self.rpcuser = kwargs.get('rpcuser', 'multichainrpc')
        self.rpcpasswd = kwargs.get('rpcpasswd',
'HFzmag67bJg2f4YuExgVDqQK5VfnvXRS5SKrByuCgiXm')
        self.rpchost = kwargs.get('rpchost', 'localhost')
        self.rpcport = kwargs.get('rpcport', '4416')
        self.chainname = kwargs.get('chainname', 'chain1')
```

We will also create a MultiChain JSON-RPC client using `Savoir`. The client will require the RPC connection information, such as the username, password, host, port, and chain name, in order to establish a connection to the RPC server. Here, the command line, `multichainrpc`, is the default RPC username, and `4416` is the default RPC port. We will use the same chain, as `chain1`, created in the earlier section.

 Note: The RPC username and password can be configured in the configuration file of the created chain. It is located at `/home/user/.multichain/chainname/multichain.conf` in a Linux machine, or the equivalent installation directory of other platforms. Additional blockchain parameters, such as port numbers, can be configured in a params file located as follows: `/home/user/.multichain/chainname/params.dat`

```
    def connect(self):
        """connects to rpc interface"""

        try:
            api = Savoir(self.rpcuser, self.rpcpasswd, self.rpchost,
self.rpcport, self.chainname)
            return api

        except Exception as e:
            return False
```

The RPC connection object is then created using the connection information provided. This object is returned to the library layer to invoke the required MultiChain APIs.

Proof of Existence library

A Proof of Existence library is a collection of methods that perform high-level tasks on a blockchain. The library contains all the operations that can be performed on a document submitted by a user. There are two main ways of performing operations on the user document, according to the design of the architecture: publish and verify.

The publish operation publishes the document digest, along with any other information passed by the user. Since we are using MultiChain streams for publishing, the data has to be formatted in a hexadecimal string, as mentioned earlier.

The following `Document` class shows the `publish` and `verify` methods, along with some methods that can be used to fetch the stream items:

```
class Document(object):

    def __init__(self):
        self.client = MultichainClient().connect()
        self.stream = 'poe'
```

The preceding constructor initializes a connection to the MultiChain node using the RPC server. This connection object can be used to invoke any MultiChain API.

The following two methods are used to fetch stream items according to their stream key and transaction ID respectively. The first uses the MultiChain API, `liststreamkeyitems`, passing the stream name and the key as arguments. In the second method, stream items are fetched using their transaction ID with the `getwallettransaction` API, which accepts the transaction ID of the published stream item as an argument:

```
    def fetch_by_key(self, key):
        """fetches the existence info of a document in blockchain"""

        return self.client.liststreamkeyitems(self.stream, key)

    def fetch_by_txid(self, tx_id):

        return self.client.getwallettransaction(tx_id)
```

Document information is stored in a key-value pair using the stream item publish API. The stream item is published in a key-value pair, where the key is the unique digest of the document and the value is an encoded hexadecimal string. The publish API will then create a transaction and insert that into the blockchain:

```
    def publish(self, key, value):
        """publishes the existence of a document in blockchain"""

        return self.client.publish(self.stream, key, value)
```

The `verify` method is invoked when the user wants to retrieve a published document's information when verifying its existence. Verification is performed with the help of the `fetch_by_key` method, as described earlier, which accepts the stream key as the argument. This method either returns a list of stream items if the key exists, or it will return an empty list:

```
def verify(self, digest):
    """verifies the existence of a document in blockchain"""

    return self.fetch_by_key(digest)
```

The latest published document information is then returned by the following method. A user can also query for a required number of documents by specifying the count. The `liststreamitems` API is used to retrieve all the items in the stream. The returned list is then reversed, and the specified number of items are retrieved. Only the requisite information is filtered from the stream item and returned:

```
def fetch_latest(self, count):

    latest_docs = []
    for doc in self.client.liststreamitems(self.stream)[::-1][:count]:
        latest_docs.append({"digest": doc.get('key'),
        "blocktime": doc.get('blocktime'),
        "confirmations": doc.get('confirmations')})
    return latest_docs
```

Proof of Existence web server

A Proof of Existence web server is an interface for communicating with the MultiChain blockchain. We will create a REST API to communicate with the blockchain application. Each user will be able to send requests to perform `publish` and `verify` operations through this web interface.

First, the packages required to encode the data and create the web server need to be imported. The default port number of the web server is set to `8000`:

```
import binascii
import json as JSON

from base64 import b64encode, b64decode
from datetime import datetime
from sanic import Sanic
from sanic.response import json
from sanic_cors import CORS, cross_origin
from poe_libs import Document
port = 8000
```

The next step is when the document object is created. This will be used to perform Proof of Existence operations. Three REST API endpoints are defined to verify, publish, and fetch the document information. We will create an implementation for all the defined API endpoints:

```
class Server(object):

    def __init__(self):

        self.app = Sanic()
        CORS(self.app)
        self.document = Document()

        self.app.add_route(self.publish, '/publish', methods=['POST'])
        self.app.add_route(self.verify, '/verify', methods=['GET'])
        self.app.add_route(self.details, '/details', methods=['GET'])
```

Publishing the document

The `publish` endpoint implementation will then be invoked when a user wants to prove the existence of a document. The `publish` implementation is an HTTP POST endpoint because it will create a new record in the blockchain through the web server interface. The user invokes this endpoint by passing the document digest, which is the hash value of the entire document. The user will also pass information such as the name, email, and message, which will be stored as metadata in the stream item. The requisite information is passed through the POST forms. The requisite values are extracted from the `request` object in order to create a dictionary:

```
async def publish(self, request):

    try:
        json_data = {'name': request.form.get('name'),
            'email': request.form.get('email'),
            'message': request.form.get('message'),
            'digest': request.form.get('digest')}
```

Since stream items store values as hexadecimal strings, the dictionary is going to be converted to a string, then base64- encoded, and finally encoded into a hexadecimal string:

```
json_string = JSON.dumps(json_data)
encoded = b64encode(json_string.encode('utf-8'))
hex_encoded = binascii.b2a_hex(encoded).decode()
```

The Proof of Existence library `publish` method is invoked, along with the digest and the computed encoded value, in order to store it in the blockchain:

```
tx_id = self.document.publish(json_data['digest'], hex_encoded)
tx_info = self.document.fetch_by_txid(tx_id)
```

Response data is then constructed to acknowledge the user's request. The user is provided with information regarding the published item, such as the transaction ID, the block hash, the timestamp, and the number of confirmations. The timestamp information is crucial in the Proof of Existence use case because it is used to prove that the document existed at that particular point in time:

```
response_data = {
    'digest': json_data['digest'],
    'transaction_id': tx_id,
    'confirmations': tx_info.get('confirmations'),
    'blockhash': tx_info.get('blockhash'),
    'blocktime': tx_info.get('blocktime'),
    'name': json_data['name'],
    'email': json_data['email'],
    'message': json_data['message'],
    'timestamp': datetime.now().timestamp(),
    'status': True}

except Exception as e:

    response_data = {'status': False}

return json(response_data)
```

Verifying the document

The user who needs to verify the existence of the document will invoke the `verify` implementation endpoint. `verify` is an HTTP GET method that accepts document digests as query strings and then responds with details regarding the document if it has already been published. By doing it this way, the user can be certain about the document's existence, provided it has already been published in the blockchain.

The value of the `digest` query string key is passed as an argument to the Proof of Existence library `verify` method. This will return a list of items if the document digest can be found in the blockchain ledger:

```
async def verify(self, request):
    """returns details about verified document"""
    digest = request.args.get('digest')
    verified_docs = self.document.verify(digest)
```

The hexadecimal-encoded value stored is decoded back to a binary string. The resulting base64-encoded string is decoded back to fetch the metadata of the submitted document:

```
response_data = []
```

```
        for doc in verified_docs:
            meta_data =
JSON.loads(b64decode(binascii.a2b_hex(doc.get('data'))).decode())
```

Transaction and block information, along with the metadata of the document, is returned to the verifier of the document:

```
            doc = {"digest": digest,
                   "transaction_id": doc.get('txid'),
                   "confirmations": doc.get('confirmations'),
                   "blocktime": doc.get('blocktime'),
                   "name": meta_data.get('name'),
                   "email": meta_data.get('email'),
                   "message": meta_data.get('message'),
                   "recorded_timestamp_UTC": doc.get('blocktime'),
                   "readable_time_UTC":
datetime.fromtimestamp(int(doc.get('blocktime'))).strftime("%c")}
            response_data.append(doc)
        return json(response_data)
```

This endpoint implementation fetches the details of the recently published document. It is an HTTP GET method that accepts the count of the document to be fetched as an argument:

```
    async def details(self, request):
        """returns details of latest inserted documents"""


        latest_docs =
self.document.fetch_latest(int(request.args.get('count')))
        return json(latest_docs)
```

Executing and deploying the application

The server side of the application is executed by running the Python web server application. The server application can be executed on any blockchain node or on any machine that has access to the blockchain JSON-RPC server. The main function of the application instantiates a web server application at the specified port, as follows:

```
if __name__ == '__main__':
    """main function to serve the api"""
    server = Server()
    server.app.run(host='0.0.0.0', port=port, debug=True)
```

The user can access the REST interface once the server has been instantiated successfully. Let's publish and verify the existence of a document using the REST endpoints.

Let's use the `curl` tool to invoke the `/publish` POST method, which runs in the local machine. We can generate the digest using any hash function. You can use the `sha256sum` tool in Linux to generate the hash value:

```
$ sha256sum index.php
86abfbd5f1a9e928935cdee9b2fd1bc2d43254b40d996e262026e9d668555613  index.php

$ curl -X POST -F 'name=user' -F 'email=test@test.com1' -F
 'message=some message' -F
 'digest=86abfbd5f1a9e928935cdee9b2fd1bc2d43254b40d996e262026e9d668555613'
 http://localhost:8000/publish
```

The POST request publishes the document through a MultiChain node. The server then responds with the following data if the publish operation was successful:

```
{
  "transaction_id":
"62eca6e6c20a4af350bd70fa3745c16de5d9a8ad70bc79cbf4c5450283424010",
  "message": "some message",
  "confirmations": 0,
  "digest":
"86abfbd5f1a9e928935cdee9b2fd1bc2d43254b40d996e262026e9d668555613",
  "name": "user",
  "email": "test@test.com1",
  "blocktime": null,
  "timestamp": 1523467920.313183,
  "status": true,
  "blockhash": null
}
```

The document's existence has successfully been published if the server responds with a transaction ID, as shown in the preceding output. `blockhash` and `blocktime` are set to null because the transaction is yet to be included in the blockchain.

The user can invoke the `/verify` GET method endpoint and use the document's digest to verify its existence, as follows:

```
$ curl
http://localhost:8000/verify?digest=86abfbd5f1a9e928935cdee9b2fd1bc2d43254b
40d996e262026e9d668555613

[
  {
    "transaction_id":
"62eca6e6c20a4af350bd70fa3745c16de5d9a8ad70bc79cbf4c5450283424010",
    "email": "test@test.com1",
    "recorded_timestamp_UTC": 1523467857,
```

```
    "blocktime": 1523467857,
    "confirmations": 22,
    "message": "some message",
    "digest":
"86abfbd5f1a9e928935cdee9b2fd1bc2d43254b40d996e262026e9d668555613",
    "name": "user",
    "readable_time_UTC": "Wed Apr 11 23:00:57 2018"
  }
]
```

The preceding response proves that the document existed at the specified timestamp. It also gives the published details of the document.

All the latest published document information can also be fetched by invoking the `/details` endpoint:

```
$ curl http://localhost:8000/details?count=3
[
  {
    "digest":
"d9d7e36d0059dfab8d7ca2ddaf9e27956e96721209d3b41cd9da46942d48f77b",
    "blocktime": "2018-04-12 00:42:38 UTC",
    "confirmations": 1
  },
  {
    "digest":
"e459c629bfdf54c5849f7718dae9db2b0035f6cb21a04cf2f8e17ffe63b60710",
    "blocktime": "2018-04-12 00:42:10 UTC",
    "confirmations": 6
  },
  {
    "digest":
"86abfbd5f1a9e928935cdee9b2fd1bc2d43254b40d996e262026e9d668555613",
    "blocktime": "2018-04-12 00:13:16 UTC",
    "confirmations": 17
  }
]
```

The details of the document show the latest published proof of the document. As we can see, the latest document information has fewer confirmations than the older information. This is due to the fact that the earlier published transactions are inserted deep in the blockchain. Unlike public blockchains, where transaction insertion depends on the priority of the transactions, MultiChain nodes treat all the transactions with high priority and are inserted in the order in which transactions arrive due to their fairly simple consensus algorithm.

As described in the architecture, the web server application communicates with the blockchain node that is connected to the MultiChain network. The web server application can either be deployed in a separate machine that is reachable by the MultiChain node, or it could be deployed in the same blockchain node. Although deploying the application in another server gives the same result, it introduces the problem of centralization due to the fact that there will only be one central web server application. Best practice is to run the application locally on the blockchain node whenever someone wishes to publish or verify the Proof of Existence of a document.

Every application needs a user interface to allow a good user experience. Our blockchain application could be integrated with a user interface in which the publish use case accepted a document and the requisite information pertaining to the document as arguments, and the verify use case only needs the document in order to check its existence. The frontend application computes the digest of the document in both scenarios.

 Note: The entire Proof of Existence project, along with integration with the frontend application, can be found in the GitHub repository of the book (`https://github.com/PacktPublishing/Foundations-of-Blockchain`). It can be used to deploy a blockchain application in a private network.

Summary

After we were introduced to the core concepts of blockchain in the earlier chapters of this book, in this chapter, we have dived into blockchain by creating a blockchain application to implement an existing use case. Throughout this chapter, we've carefully analyzed a blockchain use case and proposed an architecture to build a simple blockchain application using the MultiChain platform. The MultiChain platform's simplicity, along with other features that we discussed, allowed us to create and deploy the application with minimal effort. Getting familiar with the MultiChain platform has provided us with sufficient insights on architecting and developing a simple blockchain use case. This should serve as a foundation and motivate us to build and deploy blockchain applications within any other blockchain platforms.

Now that we have a strong background in blockchain technology by implementing a fairly simple blockchain use case, it will serve as a foundation for blockchain application development. We will now move on and dive deeper into blockchain development by familiarizing ourselves with decentralized smart contracts by implementing another blockchain use case.

Diving into Blockchain - Proof of Ownership

7

In this chapter, we'll be introduced to the wider applications of blockchain by creating a proof of ownership application. Throughout this chapter, we'll discuss the concept of smart contracts within blockchain in order to implement this application. Since we've already introduced the concepts of blockchain in the earlier chapters of this book, this chapter will mainly focus on the high-level details of smart contracts, namely proof of ownership and the creation of a decentralized application.

We're going to focus on the following topics in this chapter:

- Creating a proof of ownership application
- The concept of smart contracts within blockchain
- How to choose a smart contract platform
- Exploring the NEO blockchain platform
- Creating a decentralized application (proof of ownership) in NEO blockchain
- Exploring the Ethereum blockchain platform
- Creating a decentralized application (proof of ownership) in Ethereum blockchain

In the world of assets, it is necessary to keep track of each and every one of them if you want to claim and prove ownership of them. But assets are created by different entities in different parts of the world, and there is no single protocol for managing assets because each entity has its own system of asset management. For example, if Alice has a house and a car in a city, and she wants to sell both the house and car to Bob because she is planning to move out of the city, she has to go through different procedures to transfer ownership to Bob – she has to deal with the land registry for the house, the road transport department for the car.

In addition, she also appoints an attorney, because the procedure is quite complex. She is only able to finally transfer ownership of the car and the house to Bob after dealing with the registration office, the attorney, and the notaries. The protocol involved in the registration and management of the different assets meant Alice had to deal with different entities to perform a simple task.

The current asset management system requires approval from certain trusted authorities. The main reason for the involvement of a trusted authority is the fact that the assets exist within a trustless society. Different entities create their own set of procedures to deal with assets. Some of the entities may be using outdated technology, making it hard to use as the user has to deal with some traditional procedures.

The proof of ownership solution proposed in this chapter will use blockchain to build a decentralized application to mitigate all the issues faced by a centralized asset management system. We'll use digital identity, assets, and smart contracts to create a completely decentralized asset management system with the help of blockchain technology.

Digital assets and identity

Digital assets are programmable assets that exist in digital format. These assets can have their own value (digital tokens) or could virtually represent existing physical assets (ownership of vehicle). Digital assets have been used since the beginning of the digital age, but until now they have always existed in an environment where management was centralized. The invention of blockchain has allowed digital assets to exist in a decentralized network, where no trusted intermediary is needed to register or trade an asset. Removing the intermediaries means users don't have to pay any additional charges while trading assets.

Digital identity is essential to digital assets when dealing with asset ownership. It represents the identity of any individual or organization in a digital format. Digital identity is based on the **public key infrastructure** (**PKI**) and provides accurate identity management for the user. Unlike traditional identity documents, which could easily be forged, digital identity requires the user to authenticate via a digital signature to prove their identity. This system often uses a secured key infrastructure, which cannot be compromised easily.

We discussed claiming digital assets in the earlier chapters; you'll remember we covered the creation of an identity for the user with which the user would be able to claim an asset using a secret key. A similar approach will be used here to create and manage the digital identity of the user in the platform that we will use to build the application in this chapter.

Proof of ownership

Every asset in the world is owned by some entity. Ownership of a part of an asset might not be feasible to prove, either due to the fact that part of the ownership record is missing or due to the ambiguity in the existing record's data. Although ownership is proved digitally, or by other means, by the entities, in most cases, the ownership information is not consistent across all the systems. Proving ownership by keeping a digital record is the best solution, and digital assets and identities play a huge role in this.

Digital assets, along with digital identities, provide a convenient way to claim ownership of any goods because assets are registered digitally along with the user's identity. Whenever users need to verify and prove ownership of an asset, they can provide their identity details along with the asset that they are trying to claim. Users might often need to verify their identity by either providing some secret information or authenticating using secret information. The identity verification process depends on the third party that built the asset management system. In our previous example, where Alice wanted to sell her house and car to Bob, she would need to provide identity information to the land registry and transport departments that could then be verified by comparing it against the records on their system. The drawback of this kind of proof of ownership system is that there is no proper protocol maintained across different organizations. This is why identity management isn't secure across every system, and why organizations still use traditional systems, such as hard copies of the user's identity, to verify identities without a proper authentication mechanism, which could be easily exploited by bad actors.

A completely secure proof of ownership system could be created by using a digital identity, which uses strong authentication to prove a user's identity. Most existing systems that implement this proof of ownership model are centralized, which requires the centralized body to be trusted. Although this provenance model solves the problem, it needs the user to completely trust the third-party organization to prove and verify the ownership. Creating a decentralized proof of ownership system using blockchain is the only well-known solution that could solve all the problems regarding asset management and proof of ownership. Blockchain is the most suitable technology for asset management due to its immutability and traceability, as once some information about an asset has been appended to a blockchain, it cannot be undone. The traceability makes it easy to verify any transactions, and also allows a transaction to be restricted with a specialized blockchain if privacy is a concern.

Although proof of ownership could be achieved using a blockchain in a decentralized network, some complex agreements between participants of trades may exist in some cases. These agreements are formed between the parties by creating contracts. A concept known as **smart contracts** is used to perform this in a decentralized network. We will be using this to create a decentralized proof of ownership application.

One of the best examples of a decentralized proof of ownership application is **Everledger**, which built a proof of ownership model for the supply chain of the diamond market (`https://diamonds.everledger.io`). Everledger provides a global digital blockchain ledger to keep track of the ownership history of assets. It tries to prevent fraud in the diamond industry, which is estimated to be in the billions of dollars annually.

Smart contracts

Contracts are created between parties to enforce an agreement and to ensure that the participants cannot deny the agreement later. A smart contract is a protocol that allows contracts to be verified and enforced in a self-executing manner. In simple terms, it executes a contract agreed between parties whenever the conditions of the contract are met, without anyone's intervention. The term, smart contract, was coined by Nick Szabo, a cryptographer, in 1994. Although the smart contract was conceptualized in the early 1990s to automate the execution of traditional contracts, it wasn't implemented in a public network until the adoption of Bitcoin's underlying blockchain technology.

It was the Byzantine fault-tolerant consensus algorithms that made the execution of smart contracts possible in a decentralized public network. A number of existing blockchain platforms provide support for **Turing complete** programming languages, which makes it easier to create the logic required to build a smart contract.

A programming language is said to be Turing complete if it can be used to simulate a Turing machine. Bitcoin's scripting language was intentionally made Turing incomplete to keep the Bitcoin transaction as simple as possible.

Since smart contracts are created and deployed in the blockchain, they will benefit from all the features that blockchain provides. None of the contacts stored in the blockchain can be tampered with by anyone once they have been accepted and deployed by the parties, due to their immutability. In addition to this, deploying a smart contract in a blockchain gives complete transparency as anyone can verify the existence of the contract at any time.

Smart contracts also have several other additional benefits:

- **Faster deployment and execution**: Preparing a contract in the traditional way would require the user to spend hours of time preparing paperwork and processing it. A smart contract is nothing but a set of instructions that automate these tasks, which removes many unnecessary steps.

- **Cost-efficient deployment and execution**: Creating and executing smart contracts on a blockchain is cheaper than with traditional contracts, which need the involvement of intermediaries to be processed.
- **Secure management**: All the contracts created in a blockchain are managed securely. This is the inherent nature of the blockchain.
- **Replicated proofs**: Due to the decentralized public ledger in the network, each contract resides on every node of the network, providing multiple backups. It is impossible to lose a contract on a blockchain network.
- **Accurate execution**: Smart contracts are created with a set of instructions that execute consistently on every node in the blockchain network. This ensures that smart contracts always operate accurately. Due to the Byzantine fault-tolerant nature of blockchain, the network will ignore any faulty executions of the contract.

Choosing the smart contract platform

Smart contracts are self-executing contracts that can be deployed using any blockchain application that supports the execution of basic scripts in its transactions. Most blockchain platforms support a domain-specific language. We have already come across the language used in Bitcoin transactions, which is called **Script**, a stack-based language with limited capabilities. Although Script is a Turing-incomplete language, it only has a few options that can be used to create complex transactions. It can create multi-signature transactions, payment channels, and atomic cross-chain trading. In addition to this, Bitcoin can create a transaction with a lock time. A transaction can be created but locked for a certain amount of time in case the creator wants to invalidate the transaction before the lock time expires. Although Bitcoin's Script language provides enough flexibility to create a complex transaction, it isn't suitable for creating complex contracts.

Many blockchain platforms have been created since then that provide advanced scripting capabilities using their own domain-specific language, such as **Solidity** by Ethereum and **Plutus** by Cardano. In addition to this, most platforms have their own runtime environment, which is where the compiled smart contract is executed. The runtime environment is similar to the one used in general-purpose programming languages such as Java. Smart contracts will run on a virtual machine, which is similar to a **Java Virtual Machine (JVM)**. The blockchain virtual machine provides a way to execute untrusted code in the public network. These virtual machines also provide security against attacks such as **denial-of-service** (**DoS**) attacks, which is a necessary feature in systems that execute untrusted code.

Some of the blockchain platforms that provide these services are as follows:

- **EOS**: A smart contract platform and decentralized operating system that aims to solve the scalability issues in blockchain by conducting millions of transactions per second.
- **Ethereum**: This is the most prominent smart contract platform. It implements a nearly Turing-complete language on its blockchain. It uses a domain-specific language called Solidity, which is compiled and executed on the **Ethereum Virtual Machine (EVM)**.
- **Hyperledger Fabric**: This is a permissioned blockchain project under the Hyperledger projects hosted by The Linux Foundation. It allows execution of smart contracts called **chaincode**. It also allows a consensus mechanism to be plugged in as a component.
- **NEO**: This is a blockchain platform that allows smart contract to be written in several general-purpose programming languages, such as C#, Python, and JavaScript. We will cover NEO blockchain in detail in the next section.
- **NXT**: This is a public blockchain platform that executes a limited selection of templates for smart contracts. It doesn't have much scope for the creation of complex contracts.

Selecting a platform to create a smart contract depends on the type of application that needs to be built, required performance, smart contract language, and many other things. It is important to consider all the requirements before selecting the platform. As far as our proof of ownership application is concerned, it needs a platform that can handle digital assets and digital identity.

NEO blockchain provides a convenient way to handle digital identity and assets. In addition to this, the smart contracts can be coded in a general-purpose programming language to build the decentralized applications. We will create our smart contract in the Python programming language so that we need not master any additional programming language. Ethereum is one more platform where a wide range of use cases can be implemented conveniently. We will implement our proof of ownership use case in both the platforms since they are the most widely used blockchain platforms, and the introduction to both of these platforms will provide a solid foundation for decentralized application development.

In the coming sections, we are going to dive into both NEO and Ethereum blockchain platforms, along with proof of ownership implementation.

NEO blockchain

NEO is a blockchain platform and cryptocurrency that facilitates the creation and management of digital assets and smart contracts. The NEO project was originally launched in 2014 under the name of AntShares, until it changed its name in June, 2017. All the development resources were provided by founder, Da Hongfei, from his business blockchain solution company, called Onchain. The main motive of the NEO project is to achieve a **smart economy** with the help of digital assets, digital identity, and smart contracts in a distributed network.

The platform uses two kinds of token, called NEO and GAS. Unlike Bitcoin, a NEO token is a non-divisible token, which means that the minimum unit of NEO is 1. Holding the NEO tokens gives the right to vote during the consensus mechanism, which is explained in the, *Consensus algorithm* section. Holding the NEO token generates a new token called GAS, which is used to pay for the transaction fee. A GAS token is like a fuel that is essential if you want to deploy and execute any smart contract on the blockchain. A total of 100 million NEO tokens are generated in the genesis block. But the corresponding 100 million GAS tokens will be generated gradually in about 22 years.

Building blocks of a NEO blockchain

A NEO blockchain uses two important elements of a decentralized network to create a decentralized application and therefore construct a smart economy. These are digital assets and digital identity, which are the building blocks of any blockchain application. These concepts, along with smart contracts, are essential to the creation of any proof of ownership application, as mentioned earlier in the chapter.

NEO provides a convenient way of creating and managing the digital assets in a decentralized NEO blockchain network. NEO provides two different types of asset:

- Global assets
- Contract assets

Global assets are recorded in the system and can be identified by all the clients and smart contracts. NEO and GAS tokens are global assets. Contract assets are bound to specific contracts and cannot be identified by other contracts. Only certain compatible clients will be able to access the contract assets. NEP-5-based assets are an example of contract assets.

NEP-5 a is standard specified by NEO to create cryptographic tokens. The standard helps the developers to maintain a template while building applications related to tokens. NEP-5 tokens are similar to the ERC-20 tokens used in Ethereum. We will later implement a use case using the NEP-5 token in `Chapter 12`, *Blockchain Use Cases.*

NEO provides a way to handle connections between physical and digital assets in a blockchain with the help of digital identity. NEO implements the **X.509** public key certificate issuance standard to create digital identities. With the help of blockchain, NEO can replace the **Online Certificate Status Protocol** (**OCSP**) to manage and record the X.509 **Certificate Revocation List** (**CRL**).

NEO technology

NEO provides several functionalities to function as a scalable blockchain platform. A few of the technologies used in NEO are discussed here.

Consensus algorithm

NEO uses **Delegated Byzantine Fault Tolerance** (**dBFT**), a modified Byzantine fault-tolerant consensus algorithm. It is a mechanism that allows all the blockchain participants to reach a consensus through proxy voting. A special group of nodes called bookkeepers reach a consensus in order to generate new blocks in the network. These bookkeepers are elected by NEO token holders through voting. The dBFT algorithm has a fault tolerance of $f = \lfloor (n-1)/3 \rfloor$ of n nodes, that is, roughly 33% of the nodes. It is nearly impossible to revoke the blocks and transactions once they are generated and confirmed.

It takes around 15 to 20 seconds to generate a block in NEO, and it provides a throughput of 1,000 transactions per second, which is very high compared to Proof of Work-based implementations. NEO applications can be easily scaled due to their high transaction throughput.

NEO smart contract

Smart contracts are one of the features that highlight the NEO blockchain. Writing smart contracts in a NEO blockchain system is a fairly simple process compared to other smart contract platforms, mainly due to the support it has for a huge number of general-purpose languages in which smart contracts could be created. Unlike Ethereum, NEO doesn't need a domain-specific language to create and execute smart contracts.

NEO has a lightweight virtual machine that is similar to the JVM for Java. NEO's virtual machine executes smart contract instructions in sequence. NEO virtual machines only execute the instructions that are compiled by the NEO compilers. NEO plans to support compilers for languages such as C#, Java, C, C++, Go, JavaScript, Python, and Ruby; although not all of them have been implemented, development is underway to provide support for most languages. In addition to these compilers, NEO currently supports IDE plugins for Java and C#. This helps developers to create smart contracts without changing their development ecosystem.

Additional NEO projects

NEO is a growing community with a lot of projects in its roadmap; you'll find a sample of the most popular ones in the following list:

- **NeoX**: This feature of NEO will allow asset exchange across different chains. It will provide atomic asset exchange protocols to ensure that a transaction is either completely processed or completely rejected. Even an incompatible blockchain will be able to communicate through NeoX as long as it provides some basic smart contract functionality. Since NeoX will help to achieve cross-chain collaboration, a single smart contract could perform operations on two chains.

- **NeoFS**: This is a distributed storage mechanism that will use a **distributed hash table** (**DHT**) technology. Each document will be indexed by the digest of its content. Large documents are divided into blocks and distributed across the blockchain nodes. NeoFS plans to incentivize the nodes with tokens for storing documents that need higher reliability. NeoFS nodes can be used to store old block data from the NEO blockchain to reduce the load on full nodes.

- **NeoQS**: NEO plans to solve the challenge posed by quantum computing on cryptographic algorithms. NeoQS plans to develop quantum-safe cryptographic mechanisms.

Although all these projects are under development, the roadmap of NEO looks very promising. Both NeoFS and NeoQS will provide a research update in the third quarter of 2018, whereas NeoX is expected to run initial tests during the last quarter of 2018.

NEO nodes

Like any other blockchain platform, NEO also has nodes that hold the complete history of blockchain, which are called full nodes. These full nodes form the backbone of the network, and they communicate using the P2P protocol.

Getting started

NEO supports two variants of full nodes, one with a graphical user interface and another with just command-line support. The graphical user interface variant, called **NEO-GUI**, provides all the functionalities an end user requires. **NEO-CLI** is intended for developers who want to use the basic wallet functionality and APIs. It is quite straightforward to get started with either variant. We will be mostly dealing with NEO-CLI because it is more developer friendly.

Setting up a full node

The original NEO-CLI implementation is written in C#, and the source code can be found at `https://github.com/neo-project/neo-cli`. This implementation requires a user node with .NET Core installed to run the compiled binary. The repository explains how to set up .NET Core in different environments. A **dynamic link library** (**DLL**) file in the source code needs to be executed to run the NEO-CLI. Once .NET Core is installed on your system, the following command starts an NEO-CLI full node process:

```
$ dotnet neo-cli.dll
```

The full node uses three different ports for JSON-RPC (`10332`), P2P via TCP (`10333`), and P2P via WebSocket (`10334`). JSON-RPC has an HTTPS version (`10331`), in addition to this. NEO uses a different set of ports for test nets and private nets. It uses similar ports with the initial "1" replaced with "2" for test nets and "3" for private nets. We will be mostly dealing with private net nodes in this chapter, as we will be creating our own network to deploy the application.

The JSON-RPC interface of the node can be exposed by running the following command with the `/rpc` flag:

```
$ dotnet neo-cli.dll /rpc
```

NEO-CLI opens an interactive interface in which the user can perform all blockchain node and wallet operations:

```
NEO-CLI Version: 2.7.4.0
neo>
```

The user has to either create a wallet or open an existing one before executing any commands to manage the wallet or node. The following command inside the shell creates and opens a wallet in the NEO-CLI shell:

```
create wallet neo_wallet.db3
password: ***
address: ASxUka4WqmEkD2mJtGy37J9NeuTe8bTtYF
pubkey:  0374c66e892d7a8cbbbd4c8bd5b7b71ec83819a90c2327d7057b1234072291b5d8

open wallet neo_wallet.db3
```

The user needs to provide a password to secure the wallet, and this password will be used to unlock the wallet every time. The user can perform any wallet, transaction, or block operation after opening the wallet.

> You can refer the NEO-CLI documentation at
> `http://docs.neo.org/en-us/node/cli/cli.html` for all the commands.

NEO-CLI has support for testing, building, and deploying smart contracts in a blockchain, but currently, it doesn't support smart contracts being written in a variety of programming languages. NEO-CLI only provides a compiler for .NET and Java. We need a third-party compiler to create a smart contract in any other programming language. **neo-python** is one such project. It is backed by the City of Zion organization, which consists of a rich set of developers contributing actively. We will be using the neo-python project to build our application in this chapter.

Setting up a neo-python environment

The neo-python project provides an NEO node and an SDK that enables developers to create, test, deploy, and execute smart contracts on the NEO blockchain using Python. This project supports all the functionalities you need to manage assets in the wallet and blockchain nodes. This project aims to port the NEO-CLI implementation completely.

To set up neo-python, you need to install the Python 3.6 interpreter. neo-python can be installed on any platform, although it requires some platform-specific steps to be performed. neo-python needs the `leveldb` and `openssl` libraries to be installed before it is installed itself.

> The complete documentation of neo-python, from a quickstart to building complex smart contracts, can be found at
> `https://neo-python.readthedocs.io`.

The neo-python package can be installed from **PyPI**, just like any other Python package, or from the source repository. Once the installation is complete, neo-python's interactive shell can be launched with the `np-prompt` command. Its shell interface, as shown in the following block, is similar to that of NEO-CLI:

```
$ np-prompt
NEO cli. Type 'help' to get started
neo>
```

 neo-python can also be installed from the source by cloning the repository from `https://github.com/CityOfZion/neo-python` and installing the neo-python package in development mode. The neo-python shell can then be launched with an `np-prompt` command or simply by running the Python script `neo/bin/prompt.py`.

Any commands can be executed on the shell after opening a wallet, in a similar way to NEO-CLI.

 Although all operations performed on NEO-CLI can be executed in neo-python as well, some of the command syntax is different from NEO-CLI commands. Type `help` in the neo-python shell to list all the commands.

Setting up a JSON-RPC interface for the node

As specified in an earlier section while setting up a node, an NEO node acts as a JSON-RPC server so that it can communicate using the RPC interface. The JSON-RPC server can be instantiated in NEO-CLI by adding the `/rpc` flag, as mentioned earlier. You need to launch a different process to create an RPC server in neo-python:

```
$ np-api-server --port-rpc 10332
```

Just like Bitcoin's JSON-RPC interface, NEO provides an RPC endpoint for each of its APIs:

```
$ curl -X POST http://localhost:10332 -H 'Content-Type:
application/json' -d '{ "jsonrpc": "2.0", "id": 5, "method":
"getversion", "params": [] }'

{"jsonrpc": "2.0", "id": 5, "result": {"port": 8080, "nonce":
1439440988, "useragent": "/NEO-PYTHON:0.6.6/"}}
```

Most of the frontend application uses JSON-RPC to communicate with the decentralized applications and the blockchain itself.

neon-js, maintained by City of Zion, provides JavaScript libraries that use the RPC interface exposed by the NEO node to communicate with the blockchain.

NEO network

NEO uses a networking protocol to establish connections and communicate with each node in a duplex mode. The nodes in the network are categorized into two types based on their responsibilities: the validating nodes (bookkeeping nodes) and the ordinary peer nodes. Peer nodes help broadcast blocks and unconfirmed transactions after they've been validated, whereas bookkeeping nodes generate new blocks. NEO follows a similar networking protocol as Bitcoin to initiate connection and exchange blocks between the peers.

When we launch a NEO shell through NEO-CLI or neo-python, the node will join the network that is specified in the default configuration. A neo-python node can belong to either the main, test, or private network. The NEO node will join a test network if it is launched without specifying the network. The following command launches the node in a private network specified in the private network protocol configuration file, which can be found in `neo/data/`:

```
$ np-prompt -p
```

We will be using a private network to perform all the neo-python operations in this chapter. The node could also be initiated by explicitly specifying a network configuration file with a `-c` flag.

Test network

The NEO test network is similar to the mainnet. In the test network, users can develop, deploy, and execute programs. Instead of spending real GAS and NEO tokens, users can use test tokens, which don't have real value. Every other operation performed on the testnet is the same as on the mainnet. So, this is the perfect environment for developers to test applications before deploying them on the mainnet. Since the testnet is an active network with participants from around the world, the supply of NEO and GAS tokens is limited, and you will not be provided with any tokens when joining the network, just like in the mainnet. As a minimum of 500 GAS is required to deploy a smart contract, a user can either obtain this from other testnet users or apply for it at `https://neo.org/Testnet/Create`. Smart contracts can be deployed to the network once the user has enough GAS.

Private network

A private network is a collection of NEO nodes that achieve blockchain state consensus on their own. These NEO nodes are completely disconnected from the public nodes of the mainnet or testnet. A private network is ideal for creating a blockchain network inside an organization.

A private NEO network needs at least four nodes to achieve consensus. A private NEO network can be deployed in a local area network, and also, several nodes can be deployed on a single device by creating virtual machines. Even the nodes of a private network require GAS to create and deploy smart contracts in a private blockchain. A private node can extract all the NEO and GAS tokens from the network by creating a multi-party signature address from all the consensus nodes. The NEO and GAS can then be transferred from the contact address to a normal address.

A small private network with limited consensus nodes can be created by deploying a turnkey Docker image, which is hosted at
`https://hub.docker.com/r/cityofzion/neo-privatenet`. This Docker image deploys four NEO validating nodes, and it has pre-claimed all 100 million NEO and 16,600 GAS tokens. Any user joining the network can use the wallet that contains all the tokens to deploy smart contracts. The private network can be launched with just a couple of commands:

```
$ docker pull cityofzion/neo-privatenet
$ docker run --rm -d --name neo-privatenet -p 20333-20336:20333-
  20336/tcp -p 30333-30336:30333-30336/tcp cityofzion/neo-privatenet
```

The Docker image will create a container that has four nodes exposing both P2P (20333-20336) ports and RPC ports (30333-30336).

Any neo-python node that is in the same network can then add these four nodes as its seed nodes and start syncing the private network blockchain. Users can then use the wallet that contains all the network tokens to create transactions and deploy smart contracts.

NEO transactions

Each node on the NEO network can create transactions and perform operations in the NEO blockchain. The node has to open the wallet to create a transaction and broadcast it:

```
open wallet neo_wallet.db3
wallet
```

The `wallet` command in neo-python provides you with complete information about the opened wallet:

```
{
  "path": "neo_wallet.db3",
  "addresses": [
    {
      "version": 0,
      "script_hash": "AK2nJJpJr6o664CWJKi1QRXjqeic2zRp8y",
      "frozen": false,
      "votes": [],
      "balances": {
        "0xc56f33fc6ecfcd0c225c4ab356fee59390af8560be0e930faebe74
a6daff7c9b": "100000000.0",
        "0x602c79718b16e442de58778e148d0b1084e3b2dffd5de6b7b16cee
7969282de7": "16024.0"
      },
      "is_watch_only": false
    }
  ],
  "height": 20066,
  "percent_synced": 100,
  "synced_balances": [
    "[NEO]: 100000000.0 ",
    "[NEOGas]: 16024.0 "
  ],
  "public_keys": [
    {
      "Address": "AK2nJJpJr6o664CWJKi1QRXjqeic2zRp8y",
      "Public Key": "031a6c6fbbdf02ca351745fa86b9ba5
a9452d785ac4f7fc2b7548ca2a46c4fcf4a"
    }
  ],
  "tokens": [],
  "claims": {
    "available": "143992.0",
    "unavailable": "480.0"
  }
}
```

The wallet maintains updated details after the validation of each and every transaction. The addresses field contains details of all the keys held by the wallet. The opened wallet has only one key, whose public address is AK2nJJpJr6o664CWJKi1QRXjqeic2zRp8y. The balances field inside the addresses field shows the current NEO and GAS tokens claimed by the node. In the balances field, 0xc56f33fc6ecfcd0c225c4ab356fee59390af8560be0e930faebe74a6daff7c9b represents transaction ID of the NEO tokens, and 0x602c79718b16e442de58778e148d0b1084e3b2dffd5de6b7b16cee7969282de7 is for the GAS tokens. NEO uses these as standard IDs for NEO and GAS tokens.

Unlike Bitcoin nodes, NEO nodes can create several different types of transaction to support all the operations performed in the blockchain. The following table depicts different types of transactions that can be created in a NEO network:

Name	Description
MinerTransaction	Assign byte fees
IssueTransaction	Issuance of asset
ClaimTransaction	Claim NEO coins
EnrollmentTransaction	Enrolment for validator
VotingTransaction	Vote for validator
RegisterTransaction	Asset register
ContractTransaction	Contract transaction
AgencyTransaction	Order transaction

Table. 7.1. Transaction types in NEO

Each type of transaction will have exclusive fields to store more information about the transaction. For example, `MinerTransaction` has an additional field to store `nonce`, which is a random number.

Transferring an asset

Nodes can use transactions to perform operations on NEO assets. The transactions are created by the node using its private key, which is situated in the wallet. The user can perform any operation on the asset once the wallet is opened. A `send` command in neo-python transfers the asset by taking the asset ID, the recipient address, and the amount. The `send` command creates a transaction and relays it to the network so that it is included in the blockchain:

```
send NEO AZ81H31DMWzbSnFDLFkzh9vHwaDLayV7fU 100
[Password]> ***
Relayed Tx: 53b72dbce63a28a01432c1ddcc82aed8c28fb1fa338cab812c979
  d56cc8e4410
```

The created transaction is a `ContractTransaction`, and the details show that it houses `vout` and `vin` fields, whose functions are similar to the fields found in Bitcoin transactions. The `vin` field points to the transactions whose unspent outputs are referenced, and `vout` consists of newly created unspent outputs. The first output is the amount transacted by the user, and the second one is the change in output. Unlike Bitcoin transactions, the verification script is found under a separate script field:

```
{
  "txid": "0x53b72dbce63a28a01432c1ddcc82aed8c28fb1fa338cab812
c979d56cc8e4410",
  "type": "ContractTransaction",
  "version": 0,
  "attributes": [
    {
      "usage": 32,
      "data": "23ba2703c53263e8d6e522dc32203339dcd8eee9"
    }
  ],
  "vout": [
    {
      "n": 0,
      "asset": "0xc56f33fc6ecfcd0c225c4ab356fee59390af8560be0e930
faebe74a6daff7c9b",
      "value": "100",
      "address": "AZ81H31DMWzbSnFDLFkzh9vHwaDLayV7fU"
    },
    {
      "n": 1,
      "asset": "0xc56f33fc6ecfcd0c225c4ab356fee59390af8560be0e930
faebe74a6daff7c9b",
      "value": "99999900",
      "address": "AK2nJJpJr6o664CWJKi1QRXjqeic2zRp8y"
    }
  ],
  "vin": [
    {
      "txid": "2b8907db07ebbc3ea2244162ff3d696e7b80874d3ddc3f1fc52
e427d91cd91c3",
      "vout": 0
    }
  ],
  "sys_fee": "0",
  "net_fee": "0",
  "scripts": [
    {
      "invocation": "40f6b2e5c2ca932a536284136c254119096813ee35
d494c939d9e26a7b6247f0801284a34c39e0194c35d1db68bf54fa1de2852
b86182d86a673a206dcf64c6f04",
      "verification": "21031a6c6fbbdf02ca351745fa86b9ba5a9452d785
ac4f7fc2b7548ca2a46c4fcf4aac"
    }
  ],
  "height": 20594,
  "unspents": [
    {
```

```
        "n": 0,
        "asset": "0xc56f33fc6ecfcd0c225c4ab356fee59390af8560be0e930
   faebe74a6daff7c9b",
        "value": "100",
        "address": "AZ81H31DMWzbSnFDLFkzh9vHwaDLayV7fU"
      },
      {
        "n": 1,
        "asset": "0xc56f33fc6ecfcd0c225c4ab356fee59390af8560be0e930
   faebe74a6daff7c9b",
        "value": "99999900",
        "address": "AK2nJJpJr6o664CWJKi1QRXjqeic2zRp8y"
      }
    ]
  }
```

Creating a decentralized application

Now that we have looked into some of the basic functionalities of the NEO platform, we are ready to create our first decentralized application using the NEO blockchain. Smart contracts are the backbone of creating a decentralized application using NEO. We will become familiar with smart contracts by creating a hello world application before creating a decentralized proof of ownership application.

Basic smart contract

First, we will create a simple Python script that returns a concatenated string to greet the user:

```
from boa.builtins import concat

def main(name):
    return concat("Hello ", name)
```

The contract script uses the `concat` method provided by `boa` to concatenate two strings. Every smart contract should have a function called `main`, which will be the entry point. The smart contract needs to be compiled into byte code, which can be executed in the NeoVM. The contract can be compiled by the neo-python shell using the neo-boa compiler as follows:

```
build hello.py test 07 07 False False Alice
```

The `build` command is supplied with a `test` argument to test the sample outcome. The code immediately after the `test` flag represents the data type for the parameter and the return type. The preceding code stipulates that the contract function accepts a string parameter and returns a string value. The following table lists all the available data types and their codes:

Data types	Code
Signature	0x00
Boolean	0x01
Integer	0x02
Hash160	0x03
Hash256	0x04
ByteArray	0x05
PublicKey	0x06
String	0x07
Array	0x10
Interop Interface	0xf0
Void	0xff

Table 7.2. Data types used by contract parameters

The first Boolean values following the data types stipulate whether the contract requires local storage, and the second Boolean value indicates whether the contract has a dynamic invocation to other smart contracts whose addresses are known only during execution. Any input to the contract follows these arguments during the build process. The test invocation will show the result, along with the GAS required to invoke the contract. The result shows that the output is of a `string` type, along with the value. Most importantly, the `build` call generates the contract instructions in byte code by creating an AVM file that will be stored in the same directory:

```
Calling hello.py with arguments ['Alice']
Test deploy invoke successful
Used total of 19 operations
Result [{'type': 'String', 'value': 'Hello Alice'}]
Invoke TX gas cost: 0.0001
```

The generated AVM file needs to be imported to the NeoVM and then relayed to the blockchain network. The following `import` call performs contract importing. The `import` command takes parameters that are similar to the ones specified during the build process:

```
import contract hello.avm 07 07 False False Alice
```

The user needs to enter the details of the smart contract before it is created and relayed to the network:

```
Please fill out the following contract details:
[Contract Name] > Hello World
[Contract Version] > 1.0.0
[Contract Author] > Alice
[Contract Email] > alice@neotest.com
[Contract Description] > Basic smart contract
Creating smart contract....
{
  "hash": "0x6ed9fabe179b236ca7c22deb72a02bdf65b57b84",
  "script":
  "54c56b6a00527ac40648656c6c6f206a00c37e6c75665ec56b6a00527ac46a515
  27ac46a51c36a00c3946a52527ac46a52c3c56a53527ac4006a54527ac46a00c36
  a55527ac461616a00c36a51c39f6433006a54c36a55c3936a56527ac46a56c36a5
  3c36a54c37bc46a54c351936a54527ac46a55c36a54c3936a00527ac462c8ff616
  1616a53c36c7566",
  "parameters": "07",
  "returntype": "07"
}
Used 100.0 Gas
```

A script hash, along with the contract script, will be generated once the smart contract is created. The script hash represents the contract, and it can be used by everyone in the network to invoke the smart contract.

The GAS utilized in a transaction depends on the type of smart contract operation, and the system calls used in the smart contract. The cost of creating a smart contract is 100 GAS plus the additional fees of the system calls. If the smart contract needs a storage area, it costs an additional 400 GAS. Our earlier smart contract deployment used only 100 GAS to create the smart contract as there was no local storage required.

neo-python provides a `testinvoke` command, which can be used to test contract hashes that have already deployed in the blockchain. The `testinvoke` call will not be relayed to the network unless it is accepted by the user. It accepts only the script hash of the contract and its parameters:

```
testinvoke 0x6ed9fabe179b236ca7c22deb72a02bdf65b57b84 Alice
```

The `testinvoke` call can be executed once the node updates its local blockchain to include the relayed contract that was created earlier. Here is the output:

```
Test invoke successful
Total operations: 19
```

```
Results ['48656c6c6f20416c696365']
Invoke TX GAS cost: 0.0
Invoke TX fee: 0.0001
```

`testinvoke` invokes the contract from the blockchain and returns the computed result in an array of hexadecimal strings. The hexadecimal result `'48656c6c6f20416c696365'` translates to "Hello Alice," which is the desired output.

Proof of ownership application

We have already looked into the benefits of creating a proof of ownership application in a decentralized application earlier on in this chapter; now we're going to move on and create a proof of ownership application using NEO smart contracts in order to perform asset management in the decentralized network.

We created a Proof of Existence application to prove the existence of a document in `Chapter 6`, *Diving into Blockchain – Proof of Existence*. In this section, we will create an asset management system to register and prove the ownership of documents in this section. The goal is to create the following asset management functionalities:

- Asset registration
- Asset querying
- Asset removal
- Asset transfer

We will implement all the functionalities in a smart contract to prove the ownership of the document.

Creating the smart contract

Smart contracts created using Python contain a `main` function as the entry point. This function accepts two parameters. The first parameter accepts the type of operation, and all the additional arguments are passed to the second parameter in a list. The `operation` parameter accepts `register`, `query`, `delete`, and `transfer` so that it can perform asset management functions.

The `main` function of the smart contract parses the `operation` parameter and invokes the respective function in the smart contract to perform operations on the asset. The `main` function parses the `args` parameter and assigns the first item of the list to `asset_id`, and the others to `owner`:

```
from boa.interop.Neo.Runtime import Log, Notify
```

```
from boa.interop.Neo.Storage import Get, Put, GetContext
from boa.interop.Neo.Runtime import GetTrigger,CheckWitness
from boa.builtins import concat

def main(operation, args):
  nargs = len(args)
  if nargs == 0:
    print("No asset id supplied")
    return 0

  if operation == 'query':
    asset_id = args[0]
    return query_asset(asset_id)

  elif operation == 'delete':
    asset_id = args[0]
    return delete_asset(asset_id)

  elif operation == 'register':
    if nargs < 2:
      print("required arguments: [asset_id] [owner]")
      return 0
    asset_id = args[0]
    owner = args[1]
    return register_asset(asset_id, owner)

  elif operation == 'transfer':
    if nargs < 2:
      print("required arguments: [asset_id] [to_address]")
      return 0
    asset_id = args[0]
    to_address = args[1]
    return transfer_asset(asset_id, to_address)
```

The `register_asset` function takes `asset_id` and the owner address and creates an entry of the ownership in the blockchain. `CheckWitness` is a NEO runtime functionality check that checks whether the owner's address matches the address of the user that invoked the contract. The contract returns `False` if the asset owner who is to be registered is not the same as the user who invoked the contract. The contract verifies whether that `asset_id` is already registered by invoking the NEO storage library `Get` method. Finally, the asset is registered to the owner by storing the asset id and the owner details in a key/value pair using the `Put` storage method:

```
def register_asset(asset_id, owner):
  msg = concat("RegisterAsset: ", asset_id)
  Notify(msg)
```

```
if not CheckWitness(owner):
  Notify("Owner argument is not the same as the sender")
  return False

context = GetContext()
exists = Get(context, asset_id)
if exists:
  Notify("Asset is already registered")
  return False

Put(context, asset_id, owner)
return True
```

 NEO provides storage functionality in the blockchain by storing data in a key/value pair. Smart contracts have to specify whether the script needs contract storage space during deployment. Using storage costs extra GAS during the deployment.

The `query_asset` function queries the local storage to check whether the asset is already registered by the user. It returns the owner address if the asset is found:

```
def query_asset(asset_id):
  msg = concat("QueryAsset: ", asset_id)
  Notify(msg)

  context = GetContext()
  owner = Get(context, asset_id)
  if not owner:
    Notify("Asset is not yet registered")
    return False

  Notify(owner)
  return owner
```

The following function needs `asset_id` and the address of the asset recipient in order to transfer the asset. As the first step, it verifies the existence of the asset by checking the storage using the `Get` method. It then checks whether the asset owner is the same as the invoker. The contract also verifies that the recipient address is a valid address. Finally, the asset is updated with the new owner using the `Put` storage method:

```
def transfer_asset(asset_id, to_address):
  msg = concat("TransferAsset: ", asset_id)
  Notify(msg)

  context = GetContext()
  owner = Get(context, asset_id)
  if not owner:
```

```
      Notify("Asset is not yet registered")
      return False

  if not CheckWitness(owner):
    Notify("Sender is not the owner, cannot transfer")
    return False

  if not len(to_address) != 34:
    Notify("Invalid new owner address. Must be exactly 34
characters")
    return False

  Put(context, asset_id, to_address)
  return True
```

The `delete_asset` method implements similar functionality as `transfer_asset`, with the difference being that it deletes the asset instead of updating it. The `Delete` function call is used to delete the stored key/value pair from storage:

```
def delete_asset(asset_id):
  msg = concat("DeleteAsset: ", asset_id)
  Notify(msg)

  context = GetContext()
  owner = Get(context, asset_id)
  if not owner:
    Notify("Asset is not yet registered")
    return False

  if not CheckWitness(owner):
    Notify("Sender is not the owner, cannot transfer")
    return False

  Delete(context, asset_id)
  return True
```

Now that we have implemented all the basic functionalities of asset management, we will execute the contract using the neo-python shell in the next section.

Executing the smart contract

The smart contract is executed with similar steps as shown in the earlier section where we deployed the basic smart contract. The only differences are the parameters supplied to the contract and the corresponding return data.

As mentioned earlier, we will create a proof of ownership application to keep track of the documents. Each document can be uniquely identified by its digest. We will use the SHA256 hash value of the document as the asset ID. Let's consider a file that has the following content. The files are usually stored with an additional new line character that is not visible in raw text output:

```
This document was created by Alice.
```

And the following digest represents the SHA256 hash value of the file:

```
f572f8ce40bf97b56bad1c6f8d62552b8b066039a9835f294ea4826629278df3
```

Let's use the hash value as the asset ID to uniquely identify each document. The contract is built in the neo-python shell using the following command:

```
build poo.py test 0710 05 True False query
 ["f572f8ce40bf97b56bad1c6f8d62552b8b066039a9835f294ea4826629278
 df3"]

Test deploy invoke successful
Used total of 113 operations
Result [{'type': 'ByteArray', 'value': ''}]
Invoke TX gas cost: 0.0001
```

The `build` procedure has `0710` as a parameter type, which denotes that it takes one string (`07`) and one array (`10`) as parameters. And `05` indicates that it has a return type of `byte array`.

The contract can then be deployed using the created AVM file after a successful build:

```
import poo.avm 0710 05 True False
{
  "hash": "0x60a7ed582c6885addf1f9bec7e413d01abe54f1a",
  "script": "....",
  "parameters": "0710",
  "returntype": "05"
}
Used 500.0 Gas
```

The transaction needs an additional 400 GAS as the smart contract needs the local storage. The total GAS consumed would be `500`, as shown in the preceding code block.

The contract can be executed once the contract transaction is included in the blockchain and is synchronized in the local blockchain. Let's use the `testinvoke` command to test our created smart contract.

Let's register a document using the same SHA256 value mentioned previously as the asset ID. The `register` operation is invoked with a list of arguments consisting of the hash value and the address of the user invoking the smart contract:

```
testinvoke 0x60a7ed582c6885addf1f9bec7e413d01abe54f1a register
  ["f572f8ce40bf97b56bad1c6f8d62552b8b066039a9835f294ea4826629278
  df3", "AK2nJJpJr6o664CWJKi1QRXjqeic2zRp8y"]
```

Once the transaction is invoked and relayed to the network, other operations can be performed on the asset. Let's now transfer the document's ownership to a new owner by invoking the `transfer` operation and specifying the recipient address in the list:

```
testinvoke 0x60a7ed582c6885addf1f9bec7e413d01abe54f1a transfer
  ["f572f8ce40bf97b56bad1c6f8d62552b8b066039a9835f294ea4826629278
  df3", "AZ81H31DMWzbSnFDLFkzh9vHwaDLayV7fU"]
```

The document ownership can be verified at any time by invoking the query operation and passing the asset ID:

```
testinvoke 0x60a7ed582c6885addf1f9bec7e413d01abe54f1a query
  ["f572f8ce40bf97b56bad1c6f8d62552b8b066039a9835f294ea4826629278
  df3"]

Test invoke successful
Total operations: 118
Results ['415a3831483331444d577a62536e46444c466b7a683976487761444
  c617956376655']
Invoke TX GAS cost: 0.0
Invoke TX fee: 0.0001
```

The query returns a byte array that has a hexadecimal string. The hexadecimal result represents the address `AZ81H31DMWzbSnFDLFkzh9vHwaDLayV7fU`. Since the document's ownership was transferred to the new owner, the result shows the updated owner of the document.

We have now finished creating a smart contract to demonstrate a proof of ownership system that keeps track of the ownership of documents. Once the smart contract is deployed in a blockchain, it will stay there forever. The user has to only deal with the smart contract invocation. The RPC interface of the NEO node provides a convenient way to communicate with the blockchain. We will now look into how to conveniently communicate with the blockchain by creating an interface.

Interface for the application

The NEO community has a created few JavaScript libraries to interface with the NEO blockchain. We will be using a popular library called neon-js (`https://github.com/CityOfZion/neon-js`), which is backed by the City of Zion community.

The following script creates an interface to query the owner of the asset for our proof of ownership application:

```
queryAsset(assetID) {
  const props = {
    scriptHash: '60a7ed582c6885addf1f9bec7e413d01abe54f1a',
    operation: 'query',
    args: [assetID.hexEncode()]
  };
  const Script = Neon.create.script(props);

  rpc.Query.invokeScript(Script).execute('http://localhost:30333')
  .then((res) => {
    return res.result.stack[0].value.hexDecode()
  });
}
```

The interface created using the neon-js library builds a script for the smart contract using the `Neon.create.script` method. It then uses the RPC interface to invoke the smart contract script. After that, `queryAsset` returns the address of the user who owns the document asset.

Creating an interface to the blockchain smart contract is a crucial part of building a fully fledged decentralized application. The interface also creates a convenient way to communicate with the blockchain nodes, which enhances the user experience.

Ethereum blockchain

Ethereum is a public blockchain that was proposed by Vitalik Buterin in late 2013 and was released to the public in 2015. Ethereum was one of the initial blockchain platforms that were created to help programmers to develop and deploy decentralized applications using smart contracts. Ethereum has a rich set of frameworks and libraries to develop, test, and deploy applications. We will cover the development and deployment of proof of ownership applications using the Ethereum platform in this section. Refer to Chapter 8, *Blockchain Projects*, for more details regarding the Ethereum ecosystem.

Ethereum nodes

Similar to Bitcoin and NEO, there are several implementations of client software in different languages that can be used as an Ethereum full node. The Ethereum client implementation can be found in Java, JavaScript, Python, Go, and many other languages. The Golang implementation of Ethereum called **Go Ethereum** or **Geth** is the most popular among all.

Getting started

Setting up the node is the important step to take before diving into the application development. Although any of the Ethereum clients can be used to set up a full node, we will set up the Geth client to sync and interact with the public blockchain. Similar to the NEO blockchain, Geth client can connect to mainnet, testnet, or a private network.

Setting up a node

We will set up a Geth client that can be used to sync the entire blockchain transactions. It also provides the JSON-RPC interface to invoke any of the methods supported by the client software. The JSON-RPC interface can be used to perform several operations including deploying and invoking smart contracts.

 The Geth client can be either built or installed using packages found in most platforms. Installation instructions for different platforms can be found at
`https://github.com/ethereum/go-ethereum/wiki/Building-Ethereum`.

Geth provides a command-line interface that can be used to initiate the node. Once Geth is installed with all the dependencies, it can be launched to synchronize the local blockchain data with the public blockchain. The Geth client can be configured by supplying several parameters for the chain, transaction pool, performance tuning, account, networking, miner, and much more. The following command instantiates an Ethereum node with a few parameters: `rpc` (enable RPC server), `rpcapi` (list of APIs to be accessed through RPC interface), `cache` (memory assigned for internal caching), `rpcport` (RPC server port), and `rpcaddr` (RPC server address):

```
$ geth --rpc --rpcapi db,eth,net,web3,personal --cache=2048
  --rpcport 8545 --rpcaddr 127.0.0.1
```

The instantiated Ethereum node will try to sync the blockchain by connecting to mainnet peers. Alternatively, the Geth can be configured to connect to any of the Ethereum testnets (**Rinkeby**, **Kovan**, or **Ropsten**). The following command instantiates a node with the Rinkeby testnet blockchain:

```
$ geth -rinkeby
```

A set of Geth clients could also form their own private Ethereum network instead of connecting to the existing mainnet or testnet.

 The instructions for setting up a private network using Geth client can be found here: `https://github.com/ethereum/go-ethereum/wiki/Setting-up-private-network-or-local-cluster`.

In this chapter, we will create a private blockchain with the help of a tool provided in the **Truffle** suite framework called **Ganache CLI**, which is a JavaScript package that can be installed using the node package manager. Make sure that `node` and `npm` are installed in the system before executing the following command:

```
$ npm install -g ganache-cli
```

The private blockchain can be instantiated by launching Ganache CLI. Ganache CLI can be configured by specifying several parameters or launched without parameters, as shown in the following command:

```
$ ganache-cli
```

A successful launch will create a private blockchain along with a few accounts loaded with ethers that can be used to pay for the transaction fee for any of the transactions created. The Ganache CLI will also create a client application that will listen on the port 8545 by default. We will use the private blockchain and the application running on the port 8545 to deploy and query the smart contracts in the coming sections.

Setting up a development environment

Now that we have instantiated a local node with a private blockchain, we will set up the development environment to ease the creation and deployment of the decentralized application. Since we have to create a fully fledged decentralized application, we need to communicate with the Ethereum blockchain using scripting languages such as JavaScript. Ethereum provides a JavaScript library called **web3.js** that houses APIs to interact with the Ethereum blockchain.

The web3.js makes use of RPC calls to communicate with the Ethereum node that exposes the RPC interface (application port 8545). So, the web3.js can invoke any of the methods provided by the Ethereum node. The following code snippet can be executed on a node terminal:

```
Web3 = require('web3')
web3 = new Web3(new
 Web3.providers.HttpProvider("http://localhost:8545"));
web3.eth.getBlockNumber(console.log);
```

This code will create a `web3` instance and then add the local node as the provider. When the web3.js application executed in a web browser, the `web3` object can be injected through bridges such as MetaMask. These `web3` instances will already have the provider specified in `web3.currentProvider`. We will use MetaMask while building the proof of ownership application.

Although `web3.js` provides all the methods required to interact with the blockchain, it doesn't set up a complete development environment. This can be achieved with an Ethereum development framework called Truffle. Truffle provides a complete development environment along with convenient testing, deployment, and migration of the smart contracts. The Truffle framework can be installed using the node package manager:

```
$ npm install -g truffle
```

A Truffle project can be initiated in an empty directory to build the initial files required for application development:

```
$ truffle init
```

This will create three directories - `contracts` (smart contracts), `migrations` (deployment scripts), and `test` (test scripts) and a configuration file, `truffle.js`. We need to add the following configuration to the `truffle.js` file to point the created Truffle project to our private blockchain:

```
module.exports = {
  networks: {
    development: {
      host: '127.0.0.1',
      port: 8545,
      network_id: '*' }
  }
};
```

An interactive Truffle console can be launched from the Truffle project directory:

```
$ truffle console
```

The `web3` object will be already instantiated in the Truffle console, and any of the web3 APIs can be accessed using this object. We will use the Truffle console to query the deployed contract in the next section.

Creating a decentralized application

We can now create our first decentralized application on Ethereum platform since we have setup our development environment. We will get familiar with Ethereum smart contracts by creating and deploying a hello world application.

Basic smart contract

Ethereum makes use of a domain-specific language called as Solidity to code the logic of the smart contract. Solidity is a high-level programming language that can be compiled to produce bytecode, which is then executed on the EVM.

 Solidity is a statically typed programming language initially proposed by Gavin Wood. It was designed to be similar to ECMAScript syntax so that it can be easily adapted by the web developer community. More details about the Solidity programming language can be found at `https://solidity.readthedocs.io`.

We'll create a simple hello world smart contract using the Solidity programming language:

```
pragma solidity ^0.4.23;

contract Hello {

  function greetUser(bytes user) view public returns (bytes) {
    return abi.encodePacked("Hello ", user);

  }
}
```

The first line of the Solidity script is the version `pragma` to indicate the version of the solidity program. The preceding script should not be compiled on a Solidity compiler whose version is earlier than 0.4.23. Each contract is defined to a similar class with the contract name as the file name. All the functions are defined inside the contract. A constructor function can also be created with the same name as that of the contract. The function `greetUser` accepts a string of type `bytes` and returns a `bytes` string. The function also has public visibility, meaning it can be invoked from anywhere. The `greetUser` function will concatenate and return two strings.

We will use the Truffle framework to deploy and invoke the smart contract. We need to point the smart contract file to the Truffle framework by including the following code snippet in a new JavaScript file (`2_deploy_contracts.js`) inside the `migrations` folder, or by updating the existing `1_initial_migration.js` file:

```
var Hello = artifacts.require("./Hello.sol");
module.exports = function(deployer) {
  deployer.deploy(Hello);
};
```

The smart contract can be compiled using the following Truffle command:

```
$ truffle compile
```

It will generate an interface file called **application binary interface** (**ABI**) in the `build/contracts` folder. The generated ABI file will be in JSON format, and it provides the interface to interact with the contract in the Ethereum ecosystem.

The contract is then deployed to the blockchain by migrating it:

```
$ truffe migrate
Deploying Hello...
   ... 0x4d85f83c2ffcf1405eb7b610e0f34c99f42b4189f11fbb5ffb782b6eb4d96316
   Hello: 0x149cd2285f8b8a72a5f8b7286aceb94fb54c1aee
```

The deployed contract will generate a contract address that can be used to interact with it. We will use the Truffle console to interact with the contract:

```
$ truffle console
truffle(development)>
Hello.deployed().then((instance) => instance.greetUser("Alice"));
```

When the preceding code snippet is executed on the Truffle console to invoke the `greetUser` function of the contract with `Alice` as the parameter, the contract will return `0x48656c6c6f20416c696365`, which is a hexadecimal string for "Hello Alice."

Proof of ownership application

We will create an application with asset management functionalities to register, query, remove, and transfer the asset.

Creating the smart contract

The application logic is similar to that of one used in the NEO smart contract. But the data structure used to store the asset information is different due to the functionalities provided by the virtual machine. One major difference between NEO and Ethereum contract is that the functions in Ethereum contracts can be directly invoked with the help of ABI.

The `ProofOfOwnership` smart contract uses a mapping data structure to store the asset ownership information in a key/value pair. The asset information of type `bytes32` is mapped to the Ethereum address of the asset owner:

```
pragma solidity ^0.4.23;

contract ProofOfOwnership {
   mapping (bytes32 => address) public assetOwners;
```

The `registerAsset` function maps the address of the user who invoked the contract to the asset ID using the mapping data structure:

```
function registerAsset(bytes32 asset) public {
   if (address(assetOwners[asset]) == address(0))
     {
        assetOwners[asset] = msg.sender;
     }
}
```

The owner of the asset can be retrieved from the stored information in the mapping data structure with the help of asset ID:

```
function queryAsset(bytes32 asset) view public returns (address)
{
   return assetOwners[asset];
}
```

The `transferAsset` function transfers the ownership to the new address after verifying that the current owner of the asset is same as the one who invoked the contract:

```
function transferAsset(bytes32 asset, address owner) public {
   if (assetOwners[asset] == msg.sender)
   {
      assetOwners[asset] = owner;
   }
}
```

The `deleteAsset` function will assign an empty address to the asset when the owner of the asset invokes the contract:

```
function deleteAsset(bytes32 asset) public {
  if (assetOwners[asset] == msg.sender)
  {
    assetOwners[asset] =
0x0000000000000000000000000000000000000000;
  }
 }
}
```

Similar to the previous smart contract deployment, the following configuration should be created in a new JavaScript file (`2_deploy_contracts.js`) inside the `migrations` folder, or the existing `1_initial_migration.js` file should be updated:

```
var ProofOfOwnership= artifacts.require("./ProofOfOwnership.sol");
module.exports = function(deployer) {
  deployer.deploy(ProofOfOwnership);
};
```

The smart contract can then be compiled and migrated using the Truffle framework, as in the previous example:

```
$ truffle migrate
Deploying ProofOfOwnership...
   ... 0x0902a793d20a3846935fffa9558fb8a2f59f74edd2ef811189c9dcdd0a0aedcc
  ProofOfOwnership: 0xc58b4e456b840ca924ddc1c971932febec717e95
```

Executing the smart contract

Let's consider the same example of keeping track of document ownership that we used earlier in NEO application. We will also use the same file with the following content as the asset:

```
This document was created by Alice.
```

We will use an md5 (32 characters) hashing algorithm to calculate the asset ID of the file instead of SHA256 (64 characters). This is because the key (`bytes32`) in the mapping data structure of our contract can accept only 32 characters. The following is the 32-character or 128-bit hash value of the file generated by the md5 algorithm:

```
c9f50a3bdd2efccb7e34fbd8b42e9675
```

Once the proof of ownership smart contract is deployed to the blockchain, it can be invoked from the Truffle console. Let's register the asset using the `registerAsset` function:

```
$ truffle console
truffle(development)>
ProofOfOwnership.deployed().then((instance)=>
  instance.registerAsset("c9f50a3bdd2efccb7e34fbd8b42e9675",
  {from: "0xebe41ec4c574fde7a1d13d333d17267ca93df491"}));
```

If the invoking node has multiple accounts, a `from` address can be included in the function call to identify the user invoking the contract. Since the `registerAsset` function performs write operations, it needs GAS during the execution. The total GAS consumed will be shown once the transaction is created.

The `transferAsset` takes the asset ID along with the new owner address as arguments:

```
ProofOfOwnership.deployed().then((instance)=>
  instance.transferAsset("c9f50a3bdd2efccb7e34fbd8b42e9675",
  "0xfda013eecad647a2593aacbb3c18445f051d0f52",
  {from: "0xebe41ec4c574fde7a1d13d333d17267ca93df491"}));
```

We can query the asset at any time to check the owner of the document:

```
ProofOfOwnership.deployed().then((instance)=>
  instance.queryAsset("c9f50a3bdd2efccb7e34fbd8b42e9675"));
```

If the query returns `0xfda013eecad647a2593aacbb3c18445f051d0f52` as the current owner, we have successfully executed the `transferAsset` function.

Interface for the application

A fully fledged decentralized application can be created by integrating the frontend application with the Ethereum blockchain. We can make use of the APIs provided by the `web3.js` library to interact with the blockchain network. We have already used the Truffle development environment to deploy and invoke the smart contracts. In this section, we will make use of the Truffle libraries to communicate with the contracts.

The following code can be executed in any JavaScript runtime environment, such as Node.js. Refer to the GitHub repository of the book to find the implementation using the React library.

The `ProofOfOwnership.json` is the ABI file that was created during the compilation of the contract. This ABI is essential for communicating with the smart contract:

```
import Web3 from 'web3';
import { default as contract } from 'truffle-contract';
import contract_artifacts from
  './contracts/ProofOfOwnership.json';
```

If the code is executed in a browser where a bridging application such as MetaMask is installed, a web3 object will be injected into the browser along with the provider. The web3 object can also be created by setting the provider as local or any other remote RPC server node.

 The MetaMask browser add-on can be installed from https://metamask.io. Once the add-on is installed, an account has to be created. The user has to point MetaMask to the private blockchain that was used for the development. The accounts created by the private blockchain (via the Ganache CLI) can be imported to the MetaMask wallet so that it can be used to pay for the transaction GAS.

```
const web3 = window.web3;
if (typeof web3 !== 'undefined')
{
  this.web3 = new Web3(web3.currentProvider);
  this.user_address = this.web3.eth.accounts[0]
}
else
{
  this.web3 = new Web3
  (new Web3.providers.HttpProvider("http://localhost:8545"));
}
```

A contract instance can be created from the imported ABI. This contract instance can then be used to invoke any of the contract functions:

```
this.poo = contract(contract_artifacts);
this.poo.setProvider(this.web3.currentProvider);
```

The following function will invoke the `registerAsset` function of the contract by passing `assetID` as the argument. When the function is executed from the browser, MetaMask will bring up a window asking to confirm the transaction. The contract function will be executed after the transaction is confirmed:

```
registerAsset(assetID)
{
  try {
    let user_address = this.user_address;
    this.poo.deployed().then(function(contractInstance) {

      contractInstance.registerAsset(assetID, {gas: 1400000, from:
user_address}).then(function(c) {
        console.log(c.toLocaleString());
      });
    });
```

```
    }
  catch (err) {
    console.log(err);
  }
}
```

Similarly, the query function will invoke the `queryAsset` function of the smart contract. Since the `queryAsset` does not write to the blockchain, MetaMask will not create a new transaction:

```
queryAsset(assetID)
{
  try {
    let user_address = this.user_address;
    this.poo.deployed().then(function(contractInstance) {

      contractInstance.queryAsset
(assetID, {gas: 1400000, from: user_address}).then(function(c) {
        console.log(c.toLocaleString());
      });
    });
  }
  catch (err) {
    console.log(err);
  }
}
```

All the other functionalities of the proof of ownership application can be implemented in a similar way. Refer to the GitHub repository (`https://github.com/PacktPublishing/Foundations-of-Blockchain`) for the complete frontend implementation of the application.

Now that we have implemented the proof of ownership application using both the NEO and Ethereum blockchain platforms, we have enough information to build other applications on these platforms. Since we have also compared the functionalities of both the platforms, we can decide on a platform that is best suited to implement any use case based on the requirements.

Summary

In this chapter, we have dived deep into both creating and using smart contracts, as well as using the NEO and Ethereum platform to build a decentralized application. After creating the foundations of a NEO and Ethereum blockchain, we created a proof of ownership system to prove the ownership of the assets.

This chapter has hopefully motivated you to develop decentralized applications by introducing you to smart contracts. In the next chapter, we'll explore the real-world applications of blockchain technology by exploring projects from different domains.

8
Blockchain Projects

Although **decentralized applications** (**DApps**) can take the place of some centralized applications, their architecture, infrastructure, and implementation are quite different from that of traditional centralized applications. Not every blockchain implementation can justify its benefits compared to the existing implementations. The purpose of this chapter will be to explore a number of projects that can revolutionize decentralized networking.

In this chapter, we will be looking at both financial, and non-financial blockchain projects. Since the invention of Bitcoin, over two thousand cryptocurrencies (referred to as altcoins) have emerged and have gained a lot of attention. The widespread use of the technology gained the attention of venture capitalists and convinced them to invest in projects that were mainly focused on centralized exchanges, wallets, or creating their own cryptocurrency solutions. The application of blockchain technology was mostly biased toward the cryptocurrencies until 2015, but the adoption of decentralized applications, with the help of blockchain platforms, created immense innovation opportunities in financial as well as non-financial domains.

There was always a need for an intermediary in any centralized application. But decentralized applications no longer needed these intermediaries. The notion of eliminating intermediaries or central authorities from existing applications was appealing to many developers and investors as it could reduce the costs incurred due to these entities.

Numerous communities were created to improve the existing blockchain functionalities and also improve the end user experience in decentralized applications. This resulted in a market for appealing blockchain applications and a wide range of consumers.

It is a daunting task for a beginner to explore the ever-growing blockchain market. Moreover, it's difficult to find an application that would satisfy the users' requirements. This is mainly because the implementation you are looking for is likely to be lost in the sea of applications. Classifying and identifying a good implementation requires a lot of exploration. To begin with, we will classify the broad spectrum of applications in the following section before diving into some exciting blockchain projects.

Categorizing the blockchain projects

Different institutions have created decentralized applications or proof of concepts using blockchain technology in order to make the best use of what blockchain can offer them. Institutions that are exploring blockchain may have a financial or a non-financial use case. Based on this, we will broadly classify blockchain applications into financial and non-financial projects.

Financial projects

Any real-world asset that has an economic value can be directly mapped to a digital asset. Any project that utilizes these tradable digital assets can be classified as a financial project. Although all applications dealing with tradable assets could be classified as financial projects, they could also have non-financial use cases.

Most of the early blockchain-related projects were financial. This was mainly because the implementations were motivated by Bitcoin and Bitcoin itself was trying to decentralize the control of money on the internet. This influenced many developer communities to work on projects that were closely related to cryptocurrency. Many exchanges, token distribution platforms, and payment networks were created, which forced banking services to get directly involved so that existing banking customers could make use of cryptocurrency applications.

Although blockchain technology is also useful for non-financial applications, only the lightweight financial applications have gained a wide audience and have been able to create a resilient system due to the wide range of exposure. Although many financial applications were not necessarily restricted to cryptocurrency, many of the initial financial applications were cryptocurrencies, notably **Peercoin** and **Litecoin**, which tried to mimic Bitcoin to achieve better performance by modifying the protocol.

Non-financial projects

During the early years of Bitcoin, there were concerns about the scalability of the underlying technology, and also its future scope. Although cryptocurrency was a great invention that made the decentralization of internet money possible through its P2P-based system, its true technology hadn't been exploited completely. Several developer communities started building applications in the Bitcoin blockchain to make use of the decentralization that was achieved by Bitcoin's blockchain. Due to scalability limitations and privacy concerns of Bitcoin's blockchain, many projects were created by customizing the Bitcoin implementation and forking the Bitcoin blockchain.

As the potential of the technology became evident, it was soon implemented in digital identities, supply chains, asset management, and many other use cases to replace some of the outdated technologies. Due to the blockchain technology's limitations, not all the implementations were successful, but developers were able to find the use cases that weren't directly involved with cryptocurrency. This paved the way for organizations to explore blockchain technology in the non-financial sector. Numerous non-financial organizations that needed replacements for their existing technology started implementing blockchain as a solution. As a result, several alternative implementations of Bitcoin arose to service non-financial use cases.

We will explore some of the sub-categories of financial and non-financial projects by looking into a few applications.

Financial blockchain projects

In this section, our goal is to explore a few of the early financial implementations of blockchain in the financial domain by categorizing them.

Cryptocurrencies

The concept of blockchain has evolved since it was first introduced in Bitcoin. Although Bitcoin's underlying technology has been applied in several different fields, cryptocurrency has been recognized as the true application of the blockchain technology. Many projects have since been created, some imitating Bitcoin's implementation and others solving issues in the existing implementation.

Although many cryptocurrencies can be found that possess similar properties to Bitcoin, they don't necessarily solve the same problems. In fact, many of these currencies were created just to incentivize the actors of the network.

We will talk about these currencies in the *Crypto tokens* section. It is quite difficult to explore all the cryptocurrencies because a new implementation is created almost every day. We will try to simplify this by classifying the cryptocurrencies into **traceable** and **untraceable** currencies.

Traceable cryptocurrencies

As we know, the blocks of Bitcoin consist of collections of transactions that can be retrieved and parsed by any participant on the network. Bitcoin was created with the intention of decentralizing control over money. This came with a cost of privacy, as every transaction is public because it needed to be verified by the nodes on the network. This meant every transaction could be traced back to its origin by anyone in the network.

Bitcoin provided pseudo-anonymity because the public addresses of account holders need not be linked to their real identities. This prevented the account owner's identity from being revealed even though all the transactions were public. However, there is the risk of a user's entire transaction history being leaked if their identity is revealed. Even with these risks, transparent, publicly visible transactions don't cause much trouble because of pseudo-anonymity.

Many cryptocurrencies followed in the footsteps of Bitcoin to create completely transparent transaction ledgers. Litecoin, Namecoin, and Peercoin are some cryptocurrencies that not only mimicked the Bitcoin project but enhanced its features in one way or another.

Untraceable cryptocurrencies

Many cryptocurrencies were later developed to mask private transaction information and make the transactions untraceable, thus solving the privacy issues faced by Bitcoin and other similar cryptocurrencies. **Zcash**, **Monero**, and **Bitcoin Private** are some of the cryptocurrencies that tried to safeguard the privacy of the users by masking the private information in the transaction. We will look into how Zcash helps to achieve privacy by creating untraceable transactions.

Zcash

Zcash creates shielded transactions by hiding the sender, the recipient, and value information. Zcash was the first cryptocurrency to use the **zero-knowledge proof** cryptographic primitive in the blockchain technology, which was released in October, 2016.

A zero-knowledge proof is a system in which a user can prove that they possess knowledge without disclosing it to the verifier. Zero-knowledge proof ensures that none of the information given to the verifier compromises the privacy of the prover. In a regular transaction, users prove that they own an asset by signing transactions with the secret key. Zcash creates a zero-knowledge proof for the transaction that can be verified even though the user did not enclose much information:

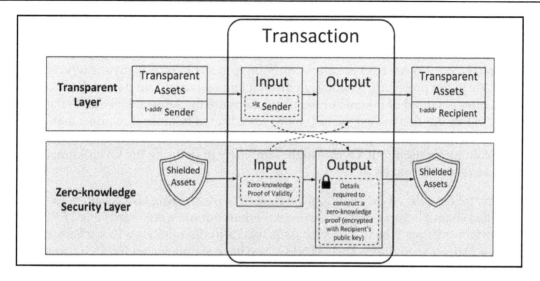

Figure 8.1: A Zcash transaction masking transaction input and output (source: https://z.cash)

Zcash uses a novel form of zero-knowledge proof called **zk-SNARK**, which stands for **Zero-Knowledge Succinct Non-Interactive Argument of Knowledge**. zk-SNARKs prove the possession of information, such as a private key, without sharing it or communicating with the verifier. This way, a shielded transaction, even if it is fully encrypted, is verifiable by using zk-SNARK proofs.

Covering the zk-SNARK protocol in depth is beyond the scope of this chapter. We will be covering it in depth in `Chapter 9`, *Blockchain Optimizations and Enhancements*.

Crypto tokens

Any type of cryptocurrency that is not created primarily to exchange values is considered a special kind of token. These tokens also possess the same capabilities as any other cryptocurrency, because they were created to function in a decentralized network. These tokens can be classified into two types:

- **Security tokens**: Security tokens represent real physical assets, such as a share in a company or any form of financial earnings. These kinds of tokens also possess a predefined economic value, which is analogous to the token's price.
- **Utility tokens**: Utility tokens are created to fuel projects and offer its holders access to the services provided by the project after launch. These tokens don't have a fixed economic value, and their price will be decided by their creator.

Coin offerings

Initial Coin Offerings (**ICO**) are created for the previously-mentioned tokens to raise the initial capital for a project. ICO is a crowd-funding process in which anyone who is willing to contribute to the project can become a part of it and own a certain part of the tokens. ICOs can offer any kind of token, but security tokens are the safest token due to their visible economic value. But this makes the ICO more complicated because it requires that you use **know your customer** (**KYC**) procedures to identify the identity of the user. Utility tokens are most commonly used in ICOs due to the simplicity of defining the token's functionality compared to security tokens.

Most of the tokens offered during ICOs are created in the existing blockchain network using a blockchain platform such as Ethereum. Ethereum has a standard called ERC-20 for smart contract creation, which is used to issue tokens in the Ethereum blockchain. Other blockchain platform providers, such as NEO, also have standardized (NEP-5) token creation to support ICO on their blockchain. We will explore more about the ICO by implementing a crowdfunding use case in `Chapter 12`, *Blockchain Use Cases*.

Ripple payment network

Ripple is a payment network that provides solutions to existing global payment systems such as SWIFT. It aids existing payment systems that suffer from the delayed, unreliable, and expensive transactions. It achieves this with a network of computers that use the ripple consensus algorithm to settle and record transactions on a distributed ledger called the Ripple Consensus Ledger (RCL).

Ripple use cases

Ripple provides a wide range of use cases, especially for global payments. We're now going to look at several examples.

Cross-border payments

Ripple provides a global payment solution, that implies that payment channels can be established in different countries. This enables banks to settle cross-border payments in real-time, with end-to-end transparency and at a low cost. The number of currencies and counterparties will grow as Ripple adoption grows, and liquidity providers need to maintain accounts with each counterparty for each currency:

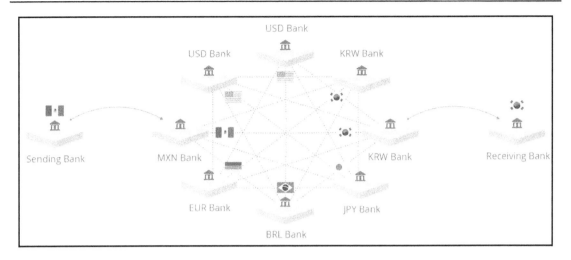

Figure 8.2: Cross-border payment channel (source: https://ripple.com)

Ripple tokens as a currency bridge

Ripple can create a currency pair between any banks with the help of Ripple's own token, which is called XRP. Unlike any other traditional intermediary currency conversion, XRP doesn't require a bank account:

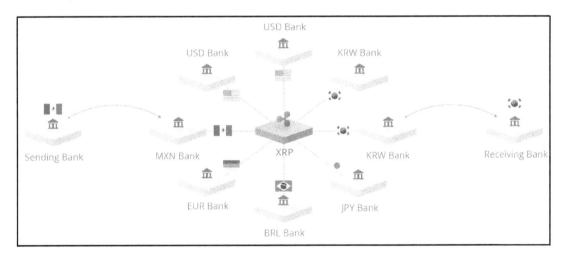

Figure 8.3: XRP as a currency bridge (source: https://ripple.com)

Ripple network

The Ripple network consists of a collection of servers that are similar to full nodes in Bitcoin. They collaborate to reach a consensus regarding the state of the network. Ripple maintains a public ledger that is constantly updated with the global truth about all the transactions.

The decentralized ledger of Ripple has two states: **last closed ledger** and **open ledger**. The last closed ledger state is the state of the most recent ledger agreed by the Ripple network. An open ledger accepts new transactions to be appended so that its state can be altered.

Each Ripple node maintains a list of a set of nodes called the **Unique Node List** (UNL), which will directly contribute to the state of the ledger. The UNL is a subset of the nodes in the Ripple network that are trusted by any server to reach consensus. The UNL members will vote for the valid transactions to be inserted to the ledger.

Ripple consensus algorithm

The **Ripple Protocol consensus algorithm (RPCA)** is a process performed every few seconds by the nodes in the network to reach a consensus in the network. The ledger will remain in the closed state after the network nodes successfully agree. The RPCA has a few mandatory steps to go through before a transaction is successfully added to the ledger:

1. Each server collects all the known valid transactions that are not already part of the ledger and makes them public. These unconfirmed transactions are called the candidate list of transactions.
2. Each server collects all the candidate lists from the UNL servers. Transactions that receive the required number of positive votes are selected for the next step.
3. Finally, it is made sure that each transaction has a minimum of 80% of a server's UNL votes. All transactions satisfying this rule are appended to the ledger.

Ripple token (XRP)

Ripple has issued a total of 100 billion XRP tokens, the majority of which are held by the Ripple community. Ripple can settle a token transaction in 3.5 seconds and can also be spent immediately. Although XRP tokens are part of the Ripple network, Ripple doesn't necessarily need XRP tokens to perform cross-border payments.

Cryptocurrency exchanges

A cryptocurrency exchange is a third-party that allows users to convert a cryptocurrency to another type of asset or a different cryptocurrency. These exchanges are mostly used to convert fiat currencies, such as US dollars, to cryptocurrencies or vice versa. Cryptocurrency exchanges are often centralized servers, and they maintain a scalable server to match users' bid and sell requests. They maintain an order-matching engine that records all the bid and sell requests and initiates a trade whenever it matches bid with a sell request. Exchanges charge a small fee for every transaction that gets executed.

One of the drawbacks of cryptocurrency exchanges is that they are a centralized model in the otherwise decentralized cryptocurrency networks. Many decentralized cryptocurrency exchanges have been created to exchange currencies directly from one user's wallet to another without transferring it to exchanges. Kyber Network, 0x, and OmiseGO are some prominent decentralized exchanges.

Decentralized exchanges

Due to the potential applications of blockchain technology, more and more people are getting involved in it. In particular, the cryptocurrency market is growing. New currencies are introduced regularly, and there are over 2,000 cryptocurrencies already in the market. This means people need to be involved with multiple currencies at the same time and exchange one currency for another. Cryptocurrency exchanges help users to exchange their tokens by placing orders on the market. Although exchanges allow users to exchange assets, they need users to transfer their assets to accounts maintained by these exchanges. This created a centralization of crypto assets in the decentralized ecosystem. This makes most of the trades that happen on centralized exchanges vulnerable to internal fraud and external hacking. A number of hacking incidents have been reported on these centralized exchanges. A hack on Mt. Gox, a Japanese exchange, is the biggest hack in the history of cryptocurrencies.

Decentralized exchanges eliminate the intermediary required during currency conversion, and they don't maintain an order book. Unlike centralized exchanges, they don't charge a fee for each trade.

Kyber Network

Kyber Network is an on-chain decentralized exchange that allows users to convert tokens effortlessly and without requiring any trust. Kyber Network functions on the Ethereum blockchain and currently supports all the Ethereum tokens. It will support cross-chain trade in the future.

Design

Some of the important components for the functioning of Kyber Network are as follows:

- **Users**: Users of the network are the backbone of the decentralized exchange. Each users' wallet acts as an interface to communicate with the network. It supports integration with existing apps, such as Status, and MetaMask, in order to manage user accounts. Integrating with these apps helps to integrate user accounts with Kyber Network without any hassle.

- MetaMask is a bridge that helps developers to integrate user interfaces with the blockchain network. MetaMask provides a browser extension so that web applications can communicate with the blockchain.

- **Smart contracts**: The logic of the way the exchange functions are coded in smart contracts and deployed to the blockchain. There are different types of contract for each of the exchange's major functions.
- **Reserves**: These act as containers of assets in the exchange. Reserves can be maintained by Kyber Network or by a third-party.
- **Reserve contributors**: These are the entities that provide capital for the reserves.
- **Reserve manager**: This is the entity responsible for maintaining the reserves and determining the exchange rates for the currencies.
- **Kyber Network operator**: This is the entity responsible for adding and removing reserve entities, as well as listing and delisting pairs of tokens in the network.

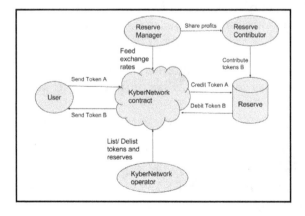

Figure 8.4: Components of Kyber Network (source: https://kyber.network/)

Figure 8.4 connects all the components of Kyber Network to create an overview of the decentralized exchange ecosystem. A user initiates an exchange operation by communicating with the Kyber Network contract with the help of the user interface provided by the user wallet. The smart contract communicates with the reserve to perform credit or debit operations. The reserve manager fetches the exchange rates, and the smart contract ensures the selection of the best exchange rates for the transaction.

Some of the properties of Kyber Network that distinguish it from existing exchanges are as follows:

- Unlike centralized exchanges, Kyber Network doesn't hold any of the users' assets. This means it's not a target for attacks.
- Since the exchange runs on a blockchain network, it will be accessible to any type of account, including contracts. Smart contracts can communicate with the exchange without any intermediary. This creates a whole new opportunity for the **decentralized autonomous organization** (**DAO**), where the rules for governing the organization can be decided by the members of the network rather than the central authority.
- All the exchange requests are executed almost instantly, and users will be able to access their converted currency immediately in their wallet.

To summarize, Kyber has a lot of potential in the blockchain ecosystem due to its decentralized model, which will fit right into any decentralized system.

Non-financial blockchain projects

Soon after the successful implementation of blockchain in the financial sector, blockchain technology saw application in the non-financial sector as well. We will explore some of these implementations by further classifying them.

Asset management

Managing an asset in the real world is a challenging task because it requires an intermediary to maintain records that contain the complete history of the asset. The intermediary needs to prove its legitimacy before it can provide users with asset information. Building trust is an expensive task, especially in a trustless network. Blockchain technology helps to achieve this trust through the decentralization of management.

The digital representation of existing physical assets is one of the key features of blockchain applications. The digital representation of a physical asset can be managed in a decentralized network.

Factom

Factom provides asset management with a precise, verifiable, and immutable audit trail, and eliminates the need for trust. Record management poses the difficult problem of protecting, synchronizing, and verifying record information. Many traditional methods still require some manual effort, which makes it more difficult to scale and to achieve accuracy.

Factom proposes a solution to the asset management problem of securing an individual's or an organization's data by publishing the encrypted data, or a fingerprint of the data, to a distributed ledger. Factom also allows users to audit and verify the data published on the blockchain. Factom achieves this by running a distributed protocol that runs on top of the Bitcoin blockchain.

Design

Factom creates a fast, cheap, and bloat-free way to develop blockchain-based applications. The main workflow of a Factom architecture involves the following steps:

1. Servers create blocks that will be recorded in Factom's own chain
2. Factom secures an anchor (a hash of the Directory Block) onto the Bitcoin blockchain

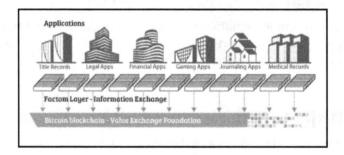

Figure 8.5: Factom ecosystem (source: https://www.factom.com)

As shown in *Figure 8.5*, the Bitcoin blockchain is the last layer in Factom's design, and it stores only the minimal information about the assets. Factom creates anchors to the Bitcoin blockchain by only storing the digest of the actual information on the immutable Bitcoin blockchain.

Factom is created by forming a hierarchy of a set of blocks, with Directory Blocks forming a connection with the Bitcoin blockchain. The hierarchy itself constitutes a chain of references as shown in *Figure 8.6*. Each reference in the Directory Block is just a hash of the Entry Block and its chain ID. These Entry Blocks have references that point to all the entries with a particular chain ID that arrived during a certain time period. The Entry Block for a chain ID is also part of a micro-chain. The bulk of the data in Factom is at the leaves, the Entries themselves. These hierarchical data structures are considered unmodifiable due to Bitcoin's immutability.

The layers and concepts in the Factom system are as follows:

- **Directory Layer**: This organizes the Merkle roots of Entry Blocks
- **Entry Block Layer**: This organizes references to entries
- **Entries**: This contains an application's raw data or a hash of its private data
- **Chains**: This is a grouping of entries specific to an application

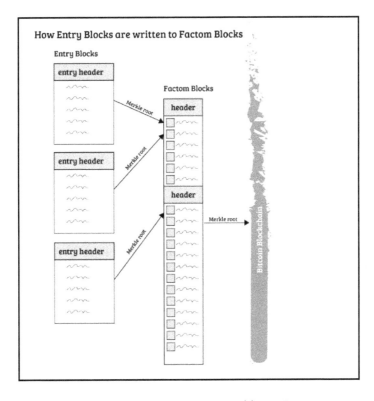

Figure 8.6: The layered architecture of Factom (source: https://www.factom.com)

Factom products

Factom provides several solutions to private enterprises as well as to the public. The following are a couple of products from Factom:

- **Factom Harmony**: This was created to solve problems in the mortgage industry. It reduces the documentation, legal, and compliance expenses incurred by using the transparency of Factom.
- **dLoc**: This is a document authentication verification system. Factom partnered with Smartrac, a leading **radio-frequency identification** (**RFID**) product manufacturer, to use the technology in any asset that can be tagged by RFID.

Social media platforms

Social media is a place where anyone can publish content, sharing their opinions, skills, or knowledge to help others who are in need of those resources. Although there are multiple social media platforms for different purposes, there are no standards defined regarding how content creators are rewarded for their contributions. The blockchain-based network helps to tokenize web content by rewarding contributors for their work on social media platforms. This is accomplished by creating reward-based decentralized social networking platforms such as Steemit, Sapient Network, Indorse, and Sola.

Steemit is a blogging platform where the content creators and the curators are rewarded fairly based on their contributions. Steemit uses the Steem blockchain to manage the reward process for every post or comment created on its platform. We will explore the Steem blockchain to understand its reward system for social media platforms.

Steem

User-generated content has always generated billions of dollars for the founders and shareholders of the social media platform giants. On the flip side, content creators are hardly recognized at all and get paid very little for their contributions. Steem supports online communities by returning most of the dividends to the contributors of the content, those who brought the value to the platform in the first place.

Steem is a blockchain-based reward system where community building and social interactions earn rewards in cryptocurrency. Steem encourages user participation in the community with a fair accounting system to reward the users accurately for their contributions. It's a Proof of Work-based currency that has a scheduled block generation time of 3 seconds.

Voting model in Steem

The Steem platform has a cryptocurrency token called STEEM. Steem operates on the basis of one STEEM, one vote. In this model, individuals who have contributed the most to the platform, as measured by their account balance, have the most influence over how contributions are scored.

Existing systems that are similar to Steem allow contributors to be paid when the consumers show their appreciation for the content by tipping, usually through a micropayment channel. The drawback of these platforms lies in the incentivization model, which doesn't necessarily always incentivize good content. Steem is designed to enable effective micropayments for all kinds of contributions. Content consumers don't have to decide how and how much they tip the content creator; instead, they vote for the content, and the Steem platform will use their votes to determine individual rewards.

Voting in Steem accurately determines the quality of the content and rewards the content creators accordingly, whereas other platforms don't necessarily provide just rewards to the creators of the content. Steem rewards those who contribute the most to the total value of a piece of content and rewards the voters proportionally to the final reward paid to the content creator.

Steem tokens

There are three main tokens in Steem: Steem (STEEM), Steem Power (SP), and Steem Backed Dollars (SBD).

STEEM

STEEM is the cryptocurrency token on the Steem blockchain. STEEM can easily be bought and sold on exchanges.

SP

SP is basically STEEM that is locked in a vesting fund for 13 weeks, providing additional benefits within the platform. The influence of Steem users on the distribution of rewards is proportional to the amount of SP they own. SP holders also receive interest from their holdings. The earliest votes get the biggest share of the reward because the rewards are distributed according to time.

SBD

The user of any currency expects its value to be stable. SBD was designed in an attempt to bring stability to the world of cryptocurrency by pegging its value to 1 USD. This token ensures the maximum benefit is given to the token holder and enables the blockchain network to grow. Due to the token's stability, it can be exchanged with other cryptocurrencies on exchanges.

Consensus in Steem

Just like other blockchain applications, a consensus mechanism is used in Steem to include any block of transactions in the public ledger. The individuals responsible for including a block are elected by the people in the Steem network. Block creation is done in rounds, and in each round 21 witnesses are selected for the created blocks. Any witness who misses a block and hasn't produced one in the last 24 hours will be disabled until they update their block signing key.

The consensus mechanism ensures that everyone has the potential to participate in block production, regardless of whether he or she is powerful enough to end up at the top. Possessing more SP improves a user's voting power.

Digital identity

Digital identity is one of the inherent features of the original blockchain implementation in Bitcoin. It identifies the owner of an asset. It can also store vital user information, which can be shared with any third-party, but only with the user's consent. The digital identity of the user stored on the blockchain can be shared with different applications, which reduces the unnecessary replication of the user's KYC operation to verify the identity. Moreover, the digital identity provided by the blockchain ensures the user's identity can be verified globally.

Many organizations are working towards the digital identity feature of the blockchain so that they can remove their dependency on using servers to maintain users' confidential data. Tech giants such as IBM and Microsoft are continuously exploring ways to standardize digital identity in the blockchain space.

ShoCard Identity Management

ShoCard is an identity management service, built with the blockchain technology, where people can own and protect their digital identity. Users can prove their identity to anyone, and they can also decide with whom they want to share their details. Third-parties can verify the authenticity of the information using blockchain without the need for a centralized validator.

The ShoCard architecture is designed to provide very high transaction throughput. It uses Proof of Work to certify a large number of users in a short time. ShoCard currently provides two products:

- Embedded model of **software as a service (SaaS)**
- **ShoBadge**, a complete enterprise-level **identity provider (IdP)** solution

ShoCard architecture

The ShoCard IM Platform provides **software development kits (SDK)** to integrate with applications. The ShoCard IM Platform is made up of the following modules:

- ShoCard SDKs
- ShoCard Service layer
- ShoCard sidechain
- Blockchain caches
- ShoCard Blockchain Adaptor

ShoCard has a service layer that lies between the application and the server. Because all the messages are encrypted, data cannot be read by the service layer during communication:

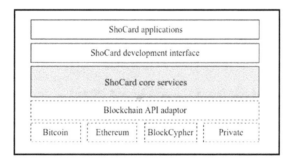

Figure 8.7: ShoCard architecture

Here are some of the responsibilities of the ShoCard services:

- The ShoCard server acts as a secure communication pipeline and simply writes the information to the blockchain.
- The ShoCard Service layer is responsible for managing the interface between all client SDKs and the blockchain.
- The ShoCard sidechains are used to increase throughput. The certification data is stored in the sidechain, and only the hashed data is stored in the public blockchain.
- The blockchain also caches the local copy of the blockchain for faster read access so that verifications can be managed independently of what happens with a public blockchain.
- The ShoCard Blockchain Adaptor abstracts the interface to the blockchain that maintains the Proof of Work, so the ShoCard Service layer can remain efficient.

ShoCard uses an immutable public blockchain to verify the users' identities, but not to store the users' details. Since public blockchain data provides a high level of transparency, the data stored in the blockchain should only be used to verify user certificates. The blockchain serves as a repository of certificates.

Some of the use cases of ShoCard are:

- Passwordless login
- Improving customers' traveling experiences at airports and hotels by creating a single travel token with a digital identity for the entire journey or stay
- Automated registration
- Identity verifications
- Proof of age

Check out the detailed list of ShoCard's identity management use cases at `https://shocard.com/identity-management-use-cases`.

Blockchain in the Internet of Things (IoT)

Many companies in the field of IoT, such as Filament, Xage, and even IBM's Watson platform, are looking for alternative techniques to achieve better connectivity and storage. The introduction of blockchain has motivated these firms to converge IoT and blockchain, and many have already successfully integrated them, gaining benefits over existing implementations.

As blockchain promises to provide a foundation for autonomous products, it guarantees to produce the **Internet of Trusted Things (IoTT)**. Some of the reasons to merge blockchain with IoT are to build trust between devices, reduce costs, and increase transaction speed. IoT, by definition, is distributed, which makes it easier to adopt use cases in the distributed blockchain ledger.

IOTA

IOTA is an open source distributed ledger created to power the future of IoT with fee-less microtransactions. Since there will be billions of devices connected to the internet that need to exchange information efficiently, a scalable solution where millions of transactions need to be processed per second is required. IOTA proposes to provide a scalable solution to machine-to-machine communication in the IoT world with a modified transaction model.

IOTA maintains its distributed ledger quite differently than existing decentralized applications. IOTA cannot be categorized as a blockchain project because it doesn't use blockchain as its underlying technology. IOTA creates and maintains transactions using a **directed acyclic graph** (**DAG**) technology instead of blocks in the blockchain. Transaction confirmation time is extremely fast, and there is no limit on the transaction throughput because it is not governed by block creation time.

IOTA is based on a newly distributed ledger called **Tangle**, which tries to tackle some of the problems of blockchain designs in an attempt to create an efficient and scalable system by introducing a new way of reaching consensus in a decentralized P2P system.

 Tangle is a distributed ledger that retains the secure transactions feature of blockchain, which eliminates double-spend but doesn't store transactions in blocks.

Design

For each new transaction, two random, unconfirmed transactions are validated in the Tangle. Each validation of a transaction increases the likelihood of a transaction being genuine. Each transaction should receive a certain number of validations in order to be accepted as a confirmed transaction. In an IOTA Tangle, a few transactions will have fewer validations, whereas others will have a sufficient number of validations.

The user must validate two other randomly selected transactions in order to send out a created transaction. This transaction should later be verified by the other users. As every node contributes to the decentralized ledger, its architecture is inherently decentralized. IOTA works with a coordinator that will confirm all transactions initially.

The coordinator can be removed once the network is large. Currently, IOTA uses **Kerl**, a version of SHA-3, as a hash function, which works with ternary (instead of binary) operations.

 IOTA uses Proof of Work in each transaction for spam protection, similar in spirit to the Proof of Work used in Hashcash.

IOTA in IoT

Although we have been hearing about IoT for quite some time, it hasn't actually contributed much to the general audience. IoT products on the market tend to increase the luxury of the users, but they don't necessarily solve real-world problems. IoT devices must replace most isolated devices, and they should be able to communicate with one another in a fairly efficient way. IOTA's architecture makes certain that communication can be scaled quite easily with the growing number of devices.

Data storage

One of the significant applications of the P2P networking protocol is the decentralization of data storage. **BitTorrent** was the first protocol to achieve the decentralization of data storage through P2P networking. The **InterPlanetary File System** (**IPFS**) protocol was later implemented to create a distributed filesystem, and it also made use of the Bitcoin blockchain technology in its later implementation.

Several blockchain projects have been created using distributed filesystems, where nodes are incentivized with tokens to contribute to storage on the network. Different consensus algorithms have been introduced that are essential to the storage, the retrieval of data, and the incentivization process.

Some blockchain-based distributed data storage projects are as follows:

- Storj
- MaidSafe
- Filecoin
- Siacoin

Filecoin

Filecoin is a distributed storage network that turns its storage network into an algorithmic market. Cryptocurrencies have proved that a critical asset such as digital money can be transacted without the need for an intermediary. But these currencies only have decentralized transaction information on the network. Decentralization of bulk data in a blockchain network is expensive and slow, and the data does not need to be verified like transactions because each piece of data is not related to the others. Many protocols have been created for decentralized data storage so that data can be fetched efficiently without the need for a third-party. IPFS is one such protocol that has proven the utility of content-addressing by decentralizing the web itself, serving billions of files used across a global P2P network

Filecoin provides an incentive model, with the help of blockchain, that is built on top of the IPFS storage protocol. Filecoin creates a marketplace for decentralized storage. The nodes that provide space for the distributed storage network are called miners, and they are analogous to the miners in Bitcoin, although they provide computing power instead. Miners are rewarded by the consumers with Filecoin for their storage contribution. The Filecoin network achieves robustness by replicating and dispersing content throughout the storage network.

The consensus in the blockchain of Filecoin is achieved by proof of spacetime, where miners who lend the storage space are eligible to create the blocks. The Filecoin protocol provides data storage and retrieval services to consumers.

IPFS

IPFS is a protocol that's designed to create addressable content and P2P methods to store media in a distributed filesystem. In 2014, IPFS adopted the Bitcoin blockchain in order to store data that needs to be immutable.

Files in IPFS are identified by their hashes, and therefore they are cached in a friendly way. IPFS uses a single massive swarm in which anyone can serve a data block to anyone else; block sharing is not limited to the peers of the file, unlike the BitTorrent protocol. IPFS files can be accessed over a variety of protocols, such as HTTP. IPFS has a name service called **Inter-Planetary Name System** (**IPNS**) that is compatible with other name services, such as DNS and .onion.

Filecoin consensus

The consensus algorithm in Bitcoin doesn't really contribute to anything other than achieving consensus about the global blockchain state.

The difficulty involved in Bitcoin mining makes it really expensive for a node to take part in the mining process. Filecoin proposes a useful work consensus mechanism that ensures that the work done by the miners to achieve consensus is useful.

Filecoin's useful consensus protocol elects a miner to create a block, and the probability of a miner being selected is proportional to its currently used storage relative to the rest of the network. Thus, this consensus protocol ensures that the amount of storage provided is also used as proof of computation.

Filecoin's decentralized storage network (DSN)

Filecoin's DSN is based on incentivizing the auditing and verifying of transactions. Clients in the network pay miners to store and retrieve data. Miners get paid only if the network audits the provided service.

Different participants in the network are **Clients**, **Storage Miners**, and **Retrieval Miners**:

- Clients pay to store data and to retrieve data in the DSN via PUT and GET requests.
- Storage Miners provide data storage to the network. Storage Miners participate in Filecoin by offering their disk space and serving PUT requests from the clients. To become Storage Miners, users must pledge their storage by depositing collateral proportional to it. Storage Miners respond to PUT requests by committing to storing the Client's data for a specified time. Storage Miners generate proofs of spacetime and submit them to the blockchain to prove that they are storing the data through time. If there are invalid or missing proofs, Storage Miners are penalized and lose part of their collateral. Storage Miners are also eligible to mine new blocks, and in doing so, they receive the mining reward for creating a block and transaction fees for the transactions included in the block.
- Retrieval Miners provide data retrieval to the network. Retrieval Miners participate in Filecoin by serving data that users request via GET. Unlike Storage Miners, they are not required to pledge, commit to storing data, or provide proof of storage. It is natural for Storage Miners to also participate as Retrieval Miners. Retrieval Miners can obtain pieces of data directly from clients, or from the Retrieval Market.

The collection of all the Filecoin nodes is referred to as the Filecoin network. The Filecoin network is responsible for the management protocol of the storage network. Management involves auditing storage proofs, repairing possible faults, managing available storage, and validating pledges.

Filecoin markets

To meet the demand and supply requests in the Filecoin network, there are two markets: a Storage Market and a Retrieval Market. The two markets have the same structure but different designs:

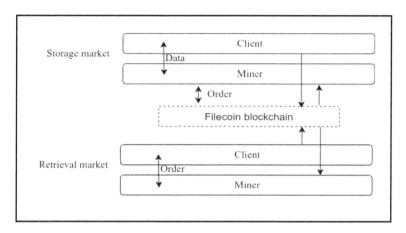

Figure 8.8: Filecoin market

Clients and miners propose a price for the services they need or provide by submitting it to the market. When the exchange matches the order, it will initiate and execute the deal.

 Filecoin exchanges services in a decentralized fashion with the help of verifiable markets. Miners and full nodes are the participants of verifiable markets. A verifiable market is a protocol with two phases: order matching and settlement.

The Storage Market is a verifiable market that allows clients to pay miners to store data. Just like any exchange, it maintains an in-chain orderbook. The orderbook is public so that the clients can always monitor prices and bid accordingly.

The Retrieval Market is a verifiable market that allows clients to pay miners to retrieve stored data. Clients request a specific piece of information, and the market allocates a miner to serve this data. Unlike Storage Miners, Retrieval Miners don't need to generate proof of storage. Any user in the network can become a Retrieval Miner by serving data in exchange for a reward in Filecoin.

BigchainDB

BigchainDB is database software that inherits many of the properties of blockchain systems. It brings together the best features of both structured databases (high transaction rates and low latency) and blockchain systems (immutability, decentralization, and identity). The initial implementation of BigchainDB did not achieve pure decentralization because it was susceptible to single points of failure. The recent release of BigchainDB achieves decentralization by ensuring **Byzantine Fault Tolerance** (**BFT**) of the nodes. This was achieved by integrating the **Tendermint** protocol, which is used for networking and consensus functionalities.

Features of BigchainDB

BigchainDB encompasses all the essential features of a distributed database and a typical blockchain-based system. Although it doesn't have the ideal features of a blockchain-based database, it is a great data storage solution and is a useful decentralized database system.

Blockchain inherited features

The blockchain-inherited features of BigchainDB include the following:

- **Decentralization**

    Each node in the network contains its own MongoDB instance, which maintains all the transactions. BigchainDB is decentralized to ensure that there is no single owner, no single point of control, and no single point of failure. Even if a third of the nodes fail in any way, the network will be resilient to this failure. BigchainDB ensures BFT by using middleware called Tendermint.

    Tendermint doesn't use Bitcoin's Proof of Work algorithm to achieve consensus for each block due to its high energy consumption. It provides BFT by achieving consensus among validating nodes. The validating nodes participate in the consensus protocol by broadcasting votes to decide on the next block to append. If the protocol achieves a majority of votes (2/3 of validators), it will commit the block to the blockchain. The Tendermint protocol needs to run this consensus procedure during each block insertion to the blockchain to determine the next block, so it is referred to as a round-based protocol.

- **Immutability:** Unlike traditional databases, BigchainDB doesn't perform an update or delete operations on the inserted data. Due to the nature of blockchain, transactions can only be appended. All the transactions at each node are maintained in a MongoDB instance in an immutable way, similar to other blockchain systems.

- **Asset ownership:** Like most asset-based blockchain applications, BigchainDB provides asset management operations such as asset creation and transfer. A user can claim an asset by owning the private key of the account to which the asset is transferred. Generally, a blockchain application such as a cryptocurrency only has a single type of asset, but BigchainDB can create as many assets as a user needs. All the asset management operations are performed by creating transactions, and it validates each transaction to make sure that it is safe from transaction attacks such as double-spend.

Database inherited features

The database-inherited features of BigchainDB include the following:

- **High transaction throughput:** BigchainDB was created as a replacement for existing distributed databases, with the added features provided by the blockchain technology. Although the database was designed with blockchain principles, it retained its database characteristics. It was able to achieve a high transaction rate even in a decentralized network. The latest version of BigchainDB processes a thousand transactions per second, which is high compared to other blockchain-based storage applications.

- **Low latency:** BigchainDB takes only a few seconds to include a transaction in a committed block. The Tendermint protocol is responsible for maintaining low latency in the decentralized network.

- **Database querying:** We all know that any structured or unstructured database uses query languages to request and retrieve the data from it. BigchainDB nodes also let users index and query stored data. Each node in the network maintains its own MongoDB instance. It is up to the node operator to decide how to expose the database to the blockchain network. The node can expose any interface. It could be a REST API or the GraphQL API.

The life cycle of BigchainDB transactions

The life cycle of BigchainDB transactions consists of the following steps:

Creating a transaction

BigchainDB transactions can be created and broadcast to the network by any user as long as the created transaction conforms to the BigchainDB Transactions Spec, which defines the expected keys and values of a transaction.

Transactions are usually created using the drivers provided by BigchainDB. There's a list of drivers available in a variety of programming languages, including Python and JavaScript.

The following JSON structure shows all the fields of the transaction. BigchainDB transactions consist of input and output, which is similar to Bitcoin transactions. Additionally, each transaction has an `operation` field, which specifies the operation performed on the asset:

```
{
  "id": "3667c0e5cbf1fd3398e375dc24f47206cc52d53d771ac68ce14ddf0
fde806a1c",
  "version": "2.0",
  "inputs": [
    {
      "fulfillment": "pGSAIEGwaKW1LibaZXx7_NZ5-V0alDLvrguGLyLRkgm
KWG73gUBJ2Wpnab0Y-4i-kSGFa_VxxYCcctpT8D6s4uTGOO c\nF-hVR2VbbxS35
NiDrwUJXYCHSH2IALYUoUZ6529Qbe2g4G",
      "fulfills": null,
      "owners_before": [
        "5RRWzmZBKPM84o63dppAttCpXG3wqYqL5niwNS1XBFyY"
      ]
    }
  ],
  "outputs": [
    {
      "amount": "1",
      "condition": {
        "details": {
          "public_key": "5RRWzmZBKPM84o63dppAttCpXG3wqYqL5niwNS1XB
FyY",
          "type": "ed25519-sha-256"
        },
        "uri": "ni:///sha-256;d-_huQ-eG-QQD-
GAJpvrSsy71LJqyNhtUAs_own7aTY?fpt=ed25519-sha-256&cost=131072"
      },
      "public_keys": [
        "5RRWzmZBKPM84o63dppAttCpXG3wqYqL5niwNS1XBFyY"
```

```
    ]
  }
],
"operation": "CREATE",
"asset": {
  "data": {
    "message": "Greetings from Berlin!"
  }
},
"metadata": null
}
```

Transmitting a transaction

Once a transaction is created, it can be transmitted to the network by invoking the HTTP API exposed by the node. When the transaction arrives at the node, it is validated to ensure that it conforms with Transactions Spec and transaction legitimacy. It is then broadcast to the network using a Tendermint instance. The following figure shows how BigchainDB's server, a MongoDB instance, and a Tendermint instance are interconnected in the network:

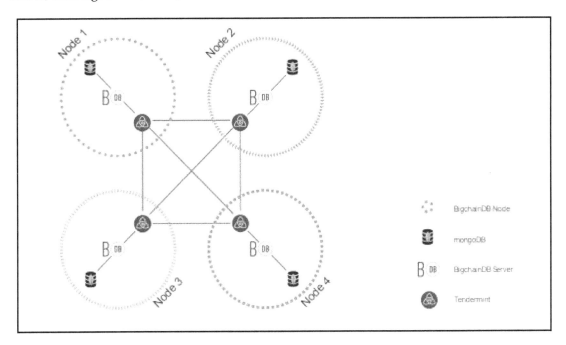

Figure 8.9: A BigchainDB network with its components (source: https://www.bigchaindb.com)

Use cases

Due to BigchainDB's blockchain and database characteristics, its applications can be witnessed in both centralized and decentralized ecosystems. In a centralized system, such as servers on the cloud, it can replace existing databases. However, its most suitable application is alongside decentralized platforms such as Ethereum. DApps created in Ethereum often make use of distributed storage mechanisms such as IPFS. BigchainDB could be used in such applications to store transaction data.

Distributed computing

In the last decade, we have witnessed tremendous growth in the computing industry. The growth in the computing industry was in terms of processing power, memory, storage, networking, design, and much more. With the increase in computing power, developers have started working on equally exciting projects to harness it. Although high-powered computing devices are available to the general public, they are not very economical. This was when distributed computing was introduced to situations where a complex problem could be solved by several computing devices by breaking the problem down into tasks.

Distributed computing is an efficient way of solving complex tasks without using any single high-powered computing machine. Just like distributed data storage, distributed computing has been integrated with blockchain platforms. **Golem** is a blockchain-based platform that provides a marketplace for computing power.

Golem

Golem is a global marketplace for distributed computing power in a P2P network. It allows anyone with redundant computing power to become a producer and monetize their computing power by contributing it to a decentralized network. Golem can be used to power decentralized microservices or any asynchronous tasks. The main advantage of Golem's marketplace is the reduction of the computing price for complex tasks such as CGI rendering, scientific calculations, and machine learning.

Golem operates in a P2P network, allowing providers with computing power to hire out their resources to customers, or in Golem parlance, requestors. Unlike existing cloud platforms, where payment is made at fixed intervals using third-party services, Golem uses a micro-payment service built with an Ethereum-based transaction system that enables direct payment between the participants in the network.

Golem ecosystem

The Golem ecosystem is formed by three main components - the resource providers, the resource requestors, and the software developers. The following figure depicts the Golem ecosystem consisting of these components:

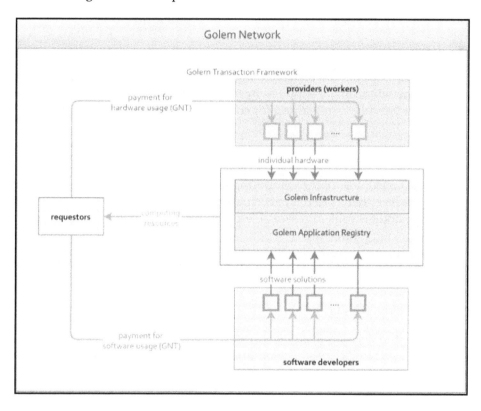

Figure 8.10: The Golem ecosystem (source: `https://golem.network`)

Application registry

The application registry is a smart contract on the Ethereum blockchain where anyone can publish applications, such as integration tools, that can run on the Golem network. This registry serves as a marketplace for requestors to look for tools.

Since it is unsafe to trust untested software in a decentralized system, Golem whitelists or blacklists applications with the help of special users called validators. When a software author publishes some software, validators review and certify the application as either safe or unsafe. All the safe applications are added to the whitelist, and others are added to the blacklist. The providers use this whitelist whenever using an application. Golem maintains a whitelist of safe applications that can be referred to by first-time users.

Providers

Computing power is supplied by providers in the Golem ecosystem. The infrastructure of the decentralized network can be supplied by anyone. Providers can even supply cycles of a single CPU. Each provider is rewarded for contributing to the requestors computing tasks.

Requestors

Requestors are the consumers of the computing resources shared by the providers. Golem is a competitive market, thanks to the participation of the providers and the requestors. This competitive market results in reasonable prices for computing resources, unlike the pricing of existing cloud platforms.

Golem allows users to act as both provider and requestor so that requestors can share their resources during idle time.

Golem Network Token (GNT)

GNT powers the entire decentralized network by facilitating the micro-payment service between the participants. GNT was created during the crowdfunding period of the project, but is mostly used in the Golem network by the requestors and providers:

- GNT is used for settlements between the providers and requestors for services provided
- Software developers receive remuneration in GNT for contributing to the application registry
- Participation in the software validation process requires GNT

Golem tokens cannot be mined and are limited to the number of tokens created during the crowdfunding period.

Blockchain platforms

As decentralized blockchain applications gained a lot of exposure in several technology sectors, individual developers and organizations began creating blockchain platforms in which applications could be created without worrying about the underlying implementations of P2P networking, consensus, or transactions. These projects have provided a platform for generic programmers to implement valid use cases just by creating business logic.

Each blockchain platform has its own blockchain and network of nodes. This isolates blockchain applications created in one blockchain platform in terms of the transactions and other data on the blockchain. There are multiple blockchain platforms, each of them trying either to solve issues in existing platforms' implementations or develop additional functionality for a particular application.

We have already looked at NEO and MultiChain platforms and created decentralized applications. Ethereum, Eris, NXT, EOS, and Hyperledger are some well-known platforms that are used to implement diverse use cases.

Ethereum

Ethereum is a widely-used platform for creating decentralized applications by providing an immutable ledger that uses a modified version of Bitcoin's consensus algorithm. Ethereum provides advanced scripting functionality with an object-oriented programming language called Solidity. Ethereum houses its own distributed virtual machine, called EVM, which can execute compiled Solidity scripts.

Ethereum was proposed in late 2013 by Vitalik Buterin, a programmer who was involved with Bitcoin at the time. Buterin had earlier proposed that Bitcoin needed an advanced scripting language to develop applications. He proposed Ethereum after failing to convince the Bitcoin development community.

Ethereum token

Ethereum contains a token called ether, which powers the functionality of the blockchain. All the transactions in Ethereum need a small ether fee to be included in the blockchain. This small unit of computation is called **gas**. Unlike NEO's GAS token, which was discussed in `Chapter 7`, *Diving into Blockchain – Proof of Ownership*, gas is not a separate token, but a small unit of ether.

Ether

Ether is a cryptocurrency used in the Ethereum ecosystem. Ether can be used as a virtual currency just like Bitcoin. It can be transacted with the help of a public key and private key that is owned by the user. Ether tokens are traded in cryptocurrency exchanges under the ETH symbol.

Gas

Gas is a small ether fee that needs to be attached when a transaction is included in the blockchain. Gas was mainly created to mitigate spam transactions in the blockchain. Any smart contract author will attach a small amount of gas when deploying it in the public ledger. This will ensure that the author is deploying a legitimate contract to the blockchain.

The price of the gas can be specified in a small amount of ether by the user while deploying the contract, and this is referred to as the gas price. The amount of gas that needs to be spent during any transaction is called the gas limit. The gas price is measured in a unit of gwei (1 ether = 10^9 gwei).

EVM

Unlike the stack-based language used in Bitcoin, Solidity is a Turing-complete language, and thus it requires a runtime environment to execute programs. EVM provides a runtime environment to execute smart contracts in Ethereum nodes. EVM runs on a node that is isolated from the Ethereum network and other processes of the host machine. Only the output of smart contracts can be broadcast and appended to the blockchain as transactions. EVM executes Solidity scripts that are compiled to Ethereum bytecode. This ensures that execution is independent of the platform so that each node on the network executes and produces the same output. EVM has been implemented in several different languages, including Go, JavaScript, and Python.

Blockchain consensus

Ethereum nodes mine blocks for the blockchain in a similar way to Bitcoin by using a Proof of Work-based algorithm. A node that appends a block ensures that a sufficient amount of computation is done on the block using a hash function. The average block creation time is limited to around 12 seconds.

Ethereum uses a Proof of Work algorithm called **Ethash**, which is an ASIC-resistant algorithm developed to overcome the centralization of the mining process. The mining requires the generation of a large dataset from the pseudorandom cache before computing the hash. Since memory is used during this process, it is resistant to ASIC-based mining devices. The verification process can be performed with low memory because it only needs part of the dataset to be regenerated.

 ASIC stands for the **application-specific integrated circuit**. The circuit will perform a specific operation. Bitcoin ASICs were developed specifically to run SHA256 hashing functions so that they make full use of the hardware's capabilities.

Ethereum has planned to replace Proof of Work-based consensus with proof of stake in the near future. Miners will no longer be able to contribute with their computation power. Instead, token holders will contribute to the consensus.

DApp development

Currently, Ethereum is the most widely-used platform for DApp development, due to its exceptional community support. There are over 2,000 active DApps on the Ethereum platform. Complete statistics can be found at `https://www.stateofthedapps.com/stats`. It provides an excellent set of tools to bootstrap DApp development. In this section, we will list some of the basic components and tools that are required to develop a DApp in the Ethereum ecosystem.

Geth

Ethereum provides client software in multiple languages, including C++, Python, and Rust. The Go programming language implementation of the client software, called **Geth**, is popular. Each piece of client software is bundled with several components:

- **Client daemon**: Just like Bitcoin Core's client daemon, the Geth daemon is a process that establishes a P2P connection with other Ethereum nodes to exchange blockchain data. The Geth daemon needs to run all the time to ensure that the client's local blockchain copy is up to date. The Geth client daemon can also validate and mine transactions. The client exposes an RPC interface to let DApps communicate with the blockchain network.

- **Client CLI**: The client software provides a **command-line interface** (**CLI**) that can be used to perform operations on the Ethereum client node. The CLI can be to manage accounts, create transactions, and query the local blockchain data, among other things.
- **Client User Interface**: Mist is the most widely-used graphical user interface software. It comes with bundled with Go and C++ implementations of the Ethereum node.

Web3.js

Like any other web applications, even DApps needs a frontend app providing the user an interface to communicate with the backend application. Since most frontend applications are executed in web browsers, Ethereum provides a JavaScript library called web3.js, which can be used in frontend applications to communicate with the decentralized blockchain network. There are libraries available in other languages, such as Web3.py for Python, that can perform similar operations if the client interface is built in Python.

Truffle framework

Truffle is a framework that helps to bootstrap the Ethereum DApp project by creating the required project structure along with basic scripts and configurations. This is similar to frameworks such as Django, Angular, and React. Truffle eases the tasks of compiling and deploying contracts onto the blockchain for developers.

MetaMask

MetaMask is an application that acts as a bridge between user interfacing applications that run generally on web browsers and Ethereum blockchain nodes. In *Figure 8.11*, MetaMask forms the bridge between the DApp user interface and blockchain nodes. MetaMask provides a plugin or extension for web browsers that enables users to manage their accounts. All transaction queries to the Ethereum blockchain are forwarded to the Ethereum network with the help of the MetaMask bridge.

MetaMask communicates with the blockchain nodes by invoking methods through the RPC interface provided by nodes:

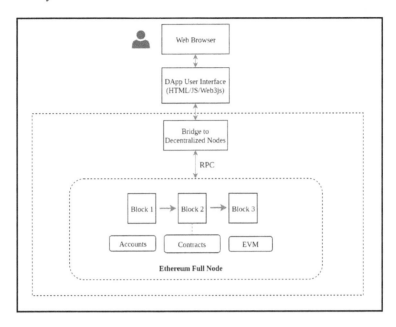

Figure 8.11: Ethereum DApp architecture

Ethereum network

Like Bitcoin, Ethereum can run on the mainnet or testnet blockchains. Both the mainnet and testnet blockchains are public blockchains. In addition to this, Ethereum nodes can set up a private or local blockchain instance. Setting up a development environment in Ethereum is a piece of cake due to the wide variety of options and community support.

Local blockchain

An Ethereum local blockchain instance can be set up in the blink of an eye. A JavaScript package called **Ganache** from the Truffle framework can set up a local instance of Ethereum. The package ships with JavaScript implementation of the Ethereum blockchain, so no Ethereum client is required for local testing. A local Ethereum blockchain instance comes with mining, account management, a blockchain explorer, and many other updated features. Ganache runs a local Ethereum client instance that also listens on the JSON-RPC port of Ethereum (8545).

Testnet blockchain

Ethereum's testnet is similar to Bitcoin's testnet. It simulates the mainnet blockchain, differing only in that it consists of an alternate blockchain whose transactions are of no real value. The testnet also needs gas to deploy smart contracts or simple transactions.

Unlike Bitcoin's testnet, there are three testnet blockchains in the Ethereum community, each of which is maintained by a different team:

- **Rinkeby testnet**: This is a proof of authority blockchain network maintained by the Geth team. Ether cannot be mined in this network.
- **Ropsten testnet**: This is a Proof of Work blockchain network where ether can be mined.
- **Kovan testnet**: This is a proof of authority blockchain network maintained by the Parity team. Ether cannot be mined in this network.

 Since gas is required to create any transaction, even in the testnet, it can be acquired by requesting it from testnet faucets where all the unused testnet Ethers are accumulated. Rinkeby testnet users can request ether from `https://faucet.rinkeby.io` by specifying the target account address.

Links for the projects

We have listed out the links for some of the projects that were mentioned throughout this chapter.

- **Zcash implementation**: `https://github.com/zcash/zcash`
- **Ripple implementation**: `https://github.com/ripple/rippled`
- **Kyber Network project**: `https://github.com/kybernetwork`
- **Factom project**: `https://github.com/FactomProject`
- **Steem blockchain**: `https://github.com/steemit/steem`
- **IOTA project**: `https://github.com/iotaledger`
- **IPFS protocol**: `https://github.com/ipfs/ipfs`
- **BigchainDB server**: `https://github.com/bigchaindb/bigchaindb`
- **Golem project**: `https://github.com/golemfactory`
- **Ethereum project**: `https://github.com/ethereum`

Summary

We've attempted to cover most blockchain applications in both the financial and non-financial sectors. This chapter has given deep insight into the growing blockchain industry and the possible future trajectory of applications in the blockchain ecosystem.

In this chapter, we initially listed out several projects under the blockchain technology by classifying them into financial and non-financial sectors. We then covered each of the projects by diving into its architecture, implementation, use cases, and much more. We made sure to understand the role of blockchain in each of the implementation covered.

Now that we know a few blockchain use cases, along with their benefits and drawbacks, we can think about optimizing the existing blockchain architecture. In the next chapter, we will cover some optimizations that we can implement when designing DApps using blockchain.

Blockchain Optimizations and Enhancements

9

Scalability is a crucial factor that is being talked about even before an application has been created. Yet, even after the application is deployed, the application will be required to be updated frequently to scale based on the application load. While scalability has been one of the concerns even in the blockchain space, it wasn't the first priority when the technology was first proposed. However, over time and due to the increased interest in the technology, people are now working toward the improvement of every aspect of blockchain technology.

In this chapter, we will explore various optimizations that can be implemented to help you achieve better performance or plan for scalability. We will also cover a few of the enhancements on the existing blockchain applications to add interesting functionalities. Most of the optimizations and enhancements discussed in this chapter are either already implemented in some blockchain projects, or are in the initial phase of implementation.

In this chapter, we'll be covering the following topics:

- Blockchain optimizations:
    - Transaction exchange
    - Off-chain transactions
    - Block size improvements
- Blockchain enhancements:
    - Sharding
    - Consensus algorithms – PoS, PoA, BFT, and PoET
    - Cross-chain network
    - Privacy enhancement

Since the original implementation of Bitcoin in 2009, it has improved tremendously in order to withstand any attacks in the trustless public network. Bitcoin undergoes improvements through a standard procedure by proposing the features through a design document called **Bitcoin Improvement Proposals** (**BIP**), which was first proposed in 2011 within the Bitcoin community. Bitcoin has nearly 200 improvement proposals (`https://github.com/bitcoin/bips`), and these proposals are responsible for its resilience in the network.

We have come across several blockchain-based projects that evolved from Bitcoin's concepts. Many other projects had to undergo huge implementation changes to shape the application for their requirements. Most of the projects improved and enhanced the existing implementation to address some of the challenges, such as scalability, security, and adaptability. The enterprises are keen on taking advantage of this technology to decentralize their existing architecture. They have been creating Proof of Concept to overcome all the existing challenges before adopting the technology. In this chapter, we'll be looking into some of the proposed optimizations and enhancements in the technology that will eradicate the challenges faced by the technology.

Blockchain optimizations

Due to the decentralized nature of the blockchain applications, it is difficult to make huge changes to the blockchain protocols of the functioning applications. The existing protocols need to be optimized carefully to achieve improvements. In this upcoming section, we will discuss a few of the possible optimizations.

Transaction exchange

Communicating and exchanging data is the essence of a decentralized P2P network. In a blockchain network, transactions are the main data that is exchanged between nodes. Optimizing the exchange of transactions could be achieved by making use of protocols that are suitable for transaction data. A few optimization techniques are described in the following sections.

Blockchain relay networks

Although the nodes in the blockchain network are equal, the nodes could opt to perform a variety of roles. A few nodes might function as fullnodes, maintaining the entire blockchain, whereas a few others function as lightweight nodes by maintaining only the required transactions. In addition to this, the nodes that are willing to create new blocks will perform mining operations. When all these nodes communicate with each other in a P2P fashion, there will be a network latency involved.

The mining nodes need to keep latency to a minimum since they are involved in time-sensitive operations. Even during a critical financial transaction, a decentralized system needs to keep latency as minimal as possible so that clients and merchants can receive notifications quickly. The Bitcoin network uses a relay network to minimize the latency during block exchange between peers, especially with mining nodes that are competing to construct the next block.

Relay nodes don't fully verify data before relaying the block/transaction to the network. Although the relay nodes are quick at relaying most of the transactions, they may not be accurate in delivering every transaction of the system. A Bitcoin Core developer called Matt Corallo created a UDP-based relay network called **Fast Internet Bitcoin Relay Engine** (**FIBRE**). It uses a compression technique provided by the compact block, which was developed by Bitcoin Core. Since the FIBRE code base is an extension to the Bitcoin Core, FIBRE nodes could be set up just like the Bitcoin core nodes.

More information about the protocol and node setup can be found at `http://bitcoinfibre.org`.

Another relay network, called **Falcon**, uses application-level cut-through routing for faster block propagation. The optimized topology claims it is faster than compression-based relay networks. These relay networks not only guarantee that network nodes will achieve higher throughput but also promise future scalability for the decentralized P2P network.

More details about the Falcon relay nodes can be found at `https://www.falcon-net.org`.

Invertible bloom lookup tables

Invertible bloom lookup tables can be used to efficiently find the difference between the two datasets. This concept has been implemented in Bitcoin to achieve lower transaction exchange latency between peers. Without any mechanism to find the difference between two sets, each Bitcoin node had to keep transferring its own transaction set to the network and expect other nodes to reply with transactions that did not exist in the transaction set. This mechanism consumed a lot of Bitcoin network bandwidth and time due to the large set of transactions in each node.

A solution is to transfer information that could be used to find the difference between datasets efficiently. Invertible bloom lookup tables solve this by creating smaller lookup tables that can find the transactional differences between the two sets.

Invertible bloom lookup tables are a variant of bloom filters. They provide a successful lookup of the key-value pairs with high probability. Unlike the bloom filters, they not only allow you to look up a particular key but also list the inserted key/value pairs. Lookup tables are a probabilistic data structure, and the probability of successful lookup increases with the size of the lookup table.

A bloom filter is a probabilistic data structure that is used to check the existence of an element in a set. Although non-existence of the element is never predicted incorrectly (false negative), existence can be falsely predicted sometimes (false positive). Bloom filters are used in Bitcoin's special kind of node, called a lightweight or **Simple Payment Verification** (**SPV**) node that is used to verify the existence of a particular transaction in a block without downloading the entire block.

Each node on the network will broadcast a lookup table for the transaction pool, which will be recognized by the other nodes in the network. The nodes in the network will only exchange the required transactions and thus reduce redundant communication. Transactions in the pool can be synchronized quickly and securely with the help of these lookup tables.

Off-chain transactions

A set of transactions that can be performed outside the blockchain is referred to as off-chain transactions. Off-chain transactions rely on several methods of validation that are different from the one used in the main blockchain. Although the main motive of the off-chain transaction is to achieve increased transaction speed, it also should provide basic security by making sure that the transactions cannot be reversed by any participant.

Off-chain state channels and **sidechains** are the popular off-chain solutions. We will have a look at both of these off-chain transaction solutions.

Off-chain state channels

A state channel is a two-way communication between the members of a system that enables the members to perform a series of transactions without committing them to the blockchain. Off-chain transactions tremendously increase the throughput by avoiding blockchain confirmation for every transaction.

Off-chain channels are ideal for micro-transactions where two parties communicate their transactions by setting up a payment channel that is independent of the blockchain state. The state channel can be closed once the transactions between the parties are concluded. The final state of the channel is then sent to the blockchain.

Figure 9.1 shows a payment channel that is created between Alice and Bob. Alice and Bob will then perform a series of transactions whose state is written to the blockchain only after the state channel is closed:

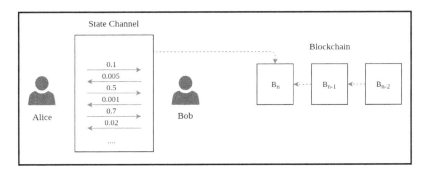

Figure 9.1: State channel transactions between two users

The Lightning Network

The Lightning Network is a second-layer payment protocol that operates on top of the Bitcoin blockchain. At the time of writing, the implementation of this protocol is running in beta mode on Bitcoin's mainnet. It is a routed bidirectional network that was proposed to solve the Bitcoin transaction scalability problem.

Design

The Lightning Network creates a routed payment channel network where communication between the nodes is bidirectional. The design has been implemented by several open source communities by following a set of standards.

A simple design of the Lightning Network involves the following steps:

1. Create a payment channel by committing the channel with the initial funds from the parties

2. Perform micropayment transactions and update the created funds of the channel

3. Close the payment channel and broadcast the final state of the channel's funds

An example of a Lightning Network

Let's consider an example where Alice wants to perform several Bitcoin payment transactions with Bob. Alice and Bob decide to open a payment channel using the Lightning Network.

Alice and Bob both create a channel, initially funding it with 2 bitcoins each. The funds can be kept in a multi-signature address account, which will ensure that both parties need to agree on the finalized fund distribution. A balance sheet will be maintained, which will update the balances of Alice and Bob after each transaction. The balance sheet is similar to the concept of keeping tabs in a restaurant or bar; instead of paying for each order, a tab is maintained that can be used to pay for all the orders together.

Alice wants to send 0.5 bitcoins to Bob, so she will create a transaction that pays 0.5 bitcoins to Bob. Instead of appending this transaction to the blockchain, the payment channel will update the balance sheet. Now the channel fund will reflect 1.5 bitcoins as Alice's balance and 2.5 bitcoins as Bob's balance:

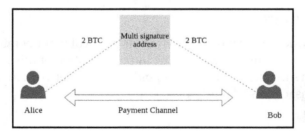

Figure 9.2: Lightning Network payment channel between Alice and Bob

Alice and Bob can perform any number of transactions without waiting for the state of the transaction because the payment channel is independent of the blockchain state. The payment channel can be closed when there are no more transactions to be performed on the created channel. The final state of the channel is then broadcasted to the blockchain network so that it gets included in the blockchain in a single transaction. The Lightning Network implementation, which securely performs off-chain transactions, increases the total transaction throughput of the blockchain network.

Routed payment network

A user in the Lightning Network doesn't need to set up a direct payment channel with every user to perform a transaction. A user can find several connected payment channels to connect to the other user in order to set up a routed payment network. Consider an example where Alice wants to set up a micro-payment channel with Carol. Alice has earlier set up a channel with Bob. She also finds out that Bob has an active channel with Carol. So, instead of setting up a new payment channel, Alice decides to create a routing payment channel with Carol via Bob, as shown in *Figure 9.3*:

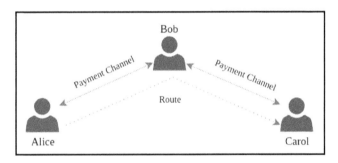

Figure 9.3: Routed payment network between Alice and Carol via Bob

Routed payment channels are established between a number of trustless nodes, and a node will not have information about the next hop in the route. Any payment channel in the network might be invalidated at any time due to faulty behavior. To tolerate faults in the network, there has to be an escrow set up for each channel in the network. Time-based script extensions (smart contracts) such as **Hash Time Lock Contract** (HTLC) can be used to set up an escrow in the payment channel.

Hash time lock contracts

HTLCs are a special type of smart contract that can be created using Bitcoin's basic programming language (Script). The participants in the network will commit their funds during a transaction with a secret that will be shared once the escrow is set up.

HTLC is similar to the locking script created during transaction creation, where a secret key generated with asymmetric cryptography is used to unlock funds. Instead of using a permanent secret key, HTLC uses a randomly generated secret that is destroyed in each transaction. The receiver of the fund will initially create a random secret, R, that is hashed using a one-way function such as SHA256. The computed hash, H, of the secret can then be shared with all the participants involved in the transaction to create HTLC scripts.

Although the fund committed to the HTLC script is redeemable by providing the secret, R, it also has a time lock, which requires the secret owner to claim the fund within a specified time. The time factor can also be specified in the number of blocks. Bitcoin uses the `CheckLockTimeVerify` extension to time-lock a contract.

The final HTLC script is prepared by combining the hashing and the time-lock conditions. Any node in the network that owns the secret could claim the fund committed to the HTLC.

Routed payment example

Let's consider a scenario by building on our previous example, where Alice wants to send 1 bitcoin to Carol instead of Bob. Since there is no active channel between Alice and Carol, Alice and Bob create a payment channel via Bob, as discussed before. Now, Carol creates a random secret, S, for the session. She creates a hash of secret S and shares it with Alice, but the secret is protected without disclosing it to anyone.

The payment channel between Alice and Bob is funded with 4 bitcoins. Similarly, the channel between Bob and Carol is also funded with 4 bitcoins. Bob has a share of 2 bitcoins on each of the payment channels. Alice begins the transaction by creating an HTLC commitment with a value of 1.1 bitcoins, payable to Bob. The additional 0.1 bitcoin is a transaction fee paid to Bob as brokerage. Bob will not be able to claim the commitment as he doesn't own the secret. Bob is now instructed to create a new transaction on the other channel. He creates an HTLC commitment with a value of 1 bitcoin, payable to Carol. As Carol owns the secret key, she claims the bitcoin and passes the key to Bob. Now Bob will be able to claim the bitcoin in the HTLC.

All the actors claim their assets without trusting the other nodes in the payment network. The final balance of the payment channel can then be written to the blockchain when any of the channels are closed:

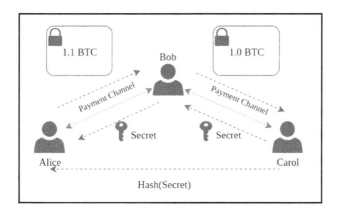

Figure 9.4: Routed payment network between Alice and Carol via Bob

Each node will perform route discovery whenever a transaction needs to be created. The information for the route discovery is collected from all the nodes in the network through the P2P networking model. Once a node has all the information, the optimal path is constructed by the sender node. After the route is discovered by the sender, each node involved in the discovered path will not be aware of all the nodes. Each node will be informed only about the node with whom they have set up a payment channel. This is achieved by implementing an onion routing protocol-based system to preserve the privacy of the transaction.

Sidechains

A sidechain is a blockchain that runs parallel to the main blockchain and is attached to the main blockchain (also referred to as the main chain) using two-way peg. Similar to the state channels, sidechains are a layer 2 solution to scale the existing blockchain network.

Any number of transactions on a set of assets can be performed on the sidechain before committing the state to the main chain. Unlike the state channel, the sidechain is a permanent chain that functions alongside the main chain. Any time an asset needs to be sent to the sidechain, the same asset needs to be locked in the main chain by transferring it to a special address. Once the asset has been locked in the main chain, the same asset can be released to the sidechain. The sidechain can then perform transactions on the asset as long as the asset is locked in the main chain. A special group called **federation** serves as an intermediary between the main chain and the sidechain.

There are several existing implementations of sidechains. Rootstock has created a sidechain that has a two-way peg with the Bitcoin blockchain. Loom (`https://loomx.io/`) has created a Proof of Stake based sidechain for the Ethereum network. Matic networks (`https://matic.network/`) is another service that has created a Proof of Stake side chain with an adapted version of the Plasma framework.

Block size improvements

A block of transactions is the basic component of any decentralized blockchain-based application. Every blockchain-based implementation will define its own structure of blocks. The Bitcoin block has a header and body section with a set of fields defined. Few of the fields have a fixed limit, and so does the block size. Bitcoin's block size is 1 MB, which was introduced in 2010. This restricts the number of transactions that can be included in a block.

As the amount of activity in the Bitcoin network increased due to its popularity, more transactions were created in each block. *Figure 9.5* shows how the average number of transactions per block has grown over the years. From last year, most Bitcoin blocks reached their threshold for the number of transactions in each block. We can conclude from the graph that the average number of transactions per block in recent years is around 2,500. Since Bitcoin has a fixed block interval of 10 minutes, the average transaction throughput that Bitcoin could achieve is about 4-5 transactions per second, which is significantly less than PayPal or Visa transactions, whose transaction throughputs are around 200 and 1,600 transactions per second respectively:

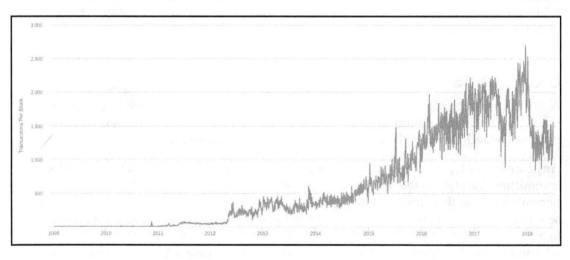

Figure 9.5: Average Bitcoin transactions per block (source: www.blockchain.info)

A straightforward solution to increase the throughput of transactions is to make full use of the block size. But, according to the graph in *Figure 9.6*, Bitcoin blocks have recently been utilizing their entire 1 MB space for transactions. Due to the increased number of recently mined blocks, there have been talks and proposals regarding an increase in the block size at several occasions. Though there was a lot of interests in the community, it failed to gain the majority required to implement the updated protocol for blocks:

 Some blocks in recent years have exceeded the limit of 1 MB, and this is due to the protocol upgrade called **Segregated Witness**, which we will discuss in a later section, *Proposed solutions*.

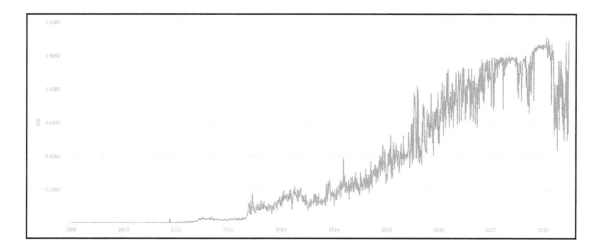

Figure 9.6: Average block size representation of Bitcoin (source: www.blockchain.info)

Motivations to increase the block size

Increasing the block size is an obvious approach to achieve higher transaction throughput. But there are several other factors that could motivate an increase in block size:

- Increased transaction activity may result in a bottleneck and thus clog the blockchain network. Some transactions might get delayed or lost forever.

- Increased waiting time for micro-payments would stop the innovation of the technology.

- Currently, users are forced to pay higher transaction fees to prioritize transactions.

Concerns on increasing the block size

Although increasing the block size is an intuitive approach to increase the transaction throughput, there are some concerns with this approach. Here are some of them:

- Exchanging block data will become more difficult because of the increased size

- Increasing the block size is an immediate solution but not a permanent one

- Changing the block size will result in a hard fork and may risk consensus failures

- Larger blocks will require higher bandwidth to exchange data, which may not excite ordinary full node users and may no longer maintain the full blockchain due to the increased maintenance cost

Proposed solutions

From the very beginning of 2010, there have been attempts to increase the block size with different proposals. There are even a number of **Bitcoin Improvement Proposals** (**BIP**) that keep track of this issue. Some of them are BIP 100 - 103 and BIP 109, and all of them are either in a draft or a rejected state.

One of the initial proposals, BIP 101 by Gavin Andreson, one of the initial developers of the Bitcoin core, suggested increasing the block size to 8 MB and doubling the limit every two years, with the size growing linearly during the two years. Although the proposal gained support from a majority of the miners, it failed to gain an economic majority as it required a hard fork. An alternate Bitcoin client called **Bitcoin XT** implemented BIP 101 in 2015, but it failed to gain consensus to implement BIP 101. The BIP implementation was later removed from Bitcoin XT.

Despite many proposed solutions, Bitcoin failed to gain a majority for new block size approval. But a solution was proposed to increase the block capacity and protect from transaction malleability in the shape of a protocol upgrade called Segregated Witness. Segregated Witness defines a new structure called a witness where all the signature information of the transaction is stored, separating it from the transaction information in the block. The transaction's validity can be verified from the information present in the witness structure.

Segregated Witness defined a new weight unit and permitted the creation of up to 4 million units. 1 byte in the new witness structure was considered as 1 unit, but 1-byte data in the old block zone was considered as 4 units. This allowed the old blocks to have a limit of 1 MB, whereas the blocks created with the upgraded protocol were not bound to the 1 MB limit. One of the biggest advantages of this proposal was that it did not require a hard fork of the blockchain to reach a consensus.

Block size improvements are only a short-term solution for the scalability issue of blockchain. The Bitcoin community continuously proposes better solutions so that they can address the network scalability issue in the long run.

Blockchain enhancements

Numerous enhancements have been built on top of the existing blockchain protocols to function more efficiently or make the blockchain application suitable to implement the desired functionality. We will discuss a few of the enhancements that require major protocol modifications.

Sharding

One of the critical issues that Bitcoin and other existing blockchain platforms face is scaling the applications in the blockchain network. Storage is the main factor that is slowing down the scalability of decentralized applications. Every full node in the blockchain stores the entire blockchain history to verify the transaction. Instead of storing redundant data on every node, data can be distributed cleverly on the network so that it will help to achieve scalability as well as decentralization. Ethereum proposed a sharding mechanism to implement a distributed behavior that could achieve scalability. We will discuss a few of the key concepts of sharding proposed by Ethereum in this section.

More details about the Ethereum's sharding roadmap can be found at
`https://github.com/ethereum/wiki/wiki/Sharding-roadmap`.

The motivation for database sharding

Sharding involves partitioning data to distribute it across multiple devices. Sharding is not a new concept to achieve a distribution of computing resources. It has been used to achieve scalability in databases. Database shards are created by horizontally partitioning tables. Each partition, or shard, is often held in a physically separated server to balance the load.

Partitioning the database table horizontally into shards will reduce the number of rows and thus reduce the index size, which would optimize searching. If the database partitioning is performed on real-world data segmentation, such as storing data related to different countries on different shards, it would be easy to query only the relevant shards.

Figure 9.7 shows how a database table that stores user details initially in a global database can be partitioned:

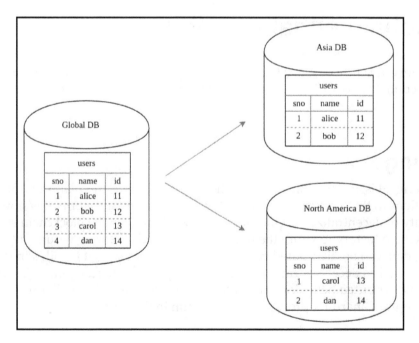

Figure 9.7: Database sharding based on physical location

The database table is horizontally sharded into two different tables, each maintaining the subset of the total rows in the original table. The tables are partitioned on the basis that the first table contains details of users from Asia, and the second table contains details of users from North America. Partitioning database tables in this way will improve the performance of querying. The database tables can also be partitioned and distributed across multiple servers by using a special type of hashing known as **consistent hashing**.

 When a hash table of N slots is resized, a majority of the keys (K) need to remapped to the slots. Consistent hashing is a special type of hashing where a change in the number of slots requires only K/N keys to be remapped.

Sharding in blockchain

A decentralized blockchain network consists of a number of nodes in order to achieve the highest possible level of decentralization. The security of the network increases with the number of nodes added to the network. But the population of nodes doesn't contribute to the scalability of the network. In fact, it is difficult to scale with an increased number of nodes. Ethereum proposed a sharding technique where the entire blockchain and its state is split into partitions called shards.

The sharding scheme in Ethereum can be partitioned into any number of shards that maintain their own history and state. Let's consider a scheme where a blockchain is partitioned into K shards based on some criteria. An example criterion for sharding could be assets, where transactions belonging to different assets are maintained on different shards. Since each shard maintains its own state, the effect of the transaction created in a shard is limited to the state of that shard.

Components in a shard

Each shard maintains data in a collation, which is analogous to the blocks in the main blockchain. Each collation contains a collection of data in the form of blobs. Each collator contains a header and body, similar to the blocks in the main chain. *Figure 9.8* depicts how the blobs are transformed into chunks, and then a Merkle proof is created for those chunks by building a Merkle tree that consists of chunks as its leaves. A chain of collations is created, which is a blockchain of the shard. The main chain still exists, which is processed by everyone, but they only store the collation headers of the shards. The longest chain of a shard is called canonical chain, and its headers will reside in the main chain:

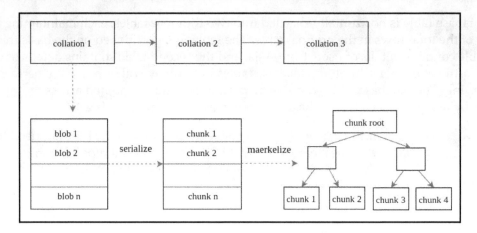

Figure 9.8: Collations and blobs in a shard

There are nodes in the shard called **proposers**. These nodes can either choose shards or select them randomly. The proposers are responsible for accepting the blobs and creating the collation. Thus they also function as collators. The **notaries** are the entities that download and verify the collations. They are assigned to the shards and randomly shuffled to a new shard every period via a random beacon chain (using some verifiable random function). They will also vote on the availability of the collation data.

A **committee** will check the votes and decide whether to include a collation header in the main chain. The collation header will establish a link to the collation data residing in the shards.

Design of a sharded blockchain

Partitioning a blockchain and distributing it across different shards needs a variety of actors, as described in the previous section. All these actors in the network will make sure that the collation data of every shard is linked to the main chain. The sharding architecture has several security concerns due to the distributed shards and several types of actors in the decentralized network.

The design of the blockchain is said to be secure if it can maintain an honest majority where more than 50 percent of the validators follow the protocol honestly. The value can be lower if there is an uncoordinated majority.

An uncoordinated majority is an act of achieving a majority, but one where no more than 50% (often between 20 to 50 percent) of validators are capable of coordinating an action.

The design of a sharded blockchain isolates the transactions of one shard from the rest of the shards in the network. If a node needs to perform a transaction with a node present on the other shard, it is not as straightforward as the classic blockchain design. Ethereum sharding uses a concept called receipt to perform cross-shard communication.

Cross-shard communication

There might be a scenario when a transaction needs to be shared between two or more shards. Ethereum uses receipts created by nodes in one shard to confirm the transaction. Let's consider a scenario in which user A present in shard M wants to send 100 coins to user B of shard N. Cross-shard communication can be established with the following steps:

1. Create a transaction on shard M for deducting the coins.

2. Create a receipt for the transaction of 100 coins from user A to B. The transaction won't be saved on the state, but the existence of the receipt can be verified by the users in shard N.

3. Create and send a transaction on shard N that includes the Merkle proof of the receipt. This transaction also confirms that the receipt is unspent. The balance of user B is increased by 100 coins in shard N.

Some complex scenarios might result in communication across multiple shards to query data from the state of other shards.

Evolution of the consensus algorithm

We have come across Bitcoin's **Proof of Work** (**PoW**) consensus algorithm in several sections of this book. The PoW algorithm is the backbone of the decentralized networking protocol. Although Bitcoin's consensus algorithm has been proven to be effective to achieve consensus in a trustless network, it is still not very efficient in terms of cost due to the computational resources spent during the mining process.

A number of alternative consensus algorithms have been developed and implemented to attain the same amount of confidence in decentralization without incurring too much expense.

Proof of Stake (PoS)

The PoS algorithm eradicates most of the issues of PoW by not depending on computational resources to achieve consensus. **PoS** uses validators, which are in contrast to the miners in PoW in that they don't perform any work to contribute to the decentralization. The contribution of the PoS validators depends on their share of the cryptocurrency coins from the total in circulation in the system. A validator with three coins is three times more likely to contribute to the validation than a validator owning a single coin. There are other factors that randomize the process to avoid one validator with a major stake monopolizing the validation process. Peercoin was the first to adopt PoS, followed by Nxt and BlackCoin. Ethereum is currently using PoW, but PoS is in active development, and it has planned to implement PoS in the mainnet in the near future.

Along with its wide-ranging benefits, it has its own set of issues in the implementation. A white paper on PoS versus PoW (`https://bitfury.com/content/downloads/pos-vs-pow-1.0.2.pdf`) published by the BitFury group lists a few of the possible attacks, such as the long-range attack, bribe attack, coin age accumulation attack, and precomputing attack. Ensuring complete security in a public decentralized network isn't a picnic. Even the resilient PoW is theoretically vulnerable to the 51% attack, which can result in double spends (we will cover the security concerns of PoW in `Chapter 10`, *Blockchain Security*). The PoS algorithm prevents validators from attacks by penalizing the nodes upon bad behavior. Ethereum requires each node to possess a minimum stake of 1,250 ethers to participate in validation. The minimum stake deposit by the validators prevents them from being dishonest in the network.

Proof of Activity (PoA)

Most cryptocurrencies and blockchain platforms that use PoW have a limited supply of tokens. For example, Bitcoin will only mint 21 million coins, and the final coin will be minted sometime during the year 2140. Miners will have to solely depend on transaction fees as their incentives when all the coins are minted. According to the current difficulty level of Bitcoin, it would reach a level when it may not be economical for miners to participate in the mining process. The existing miners may try and perform dishonest acts and spoil the blockchain system with invalid transactions for their own benefit. PoA was proposed as an alternative consensus algorithm that could be adopted by Bitcoin. It is a hybrid approach that combines PoW and PoS.

During block creation, the mining nodes perform PoW by solving the hash puzzle with computational resources. The PoW process will not add any transactions; instead, they only create the block header with the miner's details. PoS is used to further process the block by randomly selecting the validators based on the block header information. This phase of consensus is handled in a similar way to PoS-based systems. If not all the validators selected were able to sign the block, the next best block is selected, and the same process of PoS validation is applied. After each block has been included in the blockchain, both the PoW and PoS miners will receive their incentives.

Decred is a cryptocurrency that was launched in February 2016 and makes use of PoA to achieve the consensus in the network.

Byzantine Fault Tolerance (BFT) consensus models

Consensus algorithms were designed in distributed systems to tolerate Byzantine faults relating to the Byzantine generals' problem (refer to `Chapter 1`, *Introduction*, for a definition of the Byzantine generals' problem). Though PoW and PoS have tolerance to Byzantine faults, it comes at a cost. Several variants of **Byzantine Fault Tolerance** (BFT) consensus models have been proposed as solutions to this problem in untrusted distributed networks.

Practical Byzantine Fault Tolerance (PBFT)

The PBFT consensus algorithm was proposed by Miguel Castro and Barbara Liskov as a practical solution to the Byzantine generals' problem in distributed systems. It achieves consensus among nodes with a voting mechanism if the state changes. This algorithm requires at least $3f+1$ nodes in a system of f failing nodes. PBFT poses an overall overhead of about 3% to the system, which is a great improvement on the PoW consensus-based systems. Scaling PBFT in terms of nodes is still a challenge, as it will result in a greater overhead as the number of nodes increases.

The Hyperledger Fabric project uses the PBFT protocol to achieve high transaction throughput in a permissioned blockchain.

Federated Byzantine Fault Tolerance (FBFT)

FBFT is a variant of the BFT algorithm that has been implemented in payment-protocol-based blockchain platforms such as Ripple and Stellar. Both of these platforms perform critical transactions, such as cross-border payment, by dealing with fiat currencies. Due to their criticality, the consensus model should be fault resistant to avoid any attacks.

Ripple consensus protocol

An overview of the Ripple consensus protocol was covered in the previous chapter, along with its platform's architecture. Each node implements the FBFT consensus model by voting on the transactions. Each node in the network maintains a list called a **Unique Node List** (**UNL**), comprising trusted Ripple nodes. Each node broadcasts a set of transactions called a candidate set to its nodes in the UNL. Each node will validate the transactions and broadcast their votes for each transaction. Each node refines the candidate set based on the votes received for each transaction. When a particular candidate set receives 80% of votes from all the nodes in the UNL, all the transactions in the candidate set are confirmed by adding it into the blockchain ledger. The Ripple ledger goes to a closed state, and all the unconfirmed transactions will be carried over to the next round of voting.

Ripple performs a voting mechanism in rounds to achieve minimum consensus from all the nodes before the transactions are committed. FBFT achieves higher transaction rates even than a permissionless network. Hence it can be implemented in critical financial systems that need higher scalability.

Proof of Elapsed Time (PoET)

PoET is a consensus algorithm designed to solve the performance issues faced by existing consensus protocols. It solves the Byzantine Generals' problem using the trusted execution environment. Due to its trusted execution model, it is only suitable for a permissioned blockchain network. PoET consensus has been implemented in Hyperledger's Sawtooth, which is a permissioned blockchain project backed by Intel. The **trusted execution environment** (**TEE**) in the network is achieved by Intel's **Software Guard Extensions** (**SGX**), which are instruction sets that allow user code to allocate private memory regions.

Similar to the PoS algorithm, PoET elects a random peer to construct the next block with the exception that there is no staking involved. Instead, peers wait for a random amount of time before they can participate in the block creation process. Since each peer will have a random wait time, the first peer to finish the wait time will create the block. Each peer has to prove a couple of things to the network to qualify itself as the elected node:

- Prove that the node has chosen a random wait time

- Prove that the node has waited for the chosen random wait time

Each node satisfies these requirements by running the trusted code in a protected environment with the help of Intel's SGX instruction set. The node participating in the election obtains a wait time from a trusted function. The node with the shortest time will be the leader for the next block to be created. A function, say, `CreateTimer`, will set the timer and another function, say, `CheckTimer`, will create an attestation when the timer expires. This attestation proves that the node has waited for a specified wait time before creating the block. Every node on the network will use this attestation to validate the block.

Every node in the network will download the trusted code and perform an initial handshake to set up a trusted network. As a part of the handshake, the nodes will create a key pair for the trusted code and publish its public key to the entire network.

PoET promises higher performance with its time-based election mechanism to achieve consensus, and it is ideal for private enterprise blockchain networks. But the permissioned model isn't practical for a public network due to its requirement for specialized hardware to create a protected execution environment.

Cross-chain protocol

A distributed blockchain ledger is an evolving space, and many applications are implemented frequently. Just like any computer technology, which requires updates from time to time, existing blockchain systems need to be updated to evolve with the growing technology. Unlike other centralized systems, extensive changes to an existing blockchain will lead to a hard fork due to the decentralization of nodes. Existing blockchain systems suffer from restricted innovation or integration with evolved protocols.

The cross-chain protocol was developed to integrate existing blockchain applications with the newly evolved systems and enable multiple blockchain networks to communicate with each other. The cross-chain communication protocol also helps to scale blockchain networks by integrating multiple ledgers.

Several projects have been working toward the implementation of the cross-chain protocol. *Cosmos, Polkadot,* and *Interledger* are some of the projects implementing the cross-chain protocol in their own way. Cosmos and Polkadot have their own blockchain ecosystem with several components that can communicate with other independent blockchain systems. Interledger is a protocol for making payments across payment systems. In the following section, we will analyze the cross-chain protocol implementation in payment systems using Interledger.

Interledger protocol (ILP)

All the payment systems across the world are built to function in a single payment network, and all the assets and transaction details are maintained by a single ledger. Even digital currencies such as Bitcoin maintain all their transactions in a single public ledger, even though copies of the ledger are distributed throughout the network. The transactions can be easily maintained in a single ledger, but it would be difficult to vertically scale such a ledger. We have analyzed the scalability of a single ledger in the *Sharding* section of this chapter. In addition to this, the diverse payment systems will never agree on a single distributed ledger or its corresponding consensus mechanism. A protocol that can connect multiple payment systems and perform inexpensive transactions across the network would be a great solution to the vertical scaling of existing ledgers.

The Interledger protocol provides a system to securely transfer value across different ledgers, and it is also often used with other payment systems. Interledger appoints connectors between the ledgers of the participants to perform transactions. Unlike any existing payment gateway services, participants don't need to trust these connectors due to the escrow provided by the ledgers. The protocol not only enables value transfer between the blockchain-based ledgers but can also create connections with traditional payment systems such as PayPal:

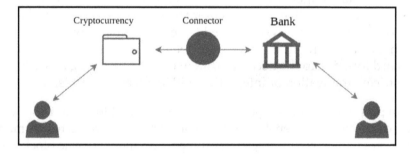

Figure 9.9: Interledger protocol (ILP) use case

Interledger components

- **Senders** send assets to the known receivers. They will initiate the payment by selecting the connectors.

- **Receivers** will expect assets from particular senders. They need to be the part of Interledger payment network.

- **Connectors** link senders with receivers to make ILP payments possible. Connectors also link up with other connectors. This is done to connect as many senders with receivers as possible, through chains of connectors that are built for each payment.

- **Ledgers** perform bookkeeping of the asset information of every participant in the network:

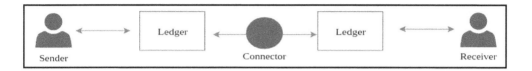

Figure 9.10: Interledger components

Design of Interledger

Current payment systems provide a way to transfer value between different ledgers in the form of payment gateways. They act as an intermediary between the payment banks. The main concerns of existing systems are security and speed. The gateways are managed by the third parties, and users need to rely on those entities to ensure security. Transaction settlement in such a payment network is slower since the gateway has to deal with multiple payment banks. Interledger introduces connectors between the ledgers, which establish links between senders and receivers. The ledger in this system creates an escrow, which is the cryptographic conditions that will secure the funds when transacting across the ledgers. The cryptographic conditions created by ledgers that act as an escrow guarantee the fund transfer to connectors only after acknowledgment from the receiver:

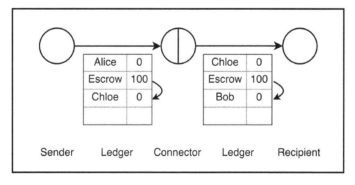

Figure 9.11: Transferring the funds to the connector (source: https://interledger.org)

A decentralized network suffers from the threat of faulty or bad actors. The conditioned escrow of the funds is a major security feature that ensures that the funds are transferred only after an acknowledgment.

 Ledger escrows use cryptographic signatures. Anyone can then validate the signature to check whether the condition has been met.

The payment process can be performed using two models in Interledger. These are atomic payments and universal payments.

Atomic payments

Interledger payments guarantee that the transfer is either executed or aborted. It uses a commitment protocol, where the readiness of the system is identified before deciding on the execution or abortion of the transaction. The commitment protocol in a decentralized system uses a set of transaction managers called notaries. These notaries are used to achieve consensus among the untrusted Byzantine nodes.

When a payment network is created before the transactions, there might be more than one connector involved between the sender and the recipient. The number of connectors depends on the selected route between the participants, which is based on the hop or the fee involved. *Figure 9.12* shows that there are $n-2$ connectors between $n-1$ ledgers while transacting between nodes $\mathbf{p_1}$ and $\mathbf{p_n}$:

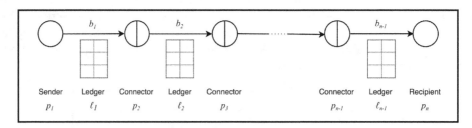

Figure 9.12: Payment route with multiple connectors (source: https://interledger.org)

All the connectors in the payment network are Byzantine nodes that could exhibit faulty behavior during the transaction. The elected group of notaries, N, need to achieve consensus among the Byzantine nodes. The trustless notaries need to be fault-tolerant in order to create an atomic transaction. The network should make sure that there are no more than f faulty notary nodes among the $3f+1$ nodes.

Before a sender can begin a transfer, a path of connectors has to be selected after considering their fees and exchange rate. Once the optimal path has been selected, the following stages can be observed during the transaction:

1. A group of notaries is elected by the participants. The election should make sure that the number of faulty notaries should be less than *f* out of a total of *3f+1* notaries.

2. The payment sender proposes a transfer request to each connector. All the connectors will verify whether the rate matches their exchange rate. The sender will start the preparation for the transfer once all the connectors confirm their approval of the proposal.

3. The sender prepares the transfer from the ledger to the connector and requests the connector to prepare for the transfer from the next ledger to its adjacent connector in the path. Each connector will prepare for the transfer as soon as it gets confirmation that the funds have been escrowed.

4. The final receiver of the fund will sign the receipt once funds at each ledger have been escrowed. If the notary receives the receipt on time, then the notary will forward the execute message to all the all the participants in the transaction.

Universal payments

Unlike the atomic payment model, there are no notaries that act as transaction managers in this model. It uses the participants inside the network to achieve consensus. Although it removes interaction with the external coordinators, it can ensure safety to only non-faulty participants in a known environment. Practical consideration of universal payments is not straightforward due to the untrusted participants of the network who display faulty behavior.

Other than providing a connection between multiple ledgers, Interledger doesn't rely on any other system, so it provides the freedom to scale the system as required. It also maintains the privacy of the transaction details. So, the cross-ledger payment protocol provided by Interledger greatly eases the communication between financial systems. More implementation details of the Interledger project can be found at
`https://github.com/interledger`.

Privacy enhancement

As we all know, Bitcoin maintains a history of the funds owned by accounts in transactions stored in blocks. Each transaction contains sensitive information, such as the sender's address, the recipient's address, and the value. All the data is used by every node in the network to verify the transaction before the block can be included in the blockchain. Bitcoin's decentralized verification forces the transparency of the transaction as there is no central authority.

Bitcoin's blockchain provides security against tampering with transactions even though they are visible to everyone. Although the blockchain secures the transactions from many attacks, it does not guarantee complete privacy to the account holders like other payment services. Anyone on the Bitcoin network can trace a transaction's history without performing any authentication. Disclosing a transaction's history could expose sensitive information about a particular account, such as recent transactions or the account balance. The limited privacy on the Bitcoin network has been one of the core concerns for the users. Since most blockchain projects evolved from Bitcoin, they followed a similar transparency model. The pseudo-anonymity feature of most blockchain applications provides some level of privacy to its users.

 Pseudo-anonymity (Pseudonymity) is the identity of an individual or a group that does not disclose its true identity. Bitcoin users are identified by their public address, which doesn't reveal their real identity.

An anonymous cryptocurrency called Zerocoin was proposed by researchers from Hopkins University. Zerocoin used zero-knowledge proofs to provide an extension to Bitcoin that enhanced its privacy by creating anonymous transactions. An improved protocol called Zerocash was later introduced, which was an independent cryptocurrency that utilized a special kind of zero-knowledge proofs called **zk-SNARKs**. Zerocash was later developed into a fully-fledged digital cryptocurrency called **Zcash**.

Since the invention of Zcash, several applications were developed to provide privacy by implementing a similar protocol. Monero, Dash, Verge, and even a fork of Bitcoin called Bitcoin Private are some privacy-based cryptocurrencies that were introduced later. We will explore Zcash in more detail, along with the underlying protocol used to ensure the privacy of its transactions in this section.

Zero-knowledge proof

A zero-knowledge proof is an important cryptographic primitive used to achieve anonymity in the implementation of Zcash. It is a method where one party, say, Alice, who owns some secret information, can prove to the other party, Bob, that she owns the information without actually revealing it. Every zero-knowledge proof will have two parties, a prover, and a verifier. The prover will always possess knowledge that is kept secret, and the verifier will verify the statement of the prover. The prover should always make use of the secret knowledge while creating the proof, which implies that the verifier should not be able to reproduce the proof to other parties without the secret knowledge. Whenever a prover creates a zero-knowledge proof, it should satisfy the following properties:

- **Completeness**: If the statement is true, an honest verifier should be convinced by the statement of an honest prover.

- **Soundness**: If the statement is false, no dishonest prover can convince the verifier that it is true. There might be a few exceptional cases that can be neglected.

- **Zero knowledge**: If the statement is true, the verifier doesn't learn anything other than the statement itself.

 Zero-knowledge proofs are probabilistic proofs. There is a small probability of a soundness error, where a dishonest prover can convince the verifier of a false statement.

General examples

Let's look at the zero-knowledge proof system with few examples.

A card trickster

Let's consider an example of a card trickster who claims that they know a trick where they can predict any card that was guessed by the spectator. In this example, the trickster is the prover, the spectator is the verifier, and the magic trick is the secret knowledge. The only way to prove that they know the trick is by performing the act. The trickster asks the spectator to think of a card. After the spectator thinks of a card, the trickster waves the magic wand and takes out a card. The spectator confirms that it was the chosen card, and they now believes that the trickster knows the trick. If the spectator still needs to confirm it, they can ask the trickster to perform the trick again.

The example simulates the zero-knowledge proof system. The trickster is the prover, and the spectator is the verifier. The trickster proves that they know the trick without actually revealing the trick, which satisfies zero knowledge. If the trickster knows the trick, they will be always able to perform the act, thus proving the completeness. If the trickster falsely claims to know the trick, performing the trick would reveal their false claim. There is a small probability, though, that the trickster will predict the card without knowing the trick. The probability is 1/52 (as there are 52 cards in a deck). This probability is small, and it would be vanishingly small if the trick was performed multiple times.

zk-SNARKs

zk-SNARK stands for **Zero-Knowledge Succinct Non-Interactive Argument of Knowledge**. As the name suggests, it is a variant of zero-knowledge proofs in which you can prove the possession of secret information without the interaction between the prover and the verifier.

Many zero-knowledge proofs required the prover and verifier to communicate continuously by setting up a channel in order to prove the knowledge. Even the example considered earlier required the continuous participation of the prover and verifier. zk-SNARK has an initial setup phase where a common string called the public parameter is shared between the prover and verifier.

 Zcash uses a forked implementation (`https://github.com/zcash/libsnark`) of the `libsnarks` (implemented in C++) library to perform zk-SNARK operations.

The zk-SNARK allows us to verify the correctness of the executed program without having to learn what was executed. Although the concept might sound simple, the internal working of the zk-SNARKs can be tricky to understand in the first glance. We will break down the implementation of zk-SNARKs into four main ingredients as suggested in the Ethereum blog:

- **Construction of quadratic arithmetic programs** (**QAPs**): The validation performed by zk-SNARK on a transaction should return true or false without revealing any of the information. This is achieved by transforming the logic of the transaction into quadratic polynomial equations that can be evaluated without revealing sensitive information.

- **Evaluation at a random point to achieve succinctness**: The polynomials used in the equations can be quite large. Therefore, the polynomials are evaluated by the verifier at a randomly chosen point. The random point chosen by the verifier should be kept as secret. The prover might generate an invalid polynomial that will satisfy only the selected point if the random point is disclosed.

- **Homomorphic encryption**: zk-SNARK also uses homomorphic encryption techniques to evaluate the polynomials without knowing the secret point. Homomorphic encryption technique ensures that performing an operation on the polynomial is the same as performing on the secret point.

- **Zero knowledge**: The prover has to make sure that zero-knowledge is achieved so that the sensitive information is not revealed and, at the same time, the transaction can be evaluated.

Zcash transactions

Zcash transactions involve senders and receivers, who can either have shielded or transparent addresses. A transaction can have any combination of addresses. A transaction with both transparent addresses is a public transaction, whereas a transaction with shielded addresses is private. In some cases, either the sender or receiver address can be shielded. If either end of the transaction was shielded, it requires the generation of a zero-knowledge proof:

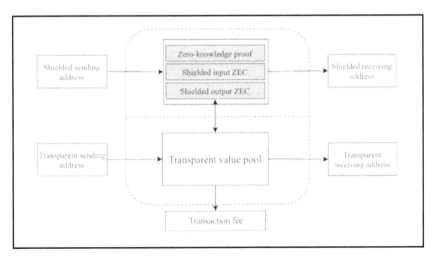

Figure 9.13: Zcash transaction with different types of address

If a user performs a transaction with a transparent address, all the unspent transaction outputs are visible to the public. A single shielded transaction address between any number of transactions involving transparent addresses can break the chain of the transaction. Thus it will be difficult to trace any transaction value back to the actual source. Even a small number of shielded addresses could result in a great deal of privacy in the blockchain network. Currently, Zcash has less than 5% of shielded transactions in their network, which still provides a good deal of privacy to its users.

Since a transaction with shielded addresses needs to create a zero-knowledge proof, it requires more resources and time (up to 40 seconds). But the verification time is negligible, which is ideal for decentralization since every node performs verification. The resource and time cost for creating shielded transactions is negligible compared to the improved privacy provided by it.

Private transactions

The main intention of zero-knowledge proofs and its variant, zk-SNARK, is to make transactions private. In a plain transaction such as in Bitcoin, a transaction value is claimed with unspent outputs (UTXOs). Each UTXO is described by the public address of the owner and the value. Let's consider that Alice has 1 bitcoin, which is represented by $UTXO_1$:

```
UTXO₁ = (PK₁)
```

PK_1 is the public key of Alice. A random number is also stored along with each UTXO, which is later used by Alice to maintain privacy:

```
UTXO₁ = (PK₁, r₁)
```

Let's now store the UTXOs in hashes for better privacy:

```
H₁ = HASH (UTXO₁)
```

These hash values are stored on each node, even after they have been spent. So, to distinguish between spent and UTXOs, a separate list called a nullifier set is maintained.

Alice wants to transfer 1 bitcoin to Bob, whose public key is PK_2. Alice creates a new UTXO addressed to Bob after spending $UTXO_1$, which has a value of 1 bitcoin:

```
UTXO₂ = (PK₂, r₂)
```

Alice creates a nullifier to spend `UTXO₁`, `nf₁` = `HASH` `(r₁)`. She also creates a hash of the `UTXO₂` and forwards it to all the public nodes (Carol in *Figure 9.14*), along with the nullifier, `nf₁`. She also forwards the newly created `UTXO₂` solely to Bob in a private channel as shown in *Figure 9.14*:

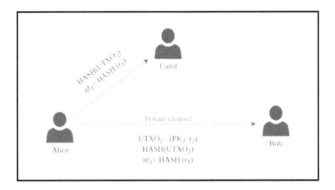

Figure 9.14: Exchanging transactions in Zcash

When Bob receives the hash of **UTXO₂** and the nullifier, **nf₁**, he makes sure that **UTXO₂** hasn't already been spent by checking his local nullifier set. He adds **nf₁** to the nullifier set if it doesn't already exist. Although Bob has verified that **UTXO₂** is legitimate, he cannot be sure that it actually belongs to Alice. The only way to make sure that the UTXO actually belongs to Alice without revealing the secret key is with the help of zero-knowledge proof.

In addition to information forwarded by Alice, as shown in *Figure 9.14*, a zero-knowledge proof string, π, is also published to convince all the nodes that she knows about **PK₁**, **sk₁**, and **r₁**, where **sk₁** is the private key corresponding to **PK₁**. Though the π string proves the knowledge, it will not reveal any of the secret information.

Summary

In this chapter, we have investigated most of the optimization and enhancement techniques of blockchain for improving the scope of this technology. We began with the basic scalability issues of Bitcoin and proposed some solutions. We covered issues and proposed solutions for networking, consensus, and the application layer of the blockchain applications. Blockchain enhancement ideas were discussed later on in the chapter to explore future possibilities in the blockchain technology.

In the coming chapter, we will be discussing the security aspect of the blockchain technology in depth.

10
Blockchain Security

After studying most of the concepts and applications of blockchain technology, it's crucial to discuss its strengths and weaknesses in order to realize the level of security that is required. In this chapter, we will be addressing some of the significant challenges faced by blockchain technology. Along this journey, we'll also point out the possible attacks you can encounter in the blockchain network and how they can be prevented.

We'll be looking at the following topics in this chapter:

- Transaction security model
- Decentralized security model
- Attacks on the blockchain, including:
    - Double-spend attacks
    - 51% attacks
    - Eclipse attacks
- The threats presented by quantum computing

Blockchain technology was adopted in decentralized public networks because of the security the technology provides, including ensuring the integrity of the data stored in the public ledger. Blockchain networks are less vulnerable to the threats faced by centralized networks. However, due to the participation of several diverse components in public networks, centralization in blockchain networks does occur. In addition to this, most blockchain platforms compromise the principles of decentralization in order to customize their applications to their needs. Due to this, the security of blockchain technology has suffered. In this chapter, we'll look into some of the security models and examine the security concerns of blockchain technology.

Transaction security model

The internet is a system of connected devices that communicate with each other using various protocols. Due to the open nature of communication on the internet, there are both individuals and groups of people trying to harm users' devices or applications by hijacking communications. These are often referred to as bad actors, and can be found in any part of the internet. It's often difficult to keep these bad actors out of any system due to the fragile nature of communication on the internet, and every application implements a security model for protection against bad actors.

Most applications ensure secure communication by encrypting the traffic between the transmitting and the receiving end. In fact, more than half of the traffic on the web is encrypted using the HTTPS protocol. Due to the increased number of attacks on the internet, encrypting traffic is of the highest priority when you're implementing a security model for an application. This is crucial for applications that deal with authentication, payment, or any other services that carry private user information.

Let's consider an example of a user performing a transaction with an online store. This transaction involves communication between the merchant's site and the respective banks. Generally, a payment gateway is used by the merchant's site to settle the transaction between the user's and the merchant's bank. Therefore, any transaction initiated by the user will reach the payment gateway through the merchant's site. Since the transaction carries private user information, such as a bank account or credit card details, it needs to be communicated in a secure way. A standard called **Payment Card Industry Data Security Standard (PCI DSS)** is used by merchants. It protects the private details provided by the users. Even after ensuring secure communication, it's still possible that any hole in security can compromise a user's data. The compromised data can be used by the attackers to steal users' funds and even steal their identities in order to perform fraudulent transactions.

All existing services, especially financial services, are centralized and are heavily dependent on encrypting traffic to provide security. Blockchain technology, on the other hand, uses a decentralized model and enables the transparency of transactions. Every transaction detail has to be public so that the networking nodes can validate the transactions. Exposing the transactions to the public doesn't reveal any confidential user information. Due to this, users don't have to encrypt the communication when broadcasting transaction information to the blockchain network.

Users use a private key to sign the transaction (analogous to an account password in banking systems) and prove their identity on a blockchain-based platform. This is the only secret information required to claim funds and create transactions. Nothing other than a private key can prove the identity of the user because the user doesn't have a real identity on the blockchain network.

If a user loses their private key, it is equivalent to losing all their assets. Users have to protect their private keys to in turn protect their identity and funds. Overall, the blockchain security model has its own pros and cons. We'll discuss some of the risks and benefits of the security model in the next section.

Risks of the security model

Ownership of a private key is sufficient to claim ownership of assets created and registered in the blockchain. Although private keys remove the burden of maintaining multiple documents to prove user's identity while performing a transaction, they increase the need for stringent security on the private key. Users cannot afford to lose their private key because it is the only proof of identity in the blockchain. This means that users have to secure their private keys, which are often stored in wallets. Users will have to secure the private key with some kind of encryption to protect it from attackers. However, there are some major risks of this system when compared to the traditional transaction model, these include:

- It's unsafe to store private key information on devices where hundreds of applications have access to the device's storage.

- Attackers will still have to carry out further attacks even after gaining access to the bank or the credit card details as they are often equipped with a two-factor authentication system. However, extracting the private key is all that an attacker has to do in a blockchain platform.

- Centralized services can help customers claim their protected assets even after losing secret information through the use of manual verification, whereas private information cannot be recovered in decentralized blockchain applications as there is no third party involved.

Securing private information in a blockchain application is the sole responsibility of the user. Various methods can be adopted by the user to secure user private key wallets, including:

- Create multiple backups of private keys on different devices

- Isolate the devices that contain private keys from the internet

- Store private keys on hardware and in paper wallets

- Scan the device used to store keys for malicious programs

Note: The information required to generate private keys that can be stored on a physical document is called a paper wallet. A paper wallet is the safest way to back up private keys because it's isolated from both electronic devices and the network.

Decentralized security model

Blockchain applications revolve around the principle of decentralization. Decentralization is achieved with the help of equally responsible nodes that are connected to form a peer-to-peer network. It's essential for most of the blockchain nodes (if not all) to exhibit similar functionality to achieve a purely decentralized network. This can be a challenging task because there is no authority in the public network to enforce rigid rules on the functionality of nodes. Many blockchain networks are being forced to centralize to improve the performance or integrate with the existing centralized entities. This exposes decentralized systems to potential issues that are already faced by existing centralized systems. We'll discuss some of the entities that have caused centralization and exposed decentralized networks to some of the potential threats.

Centralization due to cryptocurrency exchanges

Several cryptocurrencies were introduced soon after Bitcoin gained popularity. Due to the increased popularity of cryptocurrencies, there was a need for an entity where people could buy, sell, and exchange currencies. The entity acted in a similar way to the stock exchange as people placed their *asks* and *bids*. People started to trust the exchanges to maintain their private keys on the users' behalf.

Most cryptocurrency exchanges maintain users' private keys on a single server. They stored most of the key information on devices that were connected to the internet. This forced exchange account holders to trust the security of the exchange servers. The security of user accounts heavily relied on the security implemented by these servers. This is contrary to the decentralized security model of the blockchain technology, so it opened up the opportunity for intruders to perform attacks on the exchange servers using traditional methods.

A cryptocurrency wallet that is stored on a device connected to the internet is called a hot wallet. Exchanges store most of their coins in hot storage so that withdrawals can be performed instantly.

Mt. Gox

Mt. Gox was a Japanese cryptocurrency exchange, and it faced the biggest hack in the history of cryptocurrencies. In 2011, the Mt. Gox server was attacked, and around 850,000 bitcoins (valued at $450 million at the time) were stolen after their hot wallet storage was compromised. Although the exchange was able to recover some of the bitcoins, the majority of the coins were lost forever. Eventually, in February 2014, the company filed for bankruptcy.

Bitfinex

In August 2016, around 120,000 bitcoins were stolen from Bitfinex wallets. Bitfinex reduced the bitcoin funds of all their customers by 36%, including the customers whose wallets were not compromised. Newly minted BFX tokens were deposited in customers' accounts in proportion to their losses. Since these tokens did not have any intrinsic value in any other exchanges, they promised to buy back these distributed tokens eventually.

> Bitfinex is related to a controversial cryptocurrency token called *Tether*, which is traded with the ticker symbol USDT. Tether claims to own a US dollar for every Tether token issued. Tether is popular due to its fixed value, which facilitates smooth transactions between exchanges.

Coinrail

The most recent hack at the time of writing was on Coinrail during June 2018. It's one of the smallest exchanges in Korea but has a high rate of transactions. Various altcoin wallets were attacked, and an estimated 37 million US dollars was lost at that time.

Centralization in mining pools

Mining is crucial for any **Proof of Work** (**PoW**)-based blockchain platform. There has been significant growth in the mining ecosystem due to the incentive mechanism. Nodes with the mining functionality in a network have different capabilities to regular nodes. Some have high computing power, and others have limited computing power. The mining nodes with higher computing power contribute more to the block creation process, thus earn more incentives. This often discourages nodes with lower computing power from participating in mining operations. A special technique called a mining pool was created to solve this. Everyone can contribute their computational resources.

All the participants in the pool were rewarded with incentives based on their contributions. Mining pools allowed a fair distribution of incentives among the mining nodes. However, it introduced a new security threat by centralizing computational power.

Block creation in the majority of blockchain platforms is controlled by mining pools. *Figure 10.1* shows the mining pool distribution in the Ethereum network. The top three mining pools constitute more than 50% of the mining power:

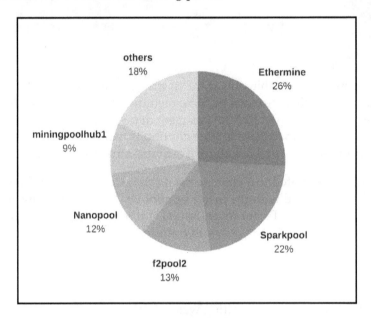

Figure 10.1: Mining pool distribution in the Ethereum network based on the mining power over 24 hours in 2018

Similarly, *Figure 10.2* shows that the top four mining pools in the Bitcoin network, combined, own the majority of the mining power:

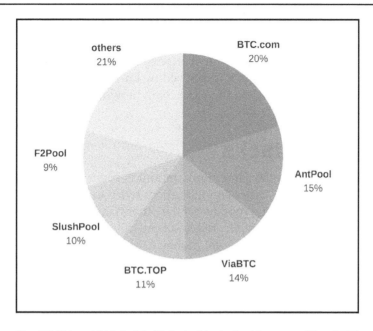

Figure 10.2: Mining pool distribution in the Bitcoin network based on the mining power over 24 hours in 2018

The centralization of computing resources is often a threat in decentralized networks as they could control the block creation process. A dishonest node could launch a 51% attack if the mining pool has enough computation power. Although the 51% attack seems unrealistic in a completely decentralized network, it's feasible to achieve this with the help of mining pools. We'll be exploring the 51% attack in depth in a later section of the chapter.

Attacks on the blockchain

Every application is vulnerable to an attack of some kind due to security issues. But the security issues of a blockchain platform are very different from those of a traditional application due to its security model. Most of the attacks that are performed on a centralized system are not applicable to a blockchain-based application. The decentralization model of a blockchain application makes it difficult to find vulnerabilities. Unlike traditional databases, blockchain data is created by achieving consensus among the network's nodes, so the only way to compromise the blockchain network is by finding vulnerabilities in the consensus mechanism.

There are a number of ways to prevent a network from reaching a valid consensus. However, attacks will not be successful on all the blockchain platforms. A resilient network such as Bitcoin will not be vulnerable to most attacks, but a blockchain network with a small number of participants can be compromised by knowledgeable intruders. We will discuss some of the feasible attacks on the blockchain network in this section.

Double-spend attacks

A double-spend attack is when the same fund amount is spent twice or several times. A physical currency such as paper cash cannot be spent twice unless a duplicate copy is created, which is expensive. Digital money, on the other hand, can easily be duplicated without any cost because they are replicated and transmitted in bits. In *Figure 10.3*, Alice sends the same 10-dollars- worth of digital money to all her friends. If her friends are unaware of other transactions, they will believe that each of their 10 dollars is legitimate:

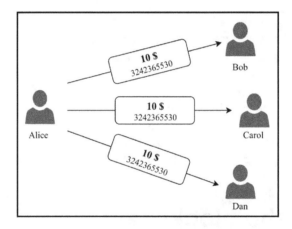

Figure 10.3: Double-spending of funds by Alice

Double-spending is a well-known problem that prevented the use of digital currency in decentralized networks. Bitcoin was the first to provide a practical solution to this problem. However, several attacks exist that can still exploit some of the vulnerabilities of the blockchain network in order to perform double-spends. Race attacks, Finney attacks, 51% attacks, and eclipse attacks are some of the attacks that can enable double-spend in a decentralized network. They can all be avoided by making sure that the transaction is buried deep in the blockchain. The chances of reversing a transaction decreases with each confirmation of the block in the blockchain. This is why Bitcoin suggests that fund receivers should wait for at least six block confirmations.

One of the simplest attacks that can be performed in a decentralized network is a race attack. A race attack is a zero-confirmation attack that can only be performed before the transaction is included in a block. Two conflicting transactions are created in this attack. One transaction will pay the victim and the second transaction will pay the same funds back to the attacker. A race attack is carried out by sending the first transaction only to the victim and broadcasting the second transaction to the rest of the network. The second transaction is likely to end up in a block before the original transaction and will thus beat the actual transaction in the race to be verified. Merchants who accept transactions before waiting for confirmation can be the victims of this attack. It's a matter of a trade-off between security and speed of transactions in Bitcoin. Only the users of blockchain platforms that have a long confirmation time, such as Bitcoin, are exposed to zero-confirmation attacks because of the long wait.

Some of the miners prioritize transactions based on the transaction fees. This prioritization could also be used to create a double-spend attack. In this section, we will construct a script to simulate a double-spend attack in the Bitcoin network by prioritizing the transaction.

Double-spending in Bitcoin transactions

We'll make use of a Python package called `python-bitcoinlib`, which has a set of libraries that provide an interface to Bitcoin's data structures and can access Bitcoin client APIs. It invokes the Bitcoin client's methods through the RPC interface.

All the required functions and data structures are imported from the `bitcoin` module, as shown here:

```
from bitcoin import SelectParams
import bitcoin.rpc
import math
import time

from bitcoin.core import b2x, b2lx, str_money_value, COIN,
CMutableTransaction, CMutableTxIn, CMutableTxOut
from bitcoin.wallet import CBitcoinAddress
```

A chain is selected to create a connection. The chain could be mainnet, testnet, or regtest. We will use Bitcoin's test network for this simulation. An RPC connection object is created to use client APIs:

```
SelectParams('testnet')

rpc = bitcoin.rpc.Proxy()
```

A Bitcoin Core daemon should be created to connect to the testnet blockchain by running the `bitcoind` with the `testnet` argument: `bitcoind -daemon -testnet`. Refer to Chapter 5, *Cryptocurrency*, for more configuration details of Bitcoin.

A few values are declared before creating a transaction. The `dust_amount` value is the minimum transaction output value that can be included in a transaction. A miner will reject the transaction if the output value is less than the `dust_amount` value. In the following code, the value of the coin is 10^8 (100 million, that is, the number of Satoshis in 1 bitcoin). The transaction fees per byte for the first and second transaction are declared. The double-spend transaction will have a higher transaction fee to increase the priority:

```
dust_amount = int(0.0001 * COIN)

feeperbyte1 = 0.000011 / 1000 * COIN
feeperbyte2 = 0.001 / 1000 * COIN
```

Opt-in **Replace-by-Fee** (**RBF**) is an option provided in Bitcoin to allow a transaction to be replaced with a different one. Some of the miners won't allow the replacement of transaction once it is placed in the transaction pool. A transaction is marked replaceable by choosing a sequence number less than MAX-1:

```
optinrbf = True
tx1_nSequence = 0xFFFFFFFF-2 if optinrbf else 0xFFFFFFFF
tx2_nSequence = tx1_nSequence
```

A payment of 0.1 **bitcoin** (**BTC**) is created that is payable to the victim address, n4Wux6bCxwFPvj7BYNb8REvtahhJ9fHJFv. Two transaction outputs are created, one with a value 0.1, and the other is a change output payed back by creating a new address. The change is initially set to 0 until the transaction inputs are selected. The `CMutableTransaction`, `CMutableTxOut`, and `CMutableTxIn` transaction objects are used to create the transaction, transaction outputs, and transaction inputs respectively in this example because they are mutable:

```
payment_address = CBitcoinAddress("n4Wux6bCxwFPvj7BYNb8REvtahhJ9fHJFv")
payment_txout = CMutableTxOut(int(0.1 * COIN),
payment_address.to_scriptPubKey())
change_txout = CMutableTxOut(0,
rpc.getnewaddress().to_scriptPubKey())

tx = CMutableTransaction()
tx.vout.append(change_txout)
tx.vout.append(payment_txout)
```

Creating the first transaction

Transaction inputs are constructed by selecting the unspent transactions that will satisfy the required transaction value (0.1 BTC) and transaction fees.

The `while` loop in the code is terminated only after enough input values are created to satisfy the output values and the minimum transaction fee for the transaction. The `delta_fee` represents the additional fee required to satisfy the transaction fee. The `delta_fee` is deducted from the `value_out` if it is a positive value, else it is added:

```
value_in = 0
value_out = sum([vout.nValue for vout in tx.vout])
unspent = sorted(rpc.listunspent(1), key=lambda x: x['amount'])
while (value_in - value_out) / len(tx.serialize()) < feeperbyte1:

    delta_fee = math.ceil((feeperbyte1 * len(tx.serialize())) - (value_in -
value_out))

    if change_txout.nValue - delta_fee > dust_amount:
        change_txout.nValue -= delta_fee
        value_out -= delta_fee
```

A new unspent transaction output is selected for spending if the input value is less than the output value. A transaction input is created for the newly selected unspent output, and the amount is added to the transaction output change. The transaction is signed each time to update `scriptSig` so that the size of the transaction is updated in each iteration:

```
if value_in - value_out < 0:
    new_outpoint = unspent[-1]['outpoint']
    new_amount = unspent[-1]['amount']
    unspent = unspent[:-1]

    print('Adding new input %s:%d with value %s BTC' % \
    (b2lx(new_outpoint.hash), new_outpoint.n,
    str_money_value(new_amount)))

    new_txin = CMutableTxIn(new_outpoint, nSequence=tx1_nSequence)
     tx.vin.append(new_txin)

    value_in += new_amount
    change_txout.nValue += new_amount
    value_out += new_amount

    r = rpc.signrawtransaction(tx)
    assert(r['complete'])

    tx.vin[-1].scriptSig = r['tx'].vin[-1].scriptSig
```

The transaction is finally signed again before it is sent to the network. This transaction is ideally sent only to the victim node in a race attack. We have broadcast the transaction in this example because we will replace this transaction by creating a higher priority for the double-spend transaction:

```
r = rpc.signrawtransaction(tx)
assert(r['complete'])
tx = CMutableTransaction.from_tx(r['tx'])

print('Payment raw transaction %s' % b2x(tx.serialize()))
print('Payment raw transaction size: %.3f KB, fees: %s, %s BTC/KB' % \
            (len(tx.serialize()) / 1000,
            str_money_value(value_in-value_out),
            str_money_value((value_in-value_out) / len(tx.serialize()) *
1000)))

txid = rpc.sendrawtransaction(tx)
print('Sent payment with txid: %s' % b2lx(txid))
```

Creating the transaction to double-spend

The double-spendable transaction is a transaction with the same value as the first transaction but with a different recipient address. The fund transfer is reversed by addressing the entire fund back to the attacker. All the transaction outputs except the transaction output carrying change are removed from the transaction. Since the change transaction output is addressed to the attacker, the entire fund value is assigned to this output transaction.

A similar process is used as before to calculate the fee for the entire transaction. A higher transaction fee per byte, `feeperbyte2`, is used when calculating the fee for the transaction:

```
tx.vout = tx.vout[0:1]
change_txout = tx.vout[0]
value_out = value_in
change_txout.nValue = value_out

while (value_in - value_out) / len(tx.serialize()) < feeperbyte2:
    delta_fee = math.ceil((feeperbyte2 * len(tx.serialize())) - (value_in -
value_out))

    if change_txout.nValue - delta_fee > dust_amount:
        change_txout.nValue -= delta_fee
        value_out -= delta_fee

    if value_in - value_out < 0:
        new_outpoint = unspent[-1]['outpoint']
```

```
new_amount = unspent[-1]['amount']
unspent = unspent[:-1]

print('Adding new input %s:%d with value %s BTC' % \
  (b2lx(new_outpoint.hash), new_outpoint.n,
   str_money_value(new_amount)))

new_txin = CMutableTxIn(new_outpoint, nSequence=tx2_nSequence)
tx.vin.append(new_txin)

value_in += new_amount
change_txout.nValue += new_amount
value_out += new_amount

r = rpc.signrawtransaction(tx)
assert(r['complete'])
tx.vin[-1].scriptSig = r['tx'].vin[-1].scriptSig
```

Once all the transaction inputs are added to the transaction, the transaction is signed and broadcast to the network:

```
r = rpc.signrawtransaction(tx)
assert(r['complete'])
tx = r['tx']

print('Double-spend raw transaction %s' % b2x(tx.serialize()))
print('Double-spend raw transaction size: %.3f KB, fees: %s, %s BTC/KB' % \
          (len(tx.serialize()) / 1000,
            str_money_value(value_in-value_out),
            str_money_value((value_in-value_out) / len(tx.serialize()) *
1000)))


txid = rpc.sendrawtransaction(tx)
print('Sent double-spend txid: %s' % b2lx(txid))
```

The transaction created for the double-spend will consist of a single transaction output that is addressed to the attacker. This transaction will replace the one created before, due to the higher transaction fee. The raw transaction and transaction ID of both the transactions are shown in the following output:

```
Adding new input
727ae80da7fc81db0304af0324907cb28d32666a6cc8a5813021ec8350a8e05f:0
with value 0.799808 BTC
Payment raw transaction
01000000015fe0a85083ec213081a5c86c6a66328db27c902403af0403db81fca70de87...
Payment raw transaction size: 0.225 KB, fees: 0.00000249, 0.00001106 BTC/KB
Sent payment with txid:
```

```
f52961ddb5881c4f5a10ca3625c978997ed46dd03da0787acb8f26e36e5e686f

Waiting for 2 seconds before double spending
Double-spend raw transaction
01000000015fe0a85083ec213081a5c86c6a66328db27c902403af0403db81fca70de87...
Double-spend raw transaction size: 0.191 KB, fees: 0.000191,
0.00099479 BTC/KB
Sent double-spend txid:
8660fc74668ea2e1fe32d2381c8f6b2512e4418677b63cecab8d7f66b5a162a4
```

The first transaction will be stored in the transaction pool of all the nodes before the second transaction is broadcast. The second transaction is created and broadcast after waiting for two seconds. *Figure 10.4* shows the first transaction information. 0.1 BTC is paid to the victim's address, and the rest is paid back to the attacker's address:

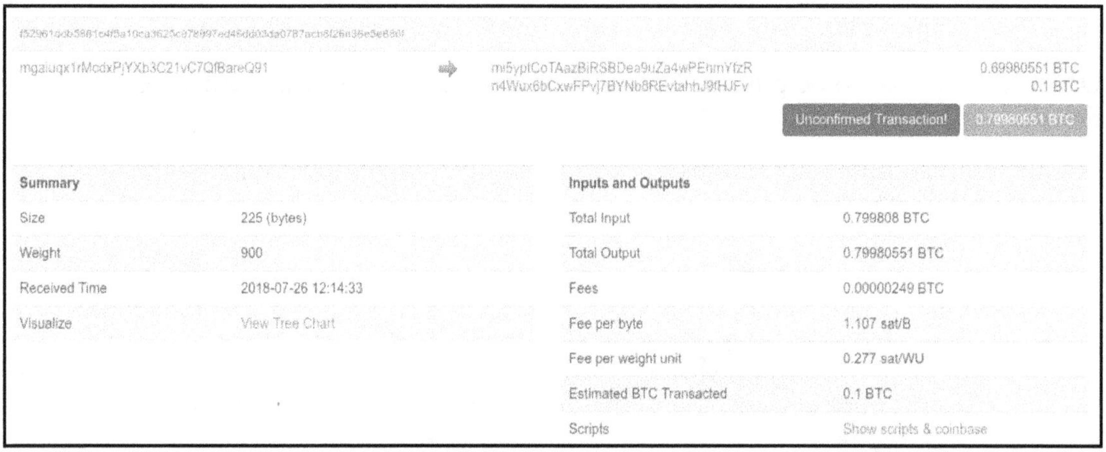

Figure 10.4: Transaction details of the first transaction (source: `blockchain.info`)

This first transaction will only be available for seconds in the network. As soon as the second transaction reaches the nodes, it will be replaced in the transaction pool. *Figure 10.5* shows the information of the transaction that replaces the initial unconfirmed transaction. This transaction has only one transaction output, which pays the entire fund back to the attacker. The transaction successfully completes the double-spend attack once it gets included in the block. When the transaction in *Figure 10.5* gets confirmed, it double-spends the same fund:

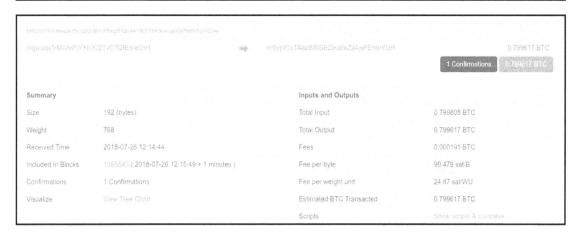

Figure 10.5: Transaction details of the double-spend transaction (source: `blockchain.info`)

Many merchants avoid double-spend attacks by waiting for a minimum number of block confirmations or by rejecting transactions that are replaceable (opt-in RBF). But some Bitcoin merchants still accept payments even if the transactions are unconfirmed. Such entities can be easily attacked with similar double-spend attacks.

 Background reading: The double-spend example used in this section is inspired by a project by Peter Todd. Refer to the project at `https://github.com/petertodd/replace-by-fee-tools` for more information on double-spend attacks.

51% attack

If a participant in the network is able to control more than 50% of the resources required to reach the consensus to create blocks, then the block creation mechanism can be manipulated by that participant. The 51% attack can be performed on any of the consensus algorithms, but it is generally used in Proof of Work-based blockchain networks.

In a PoW-based network, if a dishonest participant is able to control the majority, that is, more than 50% of the computing resources in the network, the block creation process can be manipulated by the dishonest node. The feasibility information relating to the 51% attack was also mentioned by Satoshi Nakamoto in the Bitcoin whitepaper.

Implications of the attack

When a node controls the majority of the computation power of a network, it has a better chance of creating the new blocks than the rest of the network. When an attacker gets hold of the majority of the computation power, the attacker has some control over the ordering, inclusion, and exclusion of transactions. This doesn't mean the attacker can pollute the blockchain with invalid transactions. Since all the nodes in the network verify the transactions included in the blockchain, invalid transactions would be detected by the other networking nodes and the blocks would be discarded. An attacker would be able to cause the following complications in the blockchain:

- Delay some or all of the valid transactions from being confirmed

- Prevent other miners from mining valid blocks

An attacker would not be able to cause any of the following complications:

- Steal or misplace transactions from other accounts

- Delay valid transactions from being broadcast

The preceding points prove that an attacker doesn't have much of a chance to spoil the information on the blockchain even if they control the majority of the computation. The only way the attacker makes a profit out of this attack is by manipulating their transactions by spending them several times. This is a classic attack on decentralized networks known as the double-spend attack, as we saw earlier in the chapter. The double-spend attack is basically spending the same amount twice by reversing the transaction on the blockchain. Since block creation is controlled by the attacker, the transaction can be easily reversed. The attacker might not benefit a lot even after performing a few double-spends, though they can leverage the attack by double-spending transactions on many accounts whose private keys can be stolen from hot wallets, such as exchanges. Although performing simultaneous attacks is infeasible, it's not impossible.

Controlling the majority of the computation power of a network is very expensive compared to the profits gained from the attacks. So, it is always more profitable to behave honestly and earn the incentives from valid block creation than to manipulate transactions for a small amount of profit. However, 51% of attacks could be performed by someone whose intention is not to gain profit but to defeat the consensus system for various reasons.

Some resilient platforms, such as Bitcoin, Ethereum, and Litecoin are not susceptible to these attacks. It's easier to attack smaller coins whose network's majority computation share could be easily bought. *Table 10.1* compares the attack cost for several PoW-based cryptocurrency networks:

Name	Algorithm	Hash rate (Hashes/second)	1-hour attack cost
Bitcoin	SHA-256	45,208 PH/s	$745,462
Ethereum	Ethash	241 TH/s	$325,102
Litecoin	Scrypt	280 TH/s	$50,877
ZenCash	Equihash	95 MH/s	$5,999
Bitcoin Private	Equihash	4 MH/s	$270

Table 10.1: Comparing attack cost for various PoW-based cryptocurrency networks

 Note: Hash per second is the unit used to determine the hash rate of a blockchain node. In *Table 10.1*, **Petahash per second (PH/s)**, **Terahash per second (TH/s)**, and Megahash per second are used to measure the hash rates.

Table 10.1 shows that currencies such as Bitcoin, Ethereum, and Litecoin, which require a high hash rate (difficulty) to compute the PoW hash puzzle, are costlier to attack than low hash rate networks such as ZenCash or Bitcoin Private.

Even though it is practically infeasible to perform such attacks, there have been several such attacks on small cryptocurrency networks. During early 2018, Bitcoin Gold, a fork of the Bitcoin Core project, witnessed a double-spend attack that attempted to steal money from the exchange, after the attacker controlled the majority of the hash power. Verge and MonaCoin are other currencies whose blockchain networks were compromised in 51 % attacks.

Avoiding the attack

The best way to avoid double-spends on a 51% attack is by increasing the wait time. The longer the wait, the smaller the chances of double-spends. As time passes, the transaction will get buried in the blockchain, making it difficult to reverse the transaction. This can be made sure by waiting for a specific number of block insertions (confirmations) after the transaction is included in a block. Each blockchain platform has its own suggested number of confirmations. The suggested Bitcoin block confirmation is 6, which means a wait time of around 60 minutes after the transaction is included in a block.

Eclipse attacks

Up to this point, we've explored possible attacks on the consensus of the blockchain network. But networking attacks are mostly ignored due to the difficulty involved in defeating a decentralized network that works using the peer-to-peer protocol. This doesn't mean that attacks on peer-to-peer networks are impossible. In an eclipse attack, the attacker eclipses the node from the network. The attacker makes sure that the node will not communicate with the blockchain network. The node will believe in a completely different truth than the rest of the network after the node is compromised by the attack. Generally, eclipse attacks are performed on high-profile blockchain nodes such as miners or merchants.

The eclipse attack was proposed by computer security researchers Ethan Heilman, Alison Kendler, Aviv Zohar, and Sharon Goldberg in 2015. They published a Usenix Security paper titled *Eclipse Attacks on Bitcoin's Peer-to-Peer Network*. The paper explains the possibility of an attack on Bitcoin's peer-to-peer network. Although the attack is mainly focused on Bitcoin, it can be performed on the peer-to-peer networks of another blockchain platform as well. Another paper, titled *Low-Resource Eclipse Attacks on Ethereum's Peer-to-Peer Network*, which was published in 2018, analyzed the feasibility of an eclipse attack in the Ethereum network. We will look into the details of eclipse attacks based on the first of these papers.

In a blockchain network, peers use a gossip protocol to set up an initial connection and exchange information. Each node learns about the peers in the network from the connected nodes. In an eclipse attack, the attacker prevents the victim from learning about the rest of the network by not gossiping about the other nodes. The attacker node is directly connected to the victim node, as shown in *Figure 10.6*. The attack looks similar to the man-in-the-middle attack performed between the client and the server in a centralized network. We will assume that attack takes place in Bitcoin's PoW ecosystem to understand and analyze the eclipse attack in the coming sections:

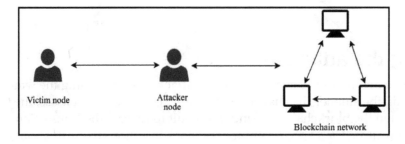

Figure 10.6: The position of the attacker in an eclipse attack

Eclipsing the node

A Bitcoin node can have a maximum of 8 outgoing and 117 incoming connections. Since there's a limit on the number of outgoing connections, the attacker can force the victim to solely establish connections to malicious nodes created by the attacker:

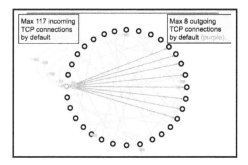

Figure 10.7: Bitcoin node with outgoing and incoming connections in a peer-to-peer network

This may look easy in theory; however, forcing the victim to only create connections to malicious nodes requires more than a single-step attack. The attacker has to learn and manipulate the victim's connection information to manipulate the user's outgoing connections. Bitcoin nodes store outgoing connection information in a peer table. The peer table is organized into buckets of addresses. Filling these buckets with the attacker's IP addresses is the idea behind the attack. An attacker will use several vulnerabilities in Bitcoin Core to achieve this. Once the peer table is filled with the attacker's node information, the victim will only attempt to connect to the attacker's nodes after the node has been rebooted.

Bitcoin has two different sets of buckets that store peer information: a set of new buckets and a set of tried buckets. New buckets consist of the addresses of newly available peers, whereas tried buckets store addresses of already-connected peers. When a node first connects to a peer, it adds the peer's information, along with a timestamp, to the tried bucket. The connected peer passes known peer information to the node, and the node stores this in the new bucket. When the node connects to the attacker's device, it will send information about the malicious peers so that the node stores those addresses in the new bucket.

When a new connection is successfully made by the node, it will add the IP address to one of the 256 tried buckets. It randomly selects a single bucket but randomizes the selection based on the network ID and the full IP address. This is also the same in the case of adding IP addresses to the new bucket. Various vulnerabilities of the Bitcoin node can be exploited to make sure that most of the addresses in the bucket are the attacker's addresses. Several vulnerabilities of the Bitcoin node are pointed out in the *Vulnerabilities and countermeasures* section.

Implications and analysis of the attack

Since the eclipse attack is performed on the network layer, it can break the security of the consensus layer too. Any attack on the consensus layer can be more effective when the node's peer-to-peer protocol is compromised. A 51% attack without the attacker owning the majority of the computing power, or the double-spend attack even after several block confirmations, can be performed when an eclipse attack is performed.

An attacker can double-spend a transaction even after n-confirmation simply by eclipsing a fraction of the miners and the victim node. The attacker can spend a fund and forward it to the eclipsed miner. When the miner includes this in a block, the attacker shows this blockchain to the victim node. The victim is convinced after looking at the confirmed transaction. The attacker also forwards a transaction to double-spend the same fund. When the attacker completes their purchase from the victim, they reveal the actual blockchain to both the eclipsed miner and the victim, thus making their blockchain obsolete.

A double-spend attack is performed in *Figure 10.8*. The attacker eclipses a miner who controls 30% of the mining power and the victim. The attacker spends a fund and sends the transaction to the eclipsed miner.

The eclipsed victim only views this version of the blockchain. The attacker then spends the same fund and creates a transaction that is viewed by the rest of the network. Since this network controls the majority (70%) of the mining power, it will create a longer blockchain, making the eclipsed miner's blockchain obsolete:

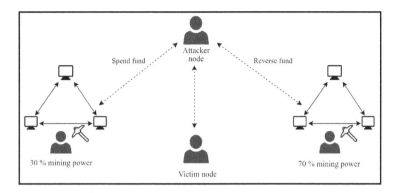

Figure 10.8: Double-spend attack by eclipsing the victim node

If an attacker is a miner, they can launch a 51% attack without owning 51% of the computing power of the network. This can be achieved by preventing the honest miners from controlling the majority of the computing power. The attacker can eclipse a few miners from rest of the network, which would prevent miners from building blocks on each other's created blocks. This will prevent honest miners from owning the majority of the power to create blocks. This will increase the chances of an attacker with less than 51% of the mining power launching a 51% attack. *Figure 10.9* shows that an attacker with 40% of the mining power eclipses two miners, each controlling only 30% of the mining power in the network. Now that attacker owns the majority of the mining power, they have a better chance of ending up with a longer chain than the other miners, who are isolated from each other. Each miner who is unaware of the rest of the network will keep building their own version of the blockchain. The attacker can publish their blockchain to the network at any time, making other versions of the blockchain obsolete:

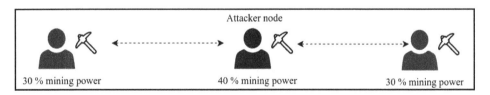

Figure 10.9: 51% attack with less than 50% of mining power

Although the eclipse attack may seem unrealistic, it isn't actually. A clever attack with the help of botnets can easily compromise a node that doesn't implement an additional layer of network security. The published paper *Eclipse Attacks on Bitcoin's Peer-to-Peer Network* explains the chances of an eclipse attack occurring with different scenarios. An experiment performed with botnets produced the following results:

- A worst-case scenario was created by filling tried bucket slots with addresses of honest nodes. An attack was performed with a total of 4,600 IP addresses for a period of 5 hours. Although the tried bucket slots were initially mostly filled with the addresses of honest nodes, 98.8% of them were replaced with the attacker's addresses after the attack. The attack had a 100% success rate.
- An attack was performed on live Bitcoin nodes that had only 7% of the tried address slots filled with legitimate addresses. The attack was simulated by attacking with 400 IP addresses and only 1 hour invested in the attack. The tried table was filled with around 57% of attacker addresses after the attack. This attack had a success rate of 84%.

Vulnerabilities and countermeasures

The attacker has to exploit a few vulnerabilities to replace legitimate peer addresses with their own addresses. Some of the vulnerabilities in Bitcoin nodes that can be exploited are as follows:

- The node selects the IP addresses from the tried bucket with recent timestamps, which increases the probability of the attacker getting selected even if the attacker owns a small portion of the tried bucket addresses. The attacker can increase the chances by increasing the attack time.
- Whenever an address bucket is filled, one of the addresses is removed randomly. Since the removed address is random, if an attacker's IP is removed from the bucket, it can be eventually inserted by repeatedly sending it to the node.

The attacker can exploit these mentioned vulnerabilities. However, these vulnerabilities can be avoided by altering the behavior of the Bitcoin node while gossiping with the peers:

- Selection of the IP address from the tried table could be randomized, which would reduce the chances of selecting an attacker peer even if it was recently connected. The attacker will not be successful even after investing a lot of time in the attack if peer selection is randomized.

- If a deterministic approach is used to insert the address of the peer into a fixed slot, it will reduce the chances of inserting the attacker's address to a different slot after it is evicted from the bucket. Deterministic insertion will ensure that repeated insertion of addresses will not add any value to an attack.

Most of the vulnerabilities in Bitcoin have been fixed. But due to the public blockchain networks and open source culture followed by most blockchain-based organizations, attackers will quickly find vulnerabilities.

Threats of quantum computing

Quantum computing is an area of computing that deals with quantum theory. We know that every single outcome of any kind of computation is represented in 0s and 1s known as bits. Quantum computing, on the other hand, uses Qubits (quantum bits) instead of bits, that exhibits several states simultaneously rather than being mutually exclusive. This technological advancement could greatly influence performance in existing computing systems.

The performance benefits gained by quantum computing can be used to solve complex computing problems, including cryptographic algorithms that could only be broken by brute-force attacks. We are already aware that blockchain technology achieves most of the functionalities with the help of cryptographic primitives. Hashing and asymmetric cryptography are the main two primitives used in the blockchain technology, as discussed in `Chapter 2`, *A Bit of Cryptography*.

The hashing primitive is the backbone of the consensus algorithm - PoW's hash puzzle. The difficulty involved in solving the hash puzzle is what makes the blockchain immutable. If the quantum computing can provide faster brute-force methods to compute the hashes or break the one-way property of some of the existing hashing algorithms, the public ledger can be easily compromised even without performing any of the attacks mentioned earlier. But the growing difficulty of PoW-based blockchain networks, especially Bitcoin, prevents any kind of threats to the consensus algorithm, at least for several years.

A digital signature that uses asymmetric cryptography is widely used in blockchain applications. Quantum computing can be a great threat to asymmetric cryptography, where the private keys could be computed from the public keys. Since the entire internet security depends on either asymmetric or symmetric cryptography, the threat is not limited to blockchain technology alone. The digital signature and encryption techniques will evolve with time to face the threat of quantum computing.

The threat of quantum computing is real, and many groups have been working on solving any of the possible threats to the blockchain technology. The NEO blockchain promises a quantum safe (NeoQS) cryptographic mechanism that uses lattice-based cryptographic mechanisms. Quantum computing has also motivated many communities to venture into non-blockchain solutions, such as Hashgraph and DAG. It is clear that quantum computing will pose some threat to blockchain technology, but it may not be in the near future. Blockchain technology will evolve with time to ensure security against quantum computing when the time comes.

Summary

This chapter explored various security aspects of blockchain technology. We covered some of the security models of the technology at the beginning of the chapter. Some issues related to the centralization caused by exchanges and mining pools were discussed as well. Various types of attacks on the blockchain network, such as double-spend attacks, 51 % attacks, and eclipse attacks were covered with some in-depth analysis. Together, we've covered how to design and deploy a blockchain platform securely.

In the next chapter, we'll will look at how the implementation of blockchain technology is being falsely hyped in most use cases and analyze why blockchain technology doesn't add value to most of these applications.

11
When Shouldn't We Use Blockchain?

So far in this book, we've learned about a number of blockchain concepts in order to understand blockchain's basic functionalities. We've also, throughout the previous chapters, dived deep into the technology in order to get familiar with decentralized applications. However, as we are looking at the foundations of blockchain technology that can help us build applications in a decentralized network, it's important for us to ask ourselves the question, *why blockchain?* It's only useful to use blockchain in a use case if that case requires the characteristics of a blockchain.

In this chapter, we'll explore the characteristics of blockchain and analyze how they influence the implementation of a blockchain use case. We'll also be looking into some of the frameworks you can use to analyze a blockchain use case.

In this chapter, we'll be covering the following topics:

- Distributed databases versus **distributed ledger technology** (**DLT**)
- What to store on a blockchain
- The differences between a centralized versus decentralized architecture
- The properties of blockchain
- Frameworks that we can use to evaluate use cases

Blockchain is an evolving technology that is continuously implemented by enthusiasts in every possible use case. Some of the characteristics of blockchain have attracted the attention of a lot of communities who have decided to build their applications in decentralized networks. In addition to this, the availability of numerous blockchain platforms has catalyzed this attraction to the technology. A number of researchers, enthusiasts, and even enterprises have started building applications in decentralized networks. Some of them propose new solutions, whereas others are trying to solve problems with traditional solutions.

But not all the proposed blockchain solutions are necessarily acceptable; in fact, a number of them are heading in the wrong direction by unnecessarily decentralizing applications. It's important to understand what blockchain has to offer to before it is adopted.

Blockchain offers many features that facilitate the building of a trustless network. However, it has its own set of limitations. Naval Ravikant, the co-founder of AngelList, who was also in the 2017 list of CoinDesk's most influential people in blockchain, said in an interview that, *"blockchain is incredibly inefficient, it's worth paying the cost when you need the decentralization, but it's not when you don't"*, addressing the concern of blockchain technology being used to build applications without proper evaluation. Most projects of this type are misguided due to the lack of a universally accepted definition of the blockchain.

In spite of the depth of knowledge of blockchain technology, we need to understand and weigh several parameters before undertaking any blockchain project. There are several evaluation models that will justify the use of a decentralized blockchain over traditional centralized systems. In this chapter, we will look into some of the parameters and also the evaluation strategy that will help us answer the question, *when shouldn't we use blockchain?*

Distributed databases versus distributed ledger technology (DLT)

The first question that pops up when we think of implementing blockchain is, *how is blockchain-powered ledger technology different from traditional databases?* Traditional databases are centralized, and most blockchain platforms use databases to store transactions locally on each node. So, the actual comparison should be between the DLT-powered by blockchain and the distributed databases, and this is what we'll focus on in this section.

Although databases are distributed in the case of distributed databases, there is still centralization involved as the databases are managed by a central trusted entity, whereas the ledger in a DLT is maintained by trustless nodes in the network. So, distributed databases don't guarantee decentralization and still promote a centralized architecture with a trusted authority. The architecture difference is clearly depicted in *Figure 11.1*.

The business use case that is trying to adopt blockchain as a storage technology has to understand the benefits and pitfalls of each of these storage technologies. Blockchain has a set of characteristics that may or may not favor the use case. We will be pointing out some of the characteristics of blockchain-based DLTs that will help us analyze the suitability of the technology for any use case under discussion:

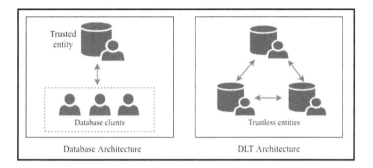

Figure 11.1: Database versus DLT architecture

Decentralized control of information

DLT decentralizes the control of information by enabling data to be shared across the boundaries of trust. Traditional databases are usually controlled by an entity, and they cannot be easily shared with the other trustless entities. One way to share the information stored on each entity's database is through an intermediary. Each entity will share information that needs to be communicated with another entity; this will be done through a central authority trusted by everyone. *Figure 11.2* shows four entities communicating with an intermediary database in order to fetch and send sharable information:

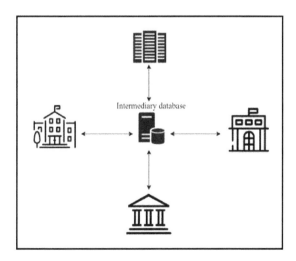

Figure 11.2: Trustless entities sharing data through an intermediary database

On the other hand, the decentralization of a DLT allows each entity to share data, while the blockchain will maintain all of the information and will be trusted by every node in the network. Each entity can verify the data on the blockchain and make sure that the information is unmodified without the need for a central trusted authority. Each entity will maintain a copy of the shared information, which is synced across the network, as shown in *Figure 11.3*:

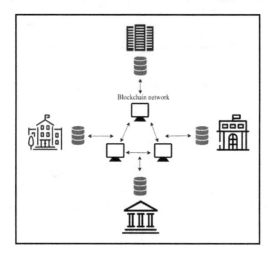

Figure 11.3: Trustless entities sharing data with each other without an intermediary

The decentralization achieved by a DLT helps to share information without trusting on a central entity. Removing the need for a central database helps to eliminate all the processes involved in maintaining it. The processes may include hiring staff to set up the infrastructure, auditing, backup, migration, and so on. The DLT eliminates the dependency on human organizations and creates a completely decentralized autonomous organization. In summary, decentralization makes perfect sense when information needs to be shared across boundaries of trust.

Confidentiality of information

Databases that are managed by centralized entities maintain the confidentiality of information by setting up authentication and authorization mechanisms. Only authenticated users who are authorized to access the resources will be able to perform operations on that information.

The security of data on the database is enhanced by using encryption techniques so that confidentiality is maintained even if the database is compromised.

A DLT is a public ledger that can be accessed by anyone without any authentication. A completely permissionless DLT doesn't enforce access control, and data will be accessible to everyone in the network. Data that is in the form of transactions has to be transparent in a decentralized network so that every node can verify them. The openness of the data stored on a blockchain is what makes decentralization possible. Bitcoin, or any other public blockchain platform (such as Ethereum), provides complete transparency for the transactions embedded in the blocks. Since identities created in the blockchain network are not mapped to real-world identities, participants are able to stay anonymous even though the transactions are public. But that may not be ideal for use cases that need complete or partial privacy.

Some advanced techniques, such as **zero-knowledge proofs** (**zk-SNARKS**) or encryption, can be used to preserve the privacy of the users. Payment channels such as the *Lightning Network*, which was discussed in `Chapter 9`, *Blockchain Optimizations and Enhancements*, can be used to commit only the desired transactions to the blockchain while performing rest of the transactions off-chain. There are other solutions, such as storing the state changes in a secure vault and storing only the reference address in the blockchain. The resources in the secure vault can only be accessed by authorized entities.

DLTs provide solutions to preserve the privacy of the entities. However, these solutions will make the implementation complex and inefficient. The proposed solutions will be against the principles of DLT. So, any use case where privacy is the primary concern would be better off using traditional databases to store information.

Robustness

DLTs will be heavily exposed to the public due to the decentralized nature of the technology. DLTs become more resilient the more they get exposed to the public network. The immutability achieved by the ledger ensures that the information cannot be easily tampered with by the intruders. The decentralization helps to achieve redundancy of information across the network, which will ensure a fault-tolerant system. The overall health of the system doesn't depend on any particular entity that will make the system robust.

Traditional databases can be replicated and partitioned. Replicating the database records will make the database fault-tolerant. The replication strategy is not an inherent feature of most databases. Although a distributed database system will replicate the records in several nodes, they are not as decentralized as a DLT.

There will be delays and synchronization issues among the nodes in the network. So, they are not as fault-tolerant as DLTs and disaster recovery mechanisms need to be employed for databases, especially for those that are centralized. A blockchain-based DLT is the preferred choice for storing records when a use case needs to achieve a fault-tolerant and robust system.

Performance

We concluded in the previous section that DLTs are more robust than traditional databases. But this fault-tolerant system comes with the cost of reduced performance. We have already come across the scalability issues faced by blockchain technology. This is due to the verification and other consensus mechanisms that are required to achieve decentralization. Bitcoin uses a **Proof of Work** (**PoW**) algorithm to achieve the consensus, which restricts the block creation time to 10 minutes. This will limit the rate at which transactions are added to the blockchain. Databases don't have any such restrictions with record insertions. Creating records in database tables is much faster than inserting transactions into blockchain.

Several blockchain platforms have solutions to improve the transaction speed. However, they cannot reach the performance achieved by traditional databases. Databases can achieve higher performance by choosing a specific type of database for a specific application. Relational database, as well as a wide range of non-relational databases such as key-value stores, tabular databases, and graphs, can be used based on the requirements of the application. Furthermore, databases can increase the performance of read operations by using in-memory storage techniques.

Databases are well suited to achieving high transaction throughput. When a use case needs fast read and write operations, databases should be the preferred choice of technology.

What can we store on a blockchain?

We previously compared blockchains with databases and analyzed their respective properties to evaluate their suitability before selecting one as our storage mechanism. We have assumed that a blockchain can store similar information that can be inserted into a database. Although it is possible to insert any data into a blockchain, it is not the preferred storage mechanism for static data. In this section, we will list out a few of the constraints on storing data on a blockchain.

Storing data as transactions

The data on a blockchain is stored in the form of atomic events called transactions. In a cryptocurrency such as Bitcoin, transactions contain scripts that help to transfer assets. However, they could also contain arbitrary information such as executable programs that act as smart contracts. A transaction should also ensure that it has an optimized set of instructions that will decide the current state of the blockchain.

Storing minimal data

Although arbitrary information can be stored in blockchain transactions, it is never recommended to dump bulky data on a blockchain. A blockchain is not a decentralized storage solution. There are several other distributed file sharing protocols, such as IPFS, that are better for storing hypermedia.

Since the transaction fee is calculated based on the size of the data in the transaction, you should try to keep the transaction as small as it needs to be in order to get the job done.

Storing data that requires minimal changes

Though the blockchain doesn't allow data to be modified, previously stored data can be updated by creating a new transaction. It's important to note that transactions are not processed quickly in blockchain networks, and it's recommended to wait for a certain number of block confirmations even after the transaction is included in the block. If a particular data item needs to be updated very often, it will take a considerable amount of time before all the interrelated transactions are processed. Many nodes might even reject such transactions that reference other unconfirmed transactions. So, it's recommended to store and process such data off-chain.

Centralized versus decentralized application architecture

We have compared DLTs and databases by analyzing their properties. But it's also important to analyze the architecture of the application before implementation. We will describe the architecture for both centralized and decentralized applications so that there will be more clarity about the components and the way in which they communicate with each other.

In an application that uses a basic centralized server architecture, there will only be a single instance of all the components involved. *Figure 11.4* shows the architecture diagram of a web server application. The user can communicate with the web server through the user interface provided by the web application. A web application is programmed using a combination of scripting languages, such as JavaScript, and markup languages, such as HTML. A simple web application will have a web server that hosts the application. However, the web server can interact with the database, file, or any other servers required for the application. Since centralized servers have a single physical address, they are mapped to domain addresses. The user can reach the **Domain Name System** (**DNS**) servers to find the physical address of the web server and then communicate using application protocols, such as HTTP.

In a centralized architecture, any number of components can function independently and communicate with each other whenever required. A typical web application will have a database, storage, and web servers as their components, as shown in *Figure 11.4*:

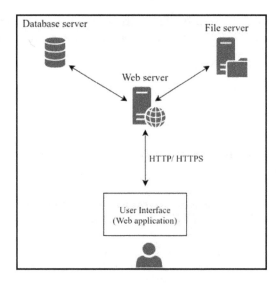

Figure 11.4: Architecture diagram of a centralized application

A decentralized application will communicate with a network of nodes that perform similar functions. A client that uses a decentralized application can communicate with any of the nodes in the network to perform any action. Unlike centralized servers, a decentralized architecture doesn't use DNS servers as there is no single server.

Figure 11.5 shows a node that is part of the blockchain network. The user communicates directly with this node to use any of the functionality of the application. As we have seen with several blockchain platforms, every node will expose a port to enable the communication using the **Remote Procedure Call** (**RPC**) protocol. JavaScript libraries are used to set up RPC connections if the client wants to communicate using the web application. Some blockchain platforms provide a bridge to facilitate communication with the decentralized network. MetaMask is a bridging application used in Ethereum.

It can be seen in the diagram of a centralized application's architecture that the infrastructure design is flexible since a single entity is responsible for maintaining the infrastructure. In a decentralized architecture, nodes don't have much flexibility when it comes to the design. A pure decentralized architecture doesn't integrate with any other centralized components as it would be against the decentralization model. An application that requires several components to be integrated would form a complex architecture, and such an architecture is not desired by a decentralized network:

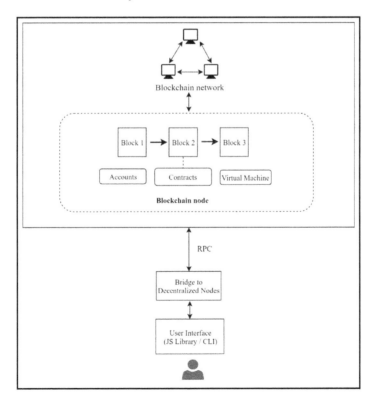

Figure 11.5: Architecture diagram of a decentralized application

As we can see in *Figure 11.5,* a client will communicate with the decentralized network without an intermediary. But there are several use cases that will require integration of centralized trusted entities with a decentralized network where functionalities are defined in smart contracts. A hybrid architecture can be created by deploying trusted entities in the form of middleware, as shown in *Figure 11.6.*

Middleware is often used as an intermediary between the client and the blockchain network. It could be a web server that can communicate with a blockchain node and create and forward the transaction whenever required. The middleware is basically a trusted entity that provides trusted data to the blockchain. The Ethereum platform makes use of special trusted entities called **oracles**. These oracles can provide trusted external information to contracts in blockchain nodes.

A hybrid architecture is often implemented by enterprises in situations where blockchain alone isn't suitable:

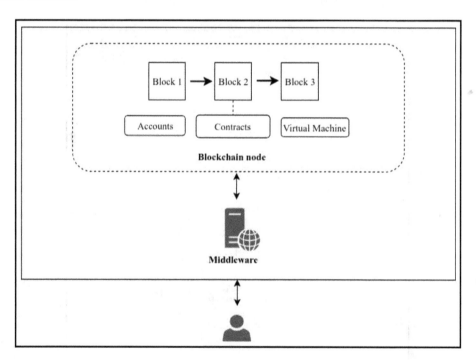

Figure 11.6: Architecture diagram of a decentralized application with middleware

Properties of blockchain

So far, we've discussed a few of the properties of blockchain while comparing DLTs with databases. But due to its decentralized nature, blockchain has a number of inherent properties that will greatly benefit some use cases while not adding value to others. In this section, we'll discuss these properties so that you are able to properly evaluate whether blockchain would be suitable in your own use case.

Immutability

Blockchain is a ledger that doesn't allow you to update or delete existing records. The data recorded on the blockchain is supposed to remain for eternity. This makes a blockchain an immutable data structure. Unlike with traditional record-keeping technologies, a record cannot be erased once it is included in the blockchain. The only way to update a record is by creating a new record that will undo the effect of the previous record. Update operations are expensive in blockchain because each record insertion consumes time and fees.

Immutability is one of the key characteristics of blockchain, so it's essential that the selected use case can make use of the immutable nature of blockchain.

Non-repudiation

Each transaction stored in a blockchain is created by an entity that signs the transaction. It is infeasible to remove a transaction once it has been added to the blockchain due to the immutability of blockchain. Due to this, the entity that signed the transaction cannot deny the existence of the transaction. Repudiation can be observed in centralized systems due to their mutability, but it is highly unlikely in decentralized systems.

Security

One of the main advantages of decentralization is enhanced security. We have already discussed the level of security provided by blockchain technology in `Chapter 10`, *Blockchain Security*. The decentralization of the blockchain network will make the system resistant to many of the traditional attacks that can be performed on the centralized systems.

Any use case implemented using a blockchain doesn't have to worry about protection of the system against many of the traditional attacks.

Redundancy

All of the blockchain records are replicated across all the nodes of the network, achieving a high level of decentralization. The redundancy achieved by the network ensures that it is a fault-tolerant system. However, redundancy will introduce latency in the network, which negatively affects performance. It is important to consider the tradeoffs between fault tolerance and performance before implementing blockchain in any use case.

Reduced cost

One of the attractive features of creating applications in a decentralized network is eliminating the costs involved in managing the organization, creation, and maintenance of the infrastructure. It is ideal to implement use cases where there is no single entity to bear the functioning cost. **Decentralized Autonomous Organizations (DAOs)** are a use case where there is no entity responsible for bearing the cost incurred.

Transparency

Every transaction included in the blockchain has to be verified by every node in the network. The verification process mandates the transparency of all the transactions stored in the blockchain. It is crucial to determine the data to be included in the blockchain when implementing a use case. An application where confidentiality is a high priority is not a good use case for a public blockchain.

Decision models for blockchain

Based on the depth of understanding of blockchain technology and its impact on real-world problems, many researchers have proposed several decision models that will help to quickly assess the suitability of blockchain in any use case. These decision models consider all the fundamental principles of the blockchain and decide whether the use case is suitable to be implemented in a blockchain-based ecosystem.

Karl Wüst and Arthur Gervais

Two computer science researchers, Karl Wüst and Arthur Gervais, proposed a decision model in the paper *Do you need a Blockchain?*, which was published in IACR Cryptology (`https://eprint.iacr.org/2017/375`). The model helps to decide between permissioned and permissionless blockchains when there are mutually mistrusting entities in the system.

Figure 11.7 depicts the flowchart for the blockchain decision model, which decides upon the suitability of blockchain in the use case and also helps to decide upon the type of blockchain. It suggests blockchain as a solution if the use case satisfies all of the following conditions:

- It needs to store the state
- There are multiple writers
- There is no online **Trusted Third Party** (TTP)
- All the writers are untrusted

It further suggests the use of a permissionless blockchain if all the writers are unknown, and recommends a permissioned blockchain otherwise. A permissioned blockchain will be public if the transactions are verified by everyone; otherwise, the blockchain could be maintained in a private network:

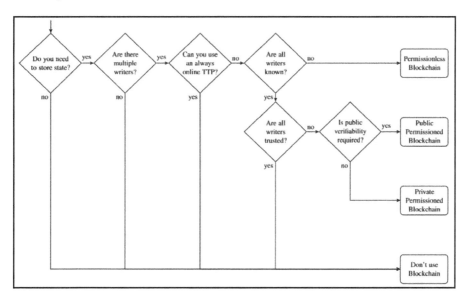

Figure 11.7: Flowchart of the blockchain decision model (source: https://eprint.iacr.org)

They also listed out the different properties of blockchains and databases to compare the implementations. *Table 11.1* shows several properties of permissionless blockchains, permissioned blockchains, and trusted databases:

	Permissionless Blockchain	Permissioned Blockchain	Central Database
Throughput	Low	High	Very High
Latency	Slow	Medium	Fast
Number of readers	High	High	High
Number of writers	High	Low	High
Number of untrusted writers	High	Low	0
Consensus mechanism	Mainly PoW, some PoS	BFT protocols (such as PBFT)	None
Centrally managed	No	Yes	Yes

Table 11.1: Comparing properties of types of blockchain and central databases

Birch-Brown-Parulava model

David Birch, Richard Brown, and Salome Parulava proposed an evaluation model in the paper *Towards ambient accountability in financial services: Shared ledgers, translucent transactions and the technological legacy of the great financial crisis*, which was published in the *Journal of Payments Strategy and Systems*. The paper proposes a model to explore the application of shared ledgers in financial services. They also envision a financial marketplace with translucent transactions.

Figure 11.8 shows the proposed decision model, which evaluates the application of blockchain in financial services. The type of blockchain to go with is classified as permissioned or permissionless based on the permissions assigned to the users of the ledger. They are also classified in a more granular way based on the level of influence of the users on the functionality of the shared ledger:

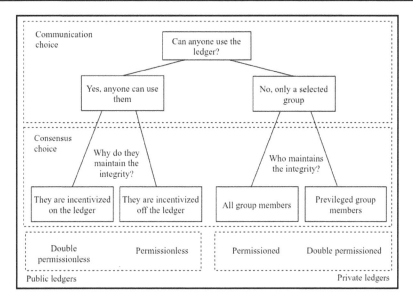

Figure 11.8: Decision model for the financial services (Source: Birch-Brown-Parulava model)

Framework to evaluate the suitability of blockchain

An evaluation framework was created by several researchers, namely Sin Kuang Lo, Xiwei Xu, Yin Kia Chiam, and Qinghua Lu, in a paper titled *Evaluating Suitability of Applying Blockchain*. The framework considers many of the properties of the blockchain to evaluate whether it matches the requirements of the use case.

The proposed framework consists of seven questions that need to be answered before evaluating the use case, as shown in *Figure 11.9*. The framework suggests using a blockchain when the following conditions are met:

- The scenario requires multiple entities
- The operation is not centralized
- The integrity of transaction history is required
- Performance is not the priority
- There is no trusted party involved
- Data transparency is desired
- Inserted data shouldn't be modifiable (immutable)

The framework further evaluates whether some properties of blockchain could be retained with alternative solutions. The framework shown in *Figure 11.9* further evaluates whether the trusted authority should be decentralized, whether data can be protected if transparency is not desired, or whether modifiable, and bulk data can be maintained off-chain. This framework is not as stringent as other decision models when evaluating the requirements of the use case:

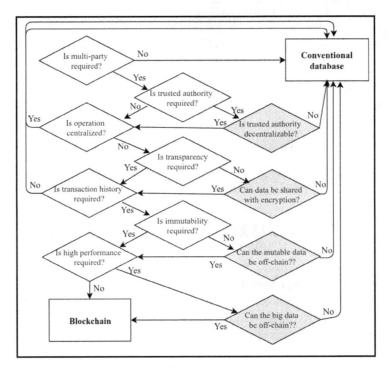

Figure 11.9: Framework for evaluation (source: Evaluating Suitability of Applying Blockchain)

This framework evaluated a few industrial use cases in the paper. After executing each use case requirement in the framework, it concluded that supply chain-and identity management-related applications could be easily adapted into a blockchain. On the other hand, information-sensitive use cases such as electronic health records and stock markets are not suitable to be implemented in a blockchain due to the transparency and low throughput of blockchain networks. In the next chapter, we'll analyze several use cases after evaluating each of them for their suitability.

Generalized decision model

We have seen several decision models proposed by blockchain researchers. Although all of them can be used to evaluate the requirements of the use case, there is no universally agreed list of conditions to decide when to use conventional technology and when to use blockchain. Based on the decision models mentioned earlier and all the properties of blockchain discussed in the earlier section, *Properties of blockchain*, we have created a generalized decision model, as shown in *Figure 11.10*:

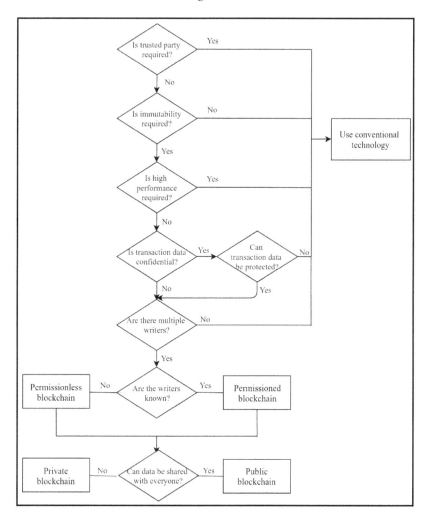

Figure 11.10: Flowchart of the generalized decision model

The decision model depicted in *Figure 11.10* considers all the properties of blockchain before deciding on the suitability of blockchain for the use case. Similar to the earlier decision models, it needs to agree on the following conditions:

- There is no trusted party involved
- The immutability of transaction data is desired
- The scenario doesn't need high performance
- The transaction data isn't confidential or could be protected by encrypting
- There are multiple writers
- The data can be shared and replicated across the network

A use case is suitable to be implemented using blockchain technology if all the conditions are satisfied. It is also crucial to determine the type of blockchain so that a suitable blockchain platform can be selected for the implementation. The decision model suggests a permissionless or permissioned based on the nature of the writing entities, as shown in *Figure 11.10*. It also suggests a public blockchain network if the data can be shared and verified by everyone in the network, or a private blockchain if there is a restriction on shared data.

We will use the decision model in the next chapter to evaluate, analyze, and choose the appropriate blockchain platform for a variety of use cases.

Summary

This chapter has provided insight into the strategies to use when deciding whether to develop a decentralized application. A comparison was drawn between distributed databases and the blockchain-based DLT to explore the properties of blockchain. Centralized and decentralized application architectures were covered in depth to explain when a blockchain-based architecture adds value. We also explored several key properties of blockchain architectures in order to give the readers the essence of blockchain. Finally, we explored some decision models that evaluate the suitability of blockchain for certain use cases that were explored.

Now that we are able to distinguish between a blockchain and a non-blockchain use cases with the help of decision models, we'll move on to discuss several financial and non-financial blockchain use cases by pointing out the issues in the current implementations and justifying the solution provided by blockchain technology.

12
Blockchain Use Cases

Now that we've dived into blockchain suitability frameworks, as seen in the last chapter, we are now equipped with the information we need to distinguish between a blockchain and a non-blockchain use case. In this chapter, we'll be focusing on defining broader blockchain use cases, which will help motivate us to create implementations for those use cases.

The following topics will be covered in this chapter:

- Provenance tracking
- Payment system
- Crowdfunding
- Decentralized autonomous organizations

The decentralization achieved by blockchain technology can provide us with a number of solutions to many of the existing problems we face with centralized systems. Although blockchain can provide solutions to many of the problems we face in existing centralized systems, it also has its own set of limitations. In the previous chapter, we came across several evaluation frameworks that helped us choose the true blockchain use cases. In this chapter, we are going to analyze the use cases that are selected by the evaluation framework, so we can justify their implementation using a decentralized architecture.

The most obvious blockchain use case involves the participation of multiple entities without a trusted authority performing centralized operations; instead, the operations are decentralized. There are several use cases that instantly qualify for the implementation because of the obvious advantages gained from implementing such use cases using blockchain. We have narrowed down the use cases after reviewing the feasibility of implementing them to provide solutions to real-world problems.

Tracking provenance in the supply chain

A supply chain is a system of entities that are involved in the process of creating a product and distributing it to consumers. This supply chain often involves suppliers, manufacturers, wholesalers, retailers, and consumers, where the product moves in the direction shown in *Figure 12.1*. The actors involved in the supply chain are often spread across several locations, which can make it challenging to keep track of the goods in the supply chain:

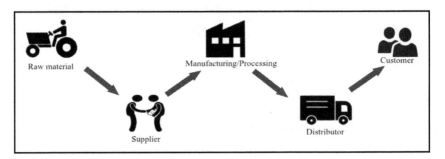

Figure 12.1: Process flow diagram of a typical supply chain

Every finished product moves along the supply chain due to the involvement of multiple entities during its production and distribution. But due to the complex nature of a supply chain, it's hard to keep track of provenance. Most existing provenance tracking is performed with the help of trusted third parties because none of the entities involved in the supply chain trust each other. Using blockchain as a shared ledger among these entities can provide us with an effective way to keep track of the provenance of any product in a supply chain. It allows trustless entities in the system to believe on the provenance data without allowing a single entity to both own and maintain it.

Pain points in a supply chain

Every product on the market has to go through several entities before it can be consumed by the end user. However, due to the lack of efficient mechanisms to track provenance, there have always been a number of concerns regarding the supply chain. Such concerns can fall under the following examples:

- End users are often misinformed about the origin of the product, and in many cases are defrauded by being supplied a sub-optimal product. Any information about the product could also be falsified by any of the entities in the supply chain, intentionally or unintentionally.

- Lower-end supply chain entities, such as suppliers and manufacturers, are exploited by the big box retailers.
- The existing process makes the supply chain opaque, and its entities fail to analyze supply and demand data.

These points summarize the main problems faced in a typical supply chain in which there is no effective mechanism for keeping track the ownership of products. This emphasizes the need for a fair way of tracking products, and this is where blockchain promises a compelling solution.

Blockchain as a solution

We've already come across the concept of proof of ownership in `Chapter 7`, *Diving into Blockchain – Proof of Ownership*. As a reminder, proof of ownership uses digital identity and digital assets to track the provenance of any asset using a public ledger. Similarly, each entity in the supply chain will have a digital identity that can own an asset at any given moment. A sophisticated solution to provenance tracking using blockchain will have the following stages:

1. The supply chain entities register as participants in the provenance tracking system
2. A digital asset with a unique identity will be created by the initial supplier, who often supplies raw materials
3. The asset is then transferred to the next supplier or manufacturer, both physically and digitally
4. The manufacturer will use the same identity for the product, along with a label for each transformed product, so that they can be traced back to the source
5. Finally, the retailers can transfer the product to the consumers when they receive the assets

When provenance tracking in the supply chain is implemented using digital assets and identities with the help of blockchain, the supply chain can benefit from many of the properties seen in blockchain. The supply chain process requires the following features:

- Multiple entities can perform both read and write operations.
- Transparency of every transaction is desired so that each entity is aware of the supply and demand information of the entire supply chain.

- The transaction history requires integrity and immutability so that a product can be tracked down to its source. Immutability ensures that no participants or potential attackers will be able to modify the provenance data.
- High transaction speed is not desired because supply chain information doesn't require real-time data.

The desired features of a supply chain show that this use case is suitable to be implemented using blockchain because it meets all the requirements of the blockchain decision model discussed in the previous chapter.

Blockchain implementation of the supply chain

Provenance tracking in a supply chain can be implemented by using many of the existing blockchain platforms, including some of the platforms we've already discussed, such as Ethereum, NEO, or MultiChain. However, one specific project, called **Hyperledger Sawtooth**, has already been widely adopted by enterprises in many supply chain use cases.

 Hyperledger Sawtooth is a project under the Hyperledger umbrella project for open source blockchain projects. The Sawtooth project was originally contributed by Intel, and it allows consensus algorithms to be plugged into the core software. The Sawtooth blockchain supports both permissioned and permissionless implementations.

Hyperledger Sawtooth has a modular architecture that allows its components to be easily manipulated. It provides a scalable solution with high transaction throughput when compared to the other blockchain platforms. The Sawtooth network mainly consists of two types of participants: **clients** and **validators**. Clients send transactions to the blockchain network, while validators ensure that they are validated and included in the blockchain. Validators follow the consensus mechanism and maintain the global state of the ledger. Sawtooth validators validate each transaction based on business logic that is specified in a component called a transaction processor. The transaction processor is the core of any distributed application created using the Sawtooth platform. It describes the application with the help of states and transaction logic. As a result, each transaction created by the client will be validated using the transaction processors.

To showcase a supply chain implementation, we are going to use an application called **Sawtooth Supply Chain**, which was built on top of Hyperledger Sawtooth. This application was created to allow users to track goods in a supply chain, thus allowing them to keep track of ownership and the other properties of the goods, such as temperature, weight, and location.

All the participants and components of Sawtooth Supply Chain can be seen in *Figure 12.2*. The client will communicate with the blockchain through the **Representational State Transfer** (**REST**) web interface, which is provided by the validator node. The transaction processor of the supply chain application, which is present in each validator node, will handle the different types of transaction, such as creating, transferring, and accepting a new asset record:

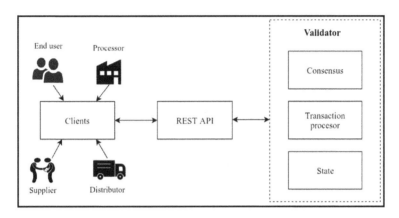

Figure 12.2: Architecture diagram of Hyperledger Sawtooth Supply Chain

 Note: The Sawtooth Supply Chain can be downloaded from the GitHub repository here:
`https://github.com/hyperledger/sawtooth-supply-chain`.

The application has several different components and can be executed using `docker-compose` by running each component as a container. Once the code has been cloned, and `docker-compose` has been set up, the containers can be initiated using `docker-compose`:

```
$ docker-compose up
```

It's worth noting that `docker-compose` will take several minutes to set up all the containers. Once everything has been set up, the following necessary components of Sawtooth Supply Chain will be created:

- The Sawtooth blockchain and the supply chain's REST API endpoints
- The supply chain transaction processor
- The database (**RethinkDB**) required for the Sawtooth node
- The client application used to interact with the blockchain

All of those components will run as independent services on each Sawtooth node. The Sawtooth Supply Chain will create a client application in which each entity of the supply chain can register and manage the assets. Sawtooth Supply Chain then launches a client application called **AssetTrack** on local port `8021`. The entities will be part of the supply chain once they are registered as agents in the application. Both public and private key pairs will then be generated for each entity, and the entity can be identified by its public key.

A logged-in entity can add an asset with a set of properties and submit transactions. The asset can only be updated with different properties and transferred to a different owner by the existing owner of the given asset. Every entity in the supply chain is also able to view all the assets and agents, but only the owner of an asset can move an asset to a different entity, thus ensuring the traceability of every asset.

At the same time, Sawtooth Supply Chain also provides us with shell access through a Docker container that we can use to run arbitrary scripts that will automatically update the supply chain data. The following Docker command can be used to log in to the shell:

```
$ docker exec -it a supply-shell bash
```

Once we are logged into the shell, a script to update some sample assets can be executed after navigating to the `server` folder with the following command:

```
$ npm run update-sample-assets
```

This example implementation will help you to understand provenance tracking by including multiple entities in a supply chain.

 More details about the Sawtooth Supply Chain transaction family can be found in the official documentation: `https://sawtooth.hyperledger.org/docs/supply-chain/`.

Financial system

Finance has always been one of the biggest use cases of blockchain, dating back to the invention of Bitcoin. Blockchain, at face value, seems to be the best fit for many of the implementations that affect the global economy, whether it's banking, stock exchanges, or payment networks. Yet, in the past, financial systems have been manipulated by centralized authorities, even in the global economy, due to the wide variety of solutions for different financial systems available across the world and the barriers between them; there is a lot of complexity involved.

Banking systems are the largest financial institutions in the world. These banking systems are regulated differently by each nation, and this has resulted in the creation of barriers when it comes to cross-border financial services. As seen in *Figure 12.3*, a banking transaction between two users, who are situated in two different regions, is regulated by different authorities, with each region having a corresponding bank that helps to communicate and settle transactions securely along the border:

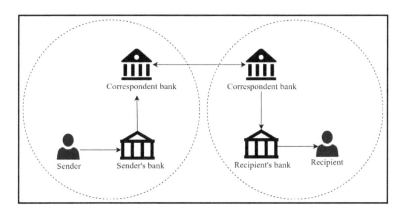

Figure 12.3: Process flow diagram of a cross-border transaction

Today, banking institutions allow their users to perform fund transfers online using different payment systems. Most countries support **Real Time Gross Settlement** (**RTGS**) payment systems in order to settle transactions between banks in real time. There are numerous other payment systems that support inter-bank transactions at a domestic level with small fees; for instance, India has **National Electronic Funds Transfer** (**NEFT**), **Immediate Payment Service** (**IMPS**), and **Unified Payments Interface** (**UPI**) as its payment systems. But when a transaction has to be performed between banks from different nations, the banks perform a wire transfer using secure systems such as **SWIFT** or **Fedwire**. Although these payment networks function as expected, they have several limitations when implemented on a global scale.

Due to all the complexities involved in creating a payment system, there is a need for a single system that can be adapted to create an efficient payment network. Blockchain technology can help us to remove the barriers between financial institutions by allowing trustless entities to communicate efficiently. Back when Bitcoin was created, it was done with the intention of providing a payment network that can be used across borders as it cannot be regulated by any single entity.

Pain points in the payment system

The complex payment system used by the banking system has a set of limitations when collaborating with different entities in the system. In the following list, you will be introduced to some of the limitations of the existing payment system:

- Not suitable for huge fund transfers due to the daily transaction limit.
- You'll often encounter high transaction fees.
- Inter-bank transactions are settled slowly. Although current payment systems provide fast transaction settlement for domestic banks, cross-border transactions are still painfully slow.
- You may find some payment systems only function during the working hours of the bank.
- Since all the payment systems are still centralized, they are susceptible to both errors and attacks.

Although banking transactions can be performed electronically, it's worth remembering that not all institutions are equipped to handle digital transactions, and for some, the use of physical currencies further complicates the financial system. The creation of an unforgeable physical currency is expensive and also has issues such as it being difficult to verify the originality of such currencies. All of these complexities have led to a corrupt financial system.

Blockchain as a solution

Blockchain was the product of Bitcoin, and was developed to replace the current payment system with peer-to-peer electronic cash. Even so, since the development of both Bitcoin and blockchain, the technology has grown to be much more than just an alternate payment system. The properties of blockchain provide a lot of scope to develop solutions to the issues in payment systems and other financial systems as well. An efficient payment system requires the following properties:

- Real-time settlement of transactions
- Low fees for domestic and international transactions
- No limitation on the amount that can be transferred
- Secure communication and record, keeping mechanisms

Blockchain, with the help of decentralized networking, could be used to build a system that removes the intermediaries in the payment system, thus achieving a fast and cheap solution. However, since liquidity can be instantly transferred to the recipient, there isn't any limit on the transaction amounts. Likewise, blockchain's consensus mechanism inherently secures the immutable ledger.

The payment system use case we have discussed satisfies the blockchain decision model since it requires most of the properties of blockchain. However, confidentiality can be a concern in the implementation of blockchain as the transaction information is transparent in a public blockchain. But you'll find that most blockchain implementations of payment systems involve both banks and other financial institutions as the end users, not the bank account holders themselves. Therefore, it provides a way to perform private transactions and obscure the private details from third-party observers. Even the payment system that performs payment transactions directly between end users could make use of anonymous transactions to preserve privacy, as discussed in `Chapter 8`, *Blockchain Projects*.

Blockchain implementations of a payment system

As we are about to discuss, there are several implementations that are trying to provide better solutions than the existing financial systems with the help of blockchain technology. Ripple and Stellar are two platforms that provide a network to act as a bridge between the participants and help remove the need for any other intermediaries. The network setup between the banks acts as a cross-border payment system and even performs currency exchange without much delay. Let's now delve more into both Ripple and Stellar.

Ripple

Ripple is a decentralized ledger-based network that allows the transfer of a digital asset known as XRP. Ripple was launched with the vision and aim of building a cryptocurrency for financial institutions, such as banks, that enables cross-border fund transfer at low cost.

Unlike other cryptocurrencies, Ripple doesn't create a parallel payment system. Instead, it provides a network called **RippleNet** for the existing payment system to settle global payments. Ripple currently provides three different types of payment solution:

- **xCurrent**: This is a software solution for sending and receiving cross-border payments between banks with end-to-end tracking; transactions are securely settled in within seconds.

- **xVia**: This allows users to send international funds through payment providers using RippleNet. It provides a set of APIs that can be directly used by the users to send payments globally.
- **xRapid**: This uses Ripple's digital asset, XRP, as the liquidity for cross-border payments. It uses exchanges to convert funds between XRP and the local currency. The greater the amount of XRP on the exchanges, the better the system works. It also removes the need for banks to own the pre-funded accounts in local currencies around the world.

 A few of the use cases for payment providers using Ripple can be found at https://ripple.com/use-cases.

Stellar

Stellar is an open source platform that supports cross-border transactions by performing an exchange of value between a pair of currencies. It was designed to connect banks, payment systems, and the end users with a more reliable system at a cheaper cost.

The Stellar network is a collection of distributed nodes called **Stellar Cores** that functions using **Stellar Consensus Protocol** (**SCP**). Any payment application can be built on top of the Stellar network. Stellar provides an HTTP API called **Horizon** to communicate with the network. To build a payment network that can perform conversion between a pair of currencies, a payment architecture that can help to perform the exchange is required. The architecture consists of trusted entities called **anchors**, which will create credits in the Stellar network for every deposit. Financial institutions such as banks are often the anchors in the payment system. To send and receive payments, Stellar needs federation and compliance servers, and a bridge server to coordinate these servers.

 More details about the Stellar network can be found at https://www.stellar.org/developers/guides/get-started/index.html.

Stellar provides several payment solutions, including faster micropayments and low-cost remittances. A great thing about Stellar is that it's already been applied in a select few real-world use cases and recently has partnered with several companies including IBM, Deloitte, SureRemit, and KlickEx to perform cross-border transactions and solve remittance challenges.

You can find out more details about Stellar use cases at `https://www.stellar.org/how-it-works/use-cases`.

Crowdfunding

Crowdfunding is a way of raising small amounts of funds from a large audience in order to support a particular cause. Crowdfunding, is often used when you need to create initial funding for start-up ideas, often ones that are in the early stages of their development. In recent years, crowdfunding has transformed the way of raising capital by getting funding from multiple participants and eliminating entities such as banks and venture capitalists.

Crowdfunding can be organized for any kind of initiative, including charity, the arts, and community-based projects. Depending on the organization's intentions, various types of crowdfunding can be used, such as the following:

- **Reward-based**, in which the supporters of the crowdfunding campaign are rewarded with goodies or early access to the product itself. Online platforms such as Kickstarter and Indiegogo offer reward-based crowdfunding.
- **Equity-based**, in which the contributor to the crowdfund is offered equity in the company based on the amount they contribute.
- **Debt-based** is similar to borrowing money from banks, but the public lends the money instead of a centralized bank. The lenders will earn interest for the investment, similar to loans in the traditional banking system. The interest rates are fair to both the borrowers and lenders.
- **Donation-based**: is something often used by charitable organizations, open source projects, or any other non-profit organizations to fundraise for different causes.

All the mentioned crowdfunding types will have at least three actors: an initiator, a platform provider, and supporters, as shown in the following figure:

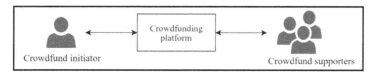

Figure 12.4: Actors in crowdfunding

Successful crowdfunding will make sure that the crowdfunding campaign is advertised in an effective manner on the platform. Crowdfunding platforms should make sure that the funding operation is seamless for both the crowdfund initiator and the supporters. Blockchain technology allows tokens to be easily created and transferred in a decentralized network without the need for any intermediary to maintain the crowdfunding platform. A crowdfund initiator will start the token distribution process, called the **initial coin offering (ICO)**. A supporter will fund the ICO, and subsequently receive tokens for the amount they contributed. These tokens will have a value during the ICO phase, and their value may vary after the ICO. The tokens could sometimes even represent the equity of an organization that offers the tokens.

Pain points in crowdfunding

Crowdfunding has many advantages over conventional funding, such as that it provides the opportunity for anyone to create or fund a project effortlessly. That being said, it does have limitations:

- Crowdfunding still needs to create agreements between the initiator and the contributor for most of the funding process if it involves reward, equity, or debt.
- Some crowdfunding formats don't provide a flexible investment option for the supporter, which results in a lack of participation.
- The supporters of a project need to trust that they will earn their equity or reward after funding the project, so they will need to trust the crowdfunding platform and the project.
- Most crowdfunding will be initiated by non-profit organizations who are following the donation model. With this method, there tends to be a limited number of supporters when using this model, and it's common that by using this method, the organizations tend to fail to reach their target.

Blockchain as a solution

Blockchain provides a token distribution mechanism in a decentralized network by creating ICOs. Executing an ICO is much simpler than any other kinds of crowdfunding. A typical ICO will involve the following stages:

1. A project looking to raise money will launch the ICO by specifying the ICO structure, such as the initial token value, the total token limit, the token sale period, and so on.

2. Once the token sale begins, supporters can invest in the project by funding the project with either a fiat currency or existing cryptocurrencies. Supporters will receive tokens equivalent to the amount invested.
3. Similar to other crowdfunding solutions, if the ICO doesn't meet the goal, the campaign is said to be unsuccessful, and funds will be returned to the investors.
4. A successful ICO can use the funds to execute the roadmap of the project.

An ICO is often compared to an **initial public offering** (**IPO**), where private organizations offer shares to the public. But there are several features that distinguish ICOs from IPOs, as mentioned here:

- ICOs are not strictly regulated by most governments across the world. Although this makes it easier to launch an ICO, it also encourages fraudulent crowdfunding.
- Since token distribution in an ICO is decentralized, there is no single party managing the funding operation, unlike IPO.
- It's cheaper and easier to launch an ICO compared to an IPO.
- ICOs are conducted by organizations that are at the initial stage, whereas IPOs are often conducted by well-established private organizations.

 IPOs are offered by corporations that are private and wish to raise capital by offering stocks to public investors. Due to the complex and lengthy procedure involved in the IPO, the companies seek the help of investment banks to help with the process.

Blockchain implementation of crowdfunding using an ICO

An ICO is created in a decentralized network with the goal to distribute tokens in order to raise funds for a given project. Since token distribution is performed in a decentralized network, the entire logic of the ICO is written in smart contracts. These contracts are then deployed in the blockchain network and executed by the blockchain nodes when performing any ICO operations.

ICOs are mostly launched on existing blockchain networks, such as Ethereum, NEO, Wanchain, and Waves. Both Ethereum and NEO are widely used to develop and deploy smart contracts with the aim to create tokens and launch ICOs. Both of these platforms have proposed standards to program the smart contracts to implement the tokens that are distributed during the ICO.

Ethereum has ERC-20, ERC-223, and ERC-721 token standards. ERC-20 is a token standard for creating fungible tokens, and it's the most widely used token for ICOs. In the following code block, we can view a code snippet showing the interface of the smart contract for ERC-20:

```
contract ERC20Interface {
  function totalSupply() public constant returns (uint);
  function balanceOf(address tokenOwner) public constant returns
  (uint balance);
  function allowance(address tokenOwner, address spender) public
  constant returns (uint remaining);
  function transfer(address to, uint tokens) public returns
  (bool success);
  function approve(address spender, uint tokens) public returns
  (bool success);
  function transferFrom(address from, address to, uint tokens)
  public returns (bool success);

  event Transfer(address indexed from, address indexed to,
  uint tokens);
  event Approval(address indexed tokenOwner, address indexed
  spender, uint tokens);
}
```

 A summary of the specification of ERC-20 as proposed in the **Ethereum Improvement Proposal** (**EIP**) 20 can be found at https://github.com/ethereum/EIPs/blob/master/EIPS/eip-20.md.

The ERC-223 token standard was designed to both provide better security and reduce the GAS usage in transactions. Both ERC-20 and ERC-223 tokens are fungible tokens, which means that every single token is identical to the others. The ERC-721 token standard was proposed to offer non-fungible tokens, where each created token is unique.

Although ERC-721 tokens are not used in typical ICOs, they are gaining popularity in several decentralized applications. Collectible crypto assets such as the ones used by CryptoKitties use ERC-721 tokens.

The NEO platform also offers a token standard, referred to as NEP5. These are fungible tokens, and the platform allows every token using the same standard to transact with others. An NEP5 token implements the following methods:

```
name() returns string;

symbol() returns string;
```

```
decimals() returns byte;

totalSupply() returns BigInteger;

balanceOf(byte[] account) returns BigInteger;

transfer(byte[] from, byte[] to, BigInteger amount) returns bool;
```

 A summary of the methods used in the NEP5 specification can be found at `https://github.com/neo-project/proposals/blob/master/nep-5.media wiki`.

To get deeper insights into ICO implementation, we are going to deploy an ICO template that creates a token that implements all the crowdfunding functionalities. Since we are already familiar with the deployment of NEO smart contracts, let's deploy a NEP5 token-based ICO template to the NEO blockchain.

 The ICO template programmed in Python that is developed by NEX, a decentralized exchange platform that can be found at `https://github.com/neonexchange/neo-ico-template`.

Firstly, we must ensure that neo-python is configured in Python 3.6. Refer to `Chapter 7`, *Diving into Blockchain – Proof of Ownership*, to find out more about configuring NEO blockchain nodes using neo-python. Likewise, we must ensure that a private blockchain is set up, as mentioned in `Chapter 7`, *Diving into Blockchain – Proof of Ownership*. The next step is to launch the NEO shell to connect to this private blockchain, which can be done by executing the following command:

```
$ np-prompt -p [private-network-node]
```

Open the sample wallet that is preloaded with NEO and GAS:

```
open wallet neo-privnet.sample.wallet
```

Once the ICO template has been cloned from `https://github.com/neonexchange/neo-ico-template`, we can go ahead with building and deploying the ICO smart contract; we need to understand some of the configurations of the smart contract.

A set of configurations can be found in the `nex/token.py` file. The configurations related to token and ICO sale include the token name, symbol, token owner, total supply, initial amount to the owner, tokens per NEO, and tokens per GAS.

The ICO smart contract has some methods that can only be executed by the owner, as shown in the sequence diagram shown in *Figure 12.5*. So, it is necessary to provide owner information (TOKEN_OWNER) in the nex/token.py file:

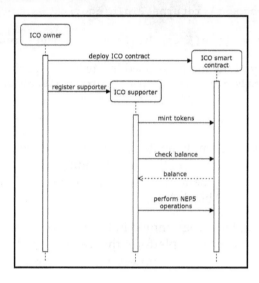

Figure 12.5: Sequence diagram of an ICO campaign

Once the smart contract has been configured, it needs to be built and deployed to the NEO blockchain:

```
build ico_template.py test 0710 05 True False name []

import contract ico_template.avm 0710 05 True False
```

After providing all the details during deployment, NEO shell outputs the hash of the contract. Here, 0xce4a9966dfd3c7c02b48646a6aac281e4c914c2d is the address of the smart contract. This address can be used to perform any ICO operations using the testinvoke command, as seen here:

```
Please fill out the following contract details:
[Contract Name] > Packt ICO
[Contract Version] > 1.0.0
[Contract Author] > Alice
[Contract Email] > alice@packtcoin.com
[Contract Description] > Basic ICO contract
Creating smart contract....
                Name: Packt ICO
                Version: 1.0.0
                Author: Alice
```

```
                    Email: alice@packtcoin.com
                    Description: Basic ICO contract
                    Needs Storage: True
                    Needs Dynamic Invoke: False
{
    "hash": "0xce4a9966dfd3c7c02b48646a6aac281e4c914c2d",
    ...
}
```

The `deploy` operation can be only performed by the token owner that we have already configured:

```
testinvoke 0xce4a9966dfd3c7c02b48646a6aac281e4c914c2d
  deploy []
```

The ICO is said to be live after the `deploy` method is invoked. Methods such as `totalSupply` and `circulation` can be invoked by any of the participants:

```
testinvoke 0xce4a9966dfd3c7c02b48646a6aac281e4c914c2d
  circulation []
```

These methods would return the total number of tokens in supply (10 million) and the total number of tokens initially assigned to the owner (2.5 million), as configured in the configuration file.

In this ICO template, the token owner has to add the participants who want to take part in the crowd sale by registering them:

```
testinvoke 0xce4a9966dfd3c7c02b48646a6aac281e4c914c2d
  crowdsale_register ["AXoZMHm7bxCF5oCkudRjJerJy5AvuRDxp2"]
```

Registered participants can then participate in the crowdfunding by attaching either NEO or GAS to mint ICO tokens:

```
testinvoke 0xce4a9966dfd3c7c02b48646a6aac281e4c914c2d
  mintTokens --attach-neo=50
```

The newly created token has to be imported to the wallet to reflect the created tokens:

```
import token 0xce4a9966dfd3c7c02b48646a6aac281e4c914c2d
```

The `wallet` command will then reflect the newly created `PCKT` token in the wallet:

```
Wallet {
  "addresses": [
    {
      ...
      "balances": {
```

```
        "0xc56f33fc6ecfcd0c225c4ab356fee59390af8560be0e930faebe74a6
    daff7c9b": "99993495.0",
        "0x602c79718b16e442de58778e148d0b1084e3b2dffd5de6b7b16cee
    7969282de7": "14033.9996"
        },
        "tokens": [
          "[ce4a9966dfd3c7c02b48646a6aac281e4c914c2d] PCKT :
    2000.00000000"
        ]
      }
    ],
    ...
    "synced_balances": [
      "[NEO]: 99993495.0 ",
      "[NEOGas]: 14033.9996 ",
      "[PCKT]: 2000 "
    ],
    ...
}
```

The newly created PCKT coin can then perform any of the NEP5 methods, such as transfer and allowance.

Creating an ICO in Ethereum would follow a similar procedure.

 A sample crowdfunding smart contract implementation using Ethereum can be found at https://www.ethereum.org/crowdsale.

There are several crypto asset issuance platforms that can help to create and manage all ICO operations without creating and deploying the smart contracts manually. Some examples include CoinLaunch, Coinfactory, and MyContract, which are some of the most popular platforms for conducting ICOs.

Non-profit autonomous organizations

Non-profit organizations are institutions that provide goods and services without seeking a profit. These organizations are run by volunteers for a particular cause, with some prime examples being charities, **non-governmental organizations** (**NGOs**), or even any voluntary organization. Although most of these organizations are operated by volunteers, each is controlled by an autonomous institution.

A non-profit project run by an autonomous organization has a lot of limitations and may not always be corruption free. However, they do tend to bring a lot of centralization to the decision-making process, which might lead to a lot of controversies. Likewise, autonomous organizations can be decentralized by introducing blockchain technology to remove any intermediaries in the organization. Decentralization in such organizations provides them with great benefits due to the fact that a non-profit organization should not be completely owned by any authority.

Pain points in non-profit autonomous organizations

As discussed, a non-profit project that is governed by an autonomous organization brings a lot of centralization to the organization's operations. Several pain points can be observed in organizations that govern volunteer-based projects:

- A lack of transparency in the organization's operations
- Centralization of power in decision-making can result in a limited set of people in the organization being involved in decision-making
- A lack of communication with external organizations

The lack of transparency and centralization of power in the autonomous organization can prevent supporters of the non-profit organization from looking into the project's progress or becoming involved in decision-making. This may result in corruption within the organization, leading to unsuccessful campaign management. You can achieve transparency and distribute power among the members of the community by creating a **decentralized autonomous organization (DAO)**.

Blockchain as a solution

Decentralizing an autonomous organization is the best way to prevent corruption in such institutions. A DAO can be constructed among trustless entities with the help of blockchain technology. In such cases, a non-profit organization should be transparent and provide distributed governance. A blockchain-based DAO could achieve this by maintaining a public ledger, thus guaranteeing transparency and disintermediation.

A non-profit DAO will have the following properties:

- Transparency of all the transactions of the organization.
- Self-governing by removing any intermediaries.

- Controlled by the shareholders. The supporters of the project could be involved in decision-making.
- Modifications to rules of the DAO must be approved by the community.
- All the properties of the non-profit DAO conform to the conditions of the blockchain decision tree, which makes DAOs an ideal use case for blockchain.

Blockchain implementation of a non-profit DAO

A non-profit DAO is implemented by maintaining a public ledger that is governed by the trustless entities in the network. The DAO can be joined by anyone who is willing to contribute to or monitor the project, and at the same time, the rules of the DAO are decided by the community, rather than the autonomous organization. All of the organization's rules are written in a smart contract and are deployed to the blockchain. Any modifications to the rules must be agreed by the entire community.

Non-profit, NGO, or government welfare projects can be implemented using DAOs to ensure complete transparency of the process.

Summary

In this chapter, we've analyzed a selection of blockchain use cases in detail, and saw how they suited being implemented using blockchain technology. We also successfully picked use cases such as provenance tracking for a supply chain, a payment system, crowdfunding, and DAOs.

By reading this chapter, we've explored how to approach and analyze a use case before selecting the right blockchain technology for its implementation. This chapter also helped to blend the essence from all the topics we have explored throughout this book about blockchain technology and quickly decide on the implementation of its use cases.

Now that we have concluded the final chapter in our journey of exploring the foundations of blockchain technology, we should be motivated enough to be a part of the continuously evolving, and intriguing, world of blockchain technology.

Other Books You May Enjoy

If you enjoyed this book, you may be interested in these other books by Packt:

Tokenomics
Sean Au
Thomas Power

ISBN: 978-1-78913-632-6

- The background of ICOs and how they came to be
- The difference between a coin and a token, a utility and a security, and all the other acronyms you're likely to ever encounter
- How these ICOs raised enormous sums of money
- Tokenomics: structuring the token with creativity
- Why it's important to play nicely with the regulators
- A sneak peak into the future of ICOs from leaders in the industry

Mastering Blockchain - Second Edition
Imran Bashir

ISBN: 978-1-78883-904-4

- Master the theoretical and technical foundations of the blockchain technology
- Understand the concept of decentralization, its impact, and its relationship with blockchain technology
- Master how cryptography is used to secure data - with practical examples
- Grasp the inner workings of blockchain and the mechanisms behind bitcoin and alternative cryptocurrencies
- Understand the theoretical foundations of smart contracts
- Learn how Ethereum blockchain works and how to develop decentralized applications using Solidity and relevant development frameworks
- Identify and examine applications of the blockchain technology - beyond currencies
- Investigate alternative blockchain solutions including Hyperledger, Corda, and many more
- Explore research topics and the future scope of blockchain technology

Leave a review - let other readers know what you think

Please share your thoughts on this book with others by leaving a review on the site that you bought it from. If you purchased the book from Amazon, please leave us an honest review on this book's Amazon page. This is vital so that other potential readers can see and use your unbiased opinion to make purchasing decisions, we can understand what our customers think about our products, and our authors can see your feedback on the title that they have worked with Packt to create. It will only take a few minutes of your time, but is valuable to other potential customers, our authors, and Packt. Thank you!

Index

www.ingramcontent.com/pod-product-compliance
Lightning Source LLC
Chambersburg PA
CBHW080613060326
40690CB00021B/4678